The First-Generation Student Experience

The First-Generation Student Experience

*Implications for Campus Practice,
and Strategies for Improving
Persistence and Success*

JEFF DAVIS

STERLING, VIRGINIA

COPYRIGHT © 2010 BY ACPA, COLLEGE STUDENT
EDUCATORS INTERNATIONAL

Published by Stylus Publishing, LLC
22883 Quicksilver Drive
Sterling, Virginia 20166-2102

Library of Congress Cataloging-in-Publication Data
Davis, Jeff, 1959–
    The first-generation student experience : implications for
campus practice, and strategies for improving persistence
and success / Jeff Davis.
        p.   cm.
    Includes bibliographical references and index.
    ISBN 978-1-57922-369-4 (cloth : alk. paper)
    ISBN 978-1-57922-370-0 (pbk. : alk. paper)
    1. First-generation college students—United States.
    2. Academic achievement—United States.   I. Title.
    LC148.2.D38   2010
    378.1'982—dc22   2009042324

13-digit ISBN: 978-1-57922-369-4 (cloth)
13-digit ISBN: 978-1-57922-370-0 (paper)

Printed in the United States of America

All first editions printed on acid free paper
that meets the American National Standards Institute
Z39–48 Standard.

Bulk Purchases

Quantity discounts are available for use in workshops
and for staff development.
Call 1–800–232–0223

First Edition, 2010

10   9   8   7   6   5   4   3

To my son Jack, who informs all my creative activities
and who will not have to struggle
as a first-generation college student.

Contents

Introduction

I T WAS NOT SO LONG AGO that the people attending American colleges and universities, besides being mostly male and White, were also, almost invariably, the children of parents who had attended colleges and universities, and that these *parents* of the people attending American colleges and universities were also very likely to have been the children of parents who had attended colleges and universities, and so on down the line. It was not until the advent of post–World War II economic prosperity and the establishment of the GI Bill that this chain of privilege began to weaken, allowing others to begin attending American colleges and universities in any significant numbers.

Since that time not so long ago, the people who run the American higher-education system—members of boards of regents, college presidents, other high-level administrators—have gradually become aware that this exclusionary ideology was more harmful than beneficial. It was not only harmful to the people who were excluded, but also harmful to the people included, they discovered, harmful to people like themselves, that is, in a number of ways that might not be so evident at first glance. To take the broad view, this exclusionary ideology was not helpful to the American economic system, for example, nor was it helpful to the ongoing project of American democracy.

The people who run the American higher-education system have become more aware of how unfair and unwise it was to hinder women from attending college, and we have achieved a certain success in the number of women enrolled in postsecondary institutions and in other areas as well (National Coalition for Women and Girls in Education, 2008). However, there is still work to be done.

Those who run the American higher-education system have become more aware of how unfair and unwise it was to make it difficult for people from ethnic minority groups to attend college, and we have achieved some success in making a college education more attainable for African Americans, Asian

Americans, Latinos, and Native Americans (Ryu, 2008). However, there is still much work to be done.

Much more recently those who run the American higher-education system also have become aware of how unfair and unwise it was to hinder people with disabilities from attending college (Harbour, 2008). There is still, however, much work to be done in this area, too.

To their credit, members of boards of regents, college presidents, and other high-level administrators not only have opened the gates of academe a little wider but also have instituted practices and programs that have made it easier for women, members of ethnic minority groups, and people with disabilities to earn college degrees. State outreach programs such as the Educational Opportunity Program in California have recruited nontraditional students to colleges and universities and have helped them with the cost of attendance and in numerous other ways once they have been accepted for enrollment. Federal grant programs like TRIO student-support-service projects have helped nontraditional college students improve their academic performance. Individual institutions have made gains in recognizing the special barriers that face nontraditional students and have adjusted their academic curricula and policies to help ensure that the path to getting a degree does not benefit traditional students disproportionately—although there is still much work to be done.

One of the by-products of these efforts to correct the inequalities of the American higher-education system has been the emergence of a relatively new category of student, one that, according to its own definition, often includes members of the underrepresented groups mentioned above but not to the exclusion of members of the so-called dominant American culture. This category is "first-generation college students." Even though the educational establishment may not have recognized first-generation students as belonging to a fully realized student category, such students have always been present on American college campuses, although their numbers were largely insignificant before the GI Bill. Certain of these students, some facing significant barriers to success, always have been able to muddle through the complex procedures of higher-education institutions, but many have fallen by the wayside, too. Student categories, to be distinguished from the students themselves, are constructed by higher-education professionals to address generalized phenomena such as retention and graduate rates, among other issues. This student *category* is the subject of this book, a category that has been in existence for only 25 years or so. Even though the phrase "first-generation college student" is uttered more often these days by college presidents and other high-level administrators in communications to the general public, the category still remains oddly emergent. First-generation college students, although educational leaders know them to be extremely important to the continued health of the education system, remain somewhat ill-defined and, more important, somewhat underserved in the sense that a well-articulated practice to help them earn college degrees more easily and efficiently has not yet been presented. Even though the research describing the issues facing first-generation college students contains gaps and areas of deficiency, we cannot wait any longer to begin addressing these issues fully. We need to get serious about practice now; we have to start making an impact on low retention and graduation rates now.

The main purpose of this volume, then, is twofold: first, it seeks to present a more mature definition of the first-generation college student, and, second, it seeks to offer a set of concrete suggestions for developing a practice that will help first-generation students earn college degrees more easily and efficiently. It is not just that first-generation students are worthy of our attention, now and in the future, but that more and more—because they are nothing less than the lifeblood of the American higher-education system, as we shall see—they are going to demand our attention. The audience for this book is not only higher-education researchers. This book was written for all education professionals who work with first-generation college students, including postsecondary institution administrators and other staff who have some say in the structure of institutional bureaucracies. It also includes the educators who work face-to-face with first-generation college students, faculty, academic advisors, and support staff professionals such as tutors and counselors. Finally, the audience for this book also includes anyone else who has a strong interest in how well the American postsecondary education system is working at the beginning of the 21st century and how it is likely to change in the near future.

CHAPTER SUMMARIES

Chapter 1 addresses the tricky business of counting the number of first-generation college students enrolled in American colleges and universities.

Counting these students is important for a number of reasons, perhaps the most important of which concerns the way state and federal money is distributed to the hundreds of public, postsecondary institutions across the country. Some kinds of students attract more money than others do, and programs that serve students with disabilities, for example, often receive funding based on how many students with disabilities institution officials can count. The number of students with disabilities is then compared to the numbers of other kinds of students who need services, and the money is divided accordingly. Higher-education researchers have had an easier time with qualitative analysis of the first-generation student experience, probably because it has been so difficult to come up with hard numbers. It is time for the quantitative analysis to catch up.

Not only has the research describing the first-generation student experience been slow to develop, but the category itself—that is, its denotative character—has been slow to develop as well. It seems almost impossible that no universally accepted definition of who is a first-generation student and who is not has fully emerged. Chapter 1 argues for a single, simple definition: *Students can claim first-generation student status if neither one of their parents or guardians possesses a four-year degree.* This simple, stripped-down definition (or another like it), which I call the "definition admissions officers can use," must be embraced by both the research community and the larger education establishment before numbers of students can be discussed accurately, and before the quantitative analysis can be realized fully.

The "definition education practitioners can use," the fuller, more personal definition that includes family background, academic preparation, barriers to success, and many other dimensions of the first-generation experience, is developed throughout the book. Education professionals need to know exactly with whom they are working because the statistics describing the success of first-generation students are not good; in fact, they are succeeding at a rate roughly half that of their non-first-generation counterparts (Chen & Carroll, 2005).

Chapter 1 also cites national statistics, state statistics for California, which has the largest postsecondary education system in the country, and introduces Sonoma State University, a fairly typical, smaller, public, four-year institution to describe the first-generation college student experience in the most personal, specific way possible. Although the material on Sonoma State may not be completely relevant to the experience of students at community colleges, for-profit schools, and private four-year institutions, the benefits of looking at the first-generation student experience through this microscope, in addition to looking at it through a telescope, so to speak, outweigh the problems inherent in using Sonoma State as a model. References to Sonoma State appear throughout the book and provide information education professionals should find valuable.

Chapters 2 and 3 build on the material in chapter 1 to describe the first-generation student experience through an examination of the research literature. Chapter 2 is divided into two major sections: Learning at College and Campus Presence.

It should be no surprise that first-generation college students are less prepared for postsecondary study than are their non-first-generation counterparts. The parents of first-generation college students did not earn a four-year degree (if they attended college at all), of course, which strongly suggests they are less knowledgeable about postsecondary education than are people who have earned a four-year degree. But it also suggests that parents of first-generation students are less knowledgeable about primary and secondary school education. In other words, they are less knowledgeable about the ways of educational institutions in general. Although some first-generation students may come from low-income areas with underperforming high schools, which also perhaps explains their lack of preparedness, chapter 2 warns against making the assumption that all or even most first-generation students are also low-income individuals.

Chapter 3 is also divided into two sections: An Extended Campus Acclimation Process and The Importance and Impact of Personal Relationships. It introduces the existential questions about college attendance, "Why are you going to college and why do you want to be a college student?" as a way to continue differentiating the concerns of first-generation college students from the concerns of their more privileged non-first-generation counterparts (and from the concerns of low-income students as well). Perceived in the American imagination as almost a fundamental rite of passage, going to college is so central to the development of identity in the United States at the beginning of the 21st century that understanding how students think about going to college is absolutely necessary to understanding the first-generation student experience. Is going to college a right of all American citizens? What does earning a college degree do to family relationships? What does one do with a college education? Chapter 3 addresses these questions and others as it attempts to delve into the psyche of individuals who are the first in their families to attend college.

In many ways chapter 4 is the heart of the book. It goes without saying that scholars and researchers interested in fully understanding the first-generation student experience must listen to first-generation students describe it. With this fundamental insight in mind, chapter 4 is a collection of 14 narratives written by first-generation students attending Sonoma State University during the last decade. Some of the student writers come from low-income backgrounds; others do not. Some write with the perspective of a first- or second-year student; others are graduate students. Some of the student writers are members of ethnic minority groups; others are members of the dominant culture. Because students with first-generation student status are also members of other student demographic categories—in fact, they run the gamut of the categories—these student writers are members of many other demographic categories as well.

Chapter 4 also addresses the question, Can any student on a college campus be a first-generation student? What the reader will find out, among other things, is that in some ways, yes, any student on a college campus could be a first-generation student. This does not mean, however, that every student walking across the quad *is* a first-generation student, just that having first-generation student status does not exclude one from belonging to any of the other demographic categories. More to the point, chapter 4 shows that there is a core first-generation student experience that all first-generation students share. The narratives these students write are striking and memorable; some will make you laugh and others will make you cry. In many cases, this is the first time these students have been asked to write about themselves in a truly meaningful way, in a way that causes them to explore the deep coding of their identity. Sometimes what the narratives reveal will make readers uncomfortable, but you can be sure that the students have considered content carefully and have told their stories with the utmost sincerity.

If the goal of chapter 4 is to present the first-generation student experience as narrative, the goal of chapter 5 is to parse this narrative into its constituent parts as an exercise in comprehending the whole. We can talk all we want about the different characteristics of first-generation students—that they have this, that they lack that—but the only way to do the students themselves justice is to see how all these separate characteristics form the whole, complete person. Told as narrative, the first-generation student experience is not quite the archetypal rags-to-riches story, nor is it exactly the story of the search for the "American dream," although it has elements of both. Most of us hear the rags-to-riches stories and the story of the search for the "American dream" not so much as finished cultural artifacts but as organic models, always evolving and growing, strongly aligned with the continuously developing American identity. Chapter 5 demonstrates, among other things, that academic advisors and student affairs professionals should study the first-generation student experience and use this knowledge to formulate a set of instructions for helping students grow stronger.

The chapter 4 narratives render in vivid, specific detail the necessarily generalized image of the first-generation college student provided by the research material presented in chapters 2 and 3. Chapter 5 goes one step further by describing those details that may not quite fit the organic model even as that model evolves and grows, describing what might be dismissed or overlooked. Reading the narratives well means marking the objective facts that are repeated, of course, but it also means appreciating the subjectivity of the writers, appreciating how students must learn to own their struggles and how they construct their own first-generation student experience. Although the subject of this book is the student "category," the reader must at least catch a glimpse of this individual student subjectivity for full understanding.

Chapter 6 gathers together the data of the first chapter, the research of the second and third, the narratives of the fourth, and the analysis of the fifth—a single piece of persuasion, let us say—and then converts it to practice. How should postsecondary institutions prepare themselves for these structural changes in higher education? What can presidents, administrators, and other officials presiding over the structural elements of their institutions do to make it easier for first-generation students to achieve four-year degrees? Chapter 6 presents 14 issues facing officials at progressive colleges and universities who want to assist first-generation students and describes a course of action to address each issue.

It will not be necessary for all postsecondary institutions to enact each of these 14 recommendations to help their first-generation students. Some colleges and universities have already begun moving in the direction of certain of the recommendations, and, of course, much will depend on the individual character of the college or university itself. The cost of identifying first-generation students will also have to be considered before applying many of these recommendations, given that most American postsecondary institutions do not yet record exactly how many first-generation students they have.

How many first-generation students attend your institution? Pondering this question puts us back at square one. The American postsecondary education system cannot afford to exclude nontraditional students by denying them access or ignoring their needs and difficulties. The first recommendation of this book, then, is for college and university officials to determine how many first-generation students attend their institution. Start making the case that it is important to count them. Some readers may not think that counting students is important enough—given the myriad difficulties facing the American postsecondary education system at the beginning of the 21st century—to be raised to the level of first priorities, but be careful if you hold this view. The author of this book and the 14 other writers who tell their stories here predict that, in the years to come, counting first-generation college students will not only be recognized as a first priority, it likely will become second nature.

1

How Many First-Generation College Students Are There?

CURRENTLY, FIRST-GENERATION COLLEGE STUDENTS are more likely to drop out, more likely to take longer to graduate if they don't drop out, and more likely to get less out of a college education than their more traditional counterparts (Chen & Carroll, 2005; Choy, 2001; Nuñez & Cuccaro-Alamin, 1998). They are also more likely to report feelings of low confidence and isolation when asked to reflect on their college experience (Engle, Bermeo, & O'Brien, 2006; Somers, Woodhouse, & Cofer, 2004). These negative characteristics, however, do not have to define first-generation college students, and it behooves educators at American postsecondary institutions to work harder toward making such reports less common. In addition to the two-part purpose described in the Introduction, this book was written as a piece of advocacy, to make the case that institutions should pay more attention to the persistence and success of first-generation college students.

Partly because the first-generation student category has only recently attracted the close attention of higher-education researchers, the word about these students has been slow to get out. Some institution officials still appear to be almost unfamiliar with the term. Stanford University Dean of Freshmen and Transfer Students Julie Lythcott-Haims, for example, was quoted in the student newspaper as saying, "Over the last five years, there's been an increased awareness among faculty, administrators, and staff of the presence of first-generation students on campus. . . . The concept of being first generation, the terminology, is a newer construct" (Fuller, 2007, p. 3). Newer

1

construct . . . ? Well, maybe. Hsiao (1992) confirmed the immature state
of the category (Bui, 2002) in her early article "First-Generation College
Students," when she made the point that most institutions do not even
count how many first-generation students they have. This was true in 1992,
and it is still true today. This lack of what might appear to be basic demographic data is not the result of sloppy record keeping or even indifference,
but more a function of the difficulties inherent in documenting first-generation student status.

This chapter begins with the first task related to documenting first-generation student status: defining just what it is we are documenting. Unfortunately, more than 15 years after Hsiao's article, postsecondary education
circles are still using more than one definition. Only after a universally
accepted definition is established can the serious counting of students com-
mence, so this chapter describes the various methods colleges and universities
may use to get this important work done. Although hard numbers are still
not easy to come by, some statistics are available that can give us an adequate
albeit blurry picture of how many first-generation students are attending
American colleges and universities now and in the near future. Finally, this
chapter ends with a brief description of California's Sonoma State University
(SSU) relative to the first-generation student experience. As mentioned in
the introduction, SSU serves as a kind of reality check in the book, as a real
place where real first-generation students, as opposed to abstract statistics,
struggle and succeed.

DEFINITIONS

Let us start with a definition *admissions officers can use*. Although it is possible
to find more than one definition of first-generation student status that
admissions officers can use—stripped down and crafted for counting heads,
so to speak—the one this author arrived at by surveying published material
is as follows: Individuals can claim first-generation student status if neither
one of their parents or guardians possesses a four-year degree. Simple
enough, and keeping the definition simple is a virtue in itself, as we shall see.
But this is hardly going to be the last word on the subject. Some researchers
suggest a variation of this definition that includes a parent's having earned a
two-year degree or having attended college without receiving a degree, and

this can be the source of no small amount of confusion, in both the academic community and the general population. For instance, most of the National Center for Education Statistics (NCES) studies (Chen & Carroll, 2005; Nuñez & Cuccaro-Alamin, 1998; Warburton, Bugarin, & Nuñez, 2001) reporting on the progress of first-generation students use a different, tripartite scheme for arriving at a definition: (1) "first-generation students," (2) "students whose parent(s) had some college," and (3) "students whose parent(s) had bachelor's or higher degree." What this method does is divide the first-generation student category (as opposed to the non-first-generation student category) into two parts, students with parents who never attended college at all and students with parents who attended "some" college. Because the parents in the "students whose parent(s) had some college" category are almost impossible to generalize about in terms of college experience, including people who attended for one semester or less and people who racked up 100 academic units or more with no degree granted, the tripartite scheme for arriving at a definition is highly problematic. Another area to consider in this context is how hiring officers have come to view a bachelor's degree in the last few decades. From the point of view of many hiring officers, the benefit of attending college is seen as an all-or-nothing proposition. Without a four-year degree, most job seekers are viewed as undereducated no matter how much they may have learned at a postsecondary institution; therefore, it is likely these non-degreed parents with "some" college (and maybe even "a lot" of college) have had to settle for jobs lower in the job market hierarchy (Ishitani, 2003). Their place in the American social strata, therefore, likely is not very high. The way bachelor's degrees have been viewed in the job market during the last few decades makes it even more likely that the households of students in the "students whose parent(s) had some college" category are more similar to than different from the households of students in the category "first-generation students," thereby negating the need to separate them into two categories. Better to call "students whose parent(s) had some college" first-generation college students, as this book does, and leave it at that . . . simplicity, again.

Why advocate for a single definition at all? Why not use multiple definitions? As mentioned earlier, the first-generation student category has remained oddly emergent for a relatively long time. The academic professionals who work with these students often have to explain what the term "first-generation student" means to the academic professionals and laypeople who ask them to describe what they do at the institution. A demographic category that has multiple, inconsistent definitions for the individual members of that category is obviously going to remain vague in many people's minds. Some might ask, can anyone be a first-generation student? Who are these people? Removing the vagueness is doubly important in this case because this is a large category, one with millions of members. The category, and, therefore, the students in that category, will receive more attention if it is clear who is a member and who is not. In the current postsecondary education funding environment, which is pitting one group against another in pursuit of shrinking resources, those groups that have trouble generating attention simply will not receive money for services, and first-generation college students are badly in need of services.

Although a stripped-down definition is necessary, and understanding why it is necessary makes for better advocacy, first-generation student status is not about the number of years a parent attended college or the number of academic units that parent accumulated. It is about being competent and comfortable navigating the higher-education landscape, about growing up in a home environment that promotes the college and university culture. This latter perspective is what *non*-first-generation students have when they begin their postsecondary education. In other words, the *absence* of the non-first-generation student experience is what first-generation student status is all about.

The people who work with first-generation students in American postsecondary institutions have known for a long time that these students are missing *something*; they know from experience that these students need extra help to succeed at the same rate as their non-first-generation counterparts. Even if the people who work with first-generation students have not studied the statistics firsthand, they must have heard the sad news by now. Academic advisors, student support professionals, faculty, and the other postsecondary education personnel who work one-on-one with students know that first-generation students can appear timid, uninformed, and even somewhat directionless. Educators try to react to these characteristics and address individual student complaints as they arise, but a more effective way to respond is needed. Advisors and others have been reactive rather than proactive in attempting to assist this student population because, among other reasons, what these students lack is not very visible or very well understood, especially by many first-generation students themselves. When a first-generation student comes into an academic advisor's office and makes obscure complaints about not fitting in, etc., it is very common for advisors to address these complaints as if they were idiomatic to the student, as if generalizing about them would not be helpful. It is also common for advisors to address these complaints using the more established assistance protocols for low-income or traditionally at-risk students. It is not that advisors have not heard first-generation student complaints before, or that the more experienced among them do not recognize them as a syndrome; it is that they do not have an established assistance protocol at their disposal. The problem is that first-generation students are not always low-income individuals, nor are they always traditionally at risk. This customary, more reactive response that treats students as if they either are an isolated case or belong to a different student population can work in certain instances with certain students, but on the whole it has not served this student population well. First-generation college students need to be treated as first-generation college students.

Academic advisors, student support professionals, and interested faculty have assisted first-generation college students, we might say, the way a repairperson repairs a misbehaving wheel on a supermarket shopping cart. You know the one; it squeaks loudly, turns in the wrong direction, and makes guiding the cart almost impossible. In the dark about the root causes of the wheel's poor performance, what does the repairperson do? The only thing he can do—he gets out his oilcan and oils the wheel, hoping there has not been so much internal damage that the wheel has become completely inoperable. What this book suggests is that academic advisors, student support professionals, and faculty should approach assisting first-generation students, not the way a repairperson would approach repairing a shopping cart wheel, but the way a maintenance engineer would approach it. The maintenance engineer knows everything about wheels on shopping carts. She knows how they are manufactured, how they are assembled, and how they perform in the field. She knows that after a certain amount of time, some wheels will be unable to perform well, in this case, because they need oil. Knowing this about some wheels, the maintenance engineer does not have to wait for the supermarket patrons to complain or the wheels to squeak; she can supply what the wheel lacks before the failure. In fact, she can ensure that all of the wheels get their proper measure of oil.

Not only does this book provide an assistance protocol for first-generation college students that academic advisors, student support professionals, and faculty can use right away to grease those squeaky wheels, chapter 6 provides a plan of action for deans, executive directors, and other high-level administrators so they can start promulgating the institutional awareness needed for meaningful long-term change. When high-level administrators see how relatively easy it can be to increase the retention and graduation rates of first-generation college students, and how doing so can dramatically increase the image and desirability of their institutions by increasing overall retention and graduation rates, they will want to be at the forefront of the next *big thing* in postsecondary student support services. First-generation students are a valuable commodity, and spending money on assisting them is money well spent.

Back to the definition. Now that we have a definition admissions officers and other administrators can use, let us use it to establish numbers of students on a national scale. The definition academic advisors, student support professionals, and faculty should use—the full definition, the more intimate definition—is fleshed out in subsequent chapters of this book. Sticking with the definition admissions officers can use for now, however, how do institution officials count how many first-generation students they have? How do they verify that neither one of a student's parents or guardians possesses a four-year degree? Currently, the answer to both these questions is: "They don't . . . because they can't." They cannot, because to verify first-generation student status in the formal sense would mean that a student's parents would have to provide documentary evidence of the absence of a four-year degree. Other student categories, such as low-income status and disability status, do not present this kind of a problem. To verify low-income status, for example, institution officials ask students to document family income by filling out the Free Application for Student Aid (FAFSA) or by submitting tax records. To verify disability status, they ask students to provide official medical records. No such documentary evidence exists for first-generation status, of course, so institutions must rely on a student's self-disclosure. Verification in the formal documentary sense, then, is not possible, and because of this, some college and university officials have not pursued counting first-generation students as avidly as they might have, as avidly as they have counted low-income students and students with disabilities.

COUNTING FIRST-GENERATION
COLLEGE STUDENTS

Even if counting first-generation students is difficult, administrators and admissions officers need to figure out how to do it, for first-generation students are lining up at the gates of academe in larger numbers than ever before. The model for establishing numbers of students described above, the formal documentary model, is not the only one educators and others use to organize students into meaningful demographic units. Sometimes, student self-disclosure is enough. For the most part, it is also not possible to verify ethnicity using the formal documentary model. In the higher education sphere, with rare exceptions, admissions officers, administrators, and student affairs professionals rely exclusively on students' self-disclosure for determining ethnic minority status. Even with regard to low-income status, student self-disclosure is sometimes enough. Although individual postsecondary institutions can and do create very current income records on their own students by means of the FAFSA, other cross-institution evaluators and research bodies, such as the Cooperative Institutional Research Program (CIRP), rely on self-disclosure to describe the lay of the land, statistically speaking.[1] This somewhat capricious attitude about verification—sometimes documentary evidence is necessary, sometimes self-disclosure is enough—suggests that verification itself is more a historical issue than a well-thought-out, functional one. Once administrators recognize that a student category such as low-income status is established and valuable, how it is documented or verified becomes a moot point.

As it turns out then, recognizing that a student category is intrinsically valuable and should be integrated into the fabric of the institutional culture can be decoupled from the need to document status. Student ethnicity, as was mentioned, is regarded as so important that how this information is gathered is not really even a consideration anymore. Is first-generation status just as important? Some readers may blanch at the suggestion that first-generation status should be considered in a similar light to ethnic minority status, but this may not be such a bad idea. At present ethnic minority status is regarded, as it should be, as being more integral to the composition of a person's identity than first-generation student status is. This is the case for many reasons, not the least of which is that ethnic minority status permeates every layer of American culture, and first-generation student status does not.

I am not suggesting that first-generation student status should be regarded as the same as ethnic minority status when considering the composition of a person's identity. I am suggesting, however, that it should be regarded as similar in the higher-education sphere.

What does it mean to suggest that first-generation student status should be regarded as similar to ethnic minority status in the higher-education sphere? One of the things it means is that, if some college and university officials regard the self-disclosure of first-generation student status with suspicion, they should rethink this suspicion. Let us not forget that because of the history of multiple definitions and for other reasons many of these students themselves are not sure they have first-generation status. Certainly, therefore, some students may not disclose their status accurately, at least at first, and some may even be intentionally dishonest about it. But the same is true of ethnic minority status; in fact, the argument can be made that there is more pressure to be dishonest about one's ethnicity, given the long history of discrimination in this country and the much shorter history of services attached to ethnic minority status, but that does not stop universities from acting on these self-disclosed numbers. Postsecondary institution officials make all kinds of important decisions, everything from religious holiday policy to curriculum guidelines, based on the numbers of ethnic minority students they have in attendance, decisions having to do with student housing activities, student club funding, campus speaker programming, and on and on. What is obviously true here is that institutions of all stripes, not just higher-education institutions, have decided that ethnic minority status is *very* important in considering how an institution presents itself to the general public, so it is useful to know how many people with ethnic minority status attend the institution. This same logic should be applied to first-generation college students. The truth is that first-generation status is *very* important in considering how a postsecondary institution represents itself to the general public. The fact that it has not been considered *very* important has been a problem. Maybe thinking about first-generation student status in the same terms as ethnic minority status is just the thing to make attending to students with first-generation status more of a priority for universities and colleges.

HOW INSTITUTIONS CAN COUNT STUDENTS

There are many methods institutions can use to count the number of first-generation students they have in attendance. Given that the mechanics of enrolling new students varies dramatically among institutions, no single method will work for every individual college or university. Some factors include how automated enrollment and class registration is, how accessible the student record database is to students themselves, and how decisions are made about what questions appear on the undergraduate application for admittance. Even though methods do vary, the following suggestions should cover most bases:

Modify undergraduate admissions applications. This is perhaps the best way to get the job done. Prospective students simply enter the level of education of their parents (or guardians) as part of the application. Many undergraduate applications already ask this question but label it optional, or ask it in such a way that determining first-generation student status by the definition this book uses is impossible. In addition, entering the correct information is one thing, but getting that information to the professionals who work with students is sometimes another. At some larger institutions, many months can go by before admissions information is transferred to the relevant campus or campuses. This complicates the process of supporting first-generation students, of course.

Survey students in courses that all students must take in their first year such as "freshman composition." This method allows institutions to begin the process of educating students about first-generation student status almost immediately. Before giving the survey, faculty can describe the barriers associated with being a first-generation college student and introduce the units on campus designed to help students overcome those barriers. Unfortunately, information collected in this way almost never involves all students when considering class waivers, complicated class schedules, and student absences.

Gather background information from students when they submit to first-semester administrative processes such as acquiring a student ID card. Since just about every student these days must acquire an ID card to access even the most basic institution services, including the library, this method has the virtue of covering all students. Also, since the student ID number generally is entered directly into the local student record database at this time, any other information gathered, in this case information determining first-generation student status, can be entered immediately and accessed immediately. This method conveys information to educators in time to support first-generation students.

Have students enter the necessary information themselves during computerized class registration. As mentioned, most undergraduate applications already ask students about their parents' level of income, but they do not put the question simply. For example, they do not ask, "Do either of your parents or guardians possess a four-year degree?" Such a question could be asked of students via the local class registration procedure before they are allowed to register for classes. If they do not answer it, they could be blocked from registering. Again, this method has the virtue of entering first-generation student status directly into an institution's student record database.

Create a campus culture where all students voluntarily enter their status directly into the institution's student record database. This is something of a variation on the previous method, but unlike the previous method, it would take many months if not years to implement fully. The idea is that all students will be educated about the difficulties of being a first-generation student and about the campus support services available to overcome those difficulties. As a by-product of this new awareness, then, students would understand why the institution wants to know their status. Via a computer password or some other technological method, students could enter their first-generation status into the student record database at any time during their first semester of study. Other background information could be entered at the same time.

Set up a first-generation student registration station in the institution's advising center. Students could enter their status via a computer workstation located in an area of the advising center that also houses information about the first-generation student experience. The first-generation student area of the center could include informational books and pamphlets, fliers advertising campus activities for first-generation students, and the locations and hours of campus units that provide the kind of assistance first-generation students need.

As this variety of methods for recording first-generation student status demonstrates, finding out how many first-generation students attend your college or university is not particularly arduous. Not being able to create a method to count students really has not been the problem; not counting them has been. In other words, if high-level institution administrators have the will, they should have little trouble determining how many first-generation students they have.

WHAT THE DATA SHOW

Although the ability to count first-generation students is still lacking at most postsecondary institutions in this country, no one disputes there are more of such students taking classes than ever before, especially in proportion to traditional, non-first-generation students, as we shall see. Just how many first-generation college students are there, anyway? According to the National Center for Education Statistics (NCES) and its major national study (Nuñez & Cuccaro-Alamin, 1998) of the many dimensions of first-generation student attendance, 43.4% of all beginning postsecondary students who entered college in the fall semester of 1989 had first-generation student status.[2] Even though this study is more than 10 years old, researchers investigating this subject still regard it as foundational groundwork for establishing national statistics. Other reports confirm the 43.4% figure or suggest it might be even higher (Chen & Carroll, 2005; Warburton et al., 2001). Choy (2001), for instance, showed that only 33.0% of the students who graduated with a high school diploma in 1992 came from non-first-generation student families, which means 67.0% of them came from first-generation student families. Two years later, 65.0% of those non-first-generation students had enrolled in a four-year institution, but only 56.0% of those first-generation students had (Choy, 2001). This means that more than 50.0% of students graduating from high school in 1992 and enrolling in four-year institutions at least two years later were first-generation college students. The numbers for two-year institutions are even higher: Phillippe and Patton (2000) showed that, of the students enrolling in two-year institutions in 1995, 67.5% reported a father who did not have a four-year degree, and 83.0% reported a mother who did not have a four-year degree.

The size of the 43.4% figure surprises many people, but it is even more impressive when we understand that it is a snapshot of the enrollment picture of almost 10 years before its publication date of 1998. This figure is likely to have climbed above the 50% threshold by now because of certain demographic trends, as we shall see.[3] Thus, it is likely that a majority of the students currently enrolled in American postsecondary institutions are first-generation students. What will this figure be in the future?

To answer this question, we have to broaden the scope of the inquiry a bit. Postsecondary education enrollment has been increasing relative to the overall American population for a while now. More than 15 million students enrolled in American degree-granting institutions for the fall 2000 semester, and 18.8 million students are projected to enroll in degree-granting institutions for the fall 2010 semester (NCES, 2007). Non-U.S. citizens whose primary residence is outside the United States—that is, international students—are included in these figures. Although the number of international students attending American colleges and universities is significant, it isn't high enough to affect any of the conclusions made here. The experience of being a first-generation college student is far different for international students from how it is for American students. International student enrollment has increased at a fairly consistent rate since the fall 1984 semester, when 342,113 international students were enrolled in American colleges and universities. In the fall 2002 semester, 586,323 international students were enrolled (Chin, 2003, p. 2).

The overall enrollment number is projected to jump to 20.2 million students for the fall 2015 semester, which represents an increase of 24.3% from 2000 to 2015[4] (NCES, 2007). During this same period, the number of college-age Americans (Americans ages 18 to 24) is predicted to decline by 21.2%: 39.2 million in 2000, 30.7 million in 2010, and 30.9 in 2015 (U.S. Census Bureau, 2008).

What these figures tell us, among other things, is that access to higher education in the United States is getting easier for many people, that the system is getting fairer. The increase in the number of students enrolled in the postsecondary school system between 2000 and 2015 is growing, while the number of college-age Americans for the same period is declining. Although comparing the difference in the growth rate and decline rate of the two categories is instructive, comparing the actual numbers of people involved is more illustrative. From 2000 to 2015, 4.9 million people will be added to the rolls of American colleges and universities, while 8.3 million people will be subtracted from the category of college-age Americans (NCES, 2007; U.S. Census Bureau, 2008).

This 4.9 million figure is important in its own right, of course, because it illustrates that large numbers of Americans are getting the chance to improve their lives through education. To grasp the meaning of these figures fully, however, to place them in the context of the goals and purposes of this book, we have to see how they demonstrate that a very high percentage of the new people enrolling in colleges and universities have been and will continue to be first-generation students.

Whenever we talk about first-generation college students, we are talking not just about the students themselves, but about their families as well. The traditional-age students who are the subject of this analysis (ages 18 to 24) are separating from their families and their home cultures and beginning their postsecondary education. Let us consider these specific families and the way the American family in general has evolved over time. During the period just before this recent increase in access to a college education, the size of the American family changed fairly dramatically (Galor & Weil, 1996; U.S. Census Bureau, 2000).

One thing we can say for sure is that the greater number of people attending college—a 24.3% increase between 2000 and 2015—is *not* the result of American families getting larger. At the end of the 1950s, the average American woman gave birth to 3.7 children; by 1990 that number was down to 1.9 (Popenoe, 1993). This number has hovered just below the long-term replacement rate of 2.0 ever since (U.S. Census Bureau, 2000). To be sure, some families are larger than the long-term replacement rate and some are smaller, but you can be just as sure that a large number of children in a single family is correlated negatively with level of income, and that level of income is strongly correlated with level of education (Easterlin, Schaeffer, & Macunovich, 1993; Galor & Weil, 1996). All of this supports the claim that during the 2000–2015 period, non-first-generation student family size in the United States has been and likely will continue to be flat or decrease in terms of the number of non-first-generation students produced. So, if the number of non-first-generation students attending college during the 2000–2015 period has been and will continue to be flat (or more likely on a downward trend), who is taking advantage of the increased access described above? If the sorts of people attending college during the 1950s and 1960s continued to attend at the same, or more likely lower, rate, what sorts of people were and are being added?

The answer is, of course, that other sorts of people from other backgrounds were and are making up the increase in college attendance—to be more specific, first-generation college student sorts of people. The increase in overall college attendance is likely the result of the gradual increase in access to the American postsecondary education for everyone, but "everyone" now consists of a much higher proportion of nontraditional students, including, of course, first-generation students. Because the number of non-first-generation students has been decreasing relative to the number of first-generation students because of the decreasing size of American families and other reasons, we can safely claim that the increased number of students—projected to be 4.9 million between 2000 and 2015—is made up of a high proportion of first-generation students.

To bolster this claim, we should also note that many of the increased number of students attending American colleges and universities have, and will continue to, come from recently immigrated American families (Hagy & Staniec, 2002). In fact, immigrants have been accounting for much of the overall increase in the American population for some time (Camarota, 2007). It should come as no surprise that children of recently immigrated families, even if their parents received an education in their country of origin, are much more likely to have first-generation student status than are children from nonimmigrant families.

There is other evidence that the continuing increase in enrollment has been and will continue to be mostly first-generation college students. Perhaps the most compelling evidence comes from the nation's community college system, which accounts for between 30.0% and 35.0% of all undergraduate students using the American postsecondary education system in any given year (U.S. Census Bureau 1999, 2006). At least 10.0% of the 24.3% increase in the number of students the postsecondary education system has been experiencing, and will continue to experience, will be realized in the community college system (Bryant, 2001). This is significant because the average student attending a community college has always been more likely to be a first-generation student than has the average student attending a public or private four-year institution (Phillippe & Patton, 2000). The research shows that this will continue to be the case, that the community college system will be the preferred destination for many people who are the first in their families to attend college (Bryant, 2001; Phelan, 2000; Phillippe & Patton, 2000). It is not unrealistic to say that nearly all of the 10.0% of the 24.3% increase in numbers who will be attending community colleges will be first-generation college students.

FIRST-GENERATION STUDENT STATUS AS A PROXY FOR ETHNICITY

There are many good reasons for knowing how many first-generation students attend a particular college or university. If institution officials know exactly how many of their students are first-generation students, they are better able to structure campus services and manage the limited resources available for those services. Knowing how many first-generation students attend the institution is a good first step, for example, for devising an institution-wide plan to increase the graduation rate. There are other good reasons as well. New demographic analysis is often the starting point for initiating meaningful change at any institution or organization. One of the more intriguing new ideas becoming associated with counting first-generation students has to do with the desire to provide academic opportunities for ethnic minority students in this era when affirmative action policies are coming under scrutiny and, in most cases, are being rolled back and even abolished. Some education researchers are floating the idea that the first-generation student category might be able to serve as a proxy for ethnicity and race.

Duggan (2001) at least confirmed this rationale, pointing out that "race may have, for all practical purposes, been eliminated by recent federal court decisions as a determining factor in admissions decisions" (p. 2). The politics surrounding the use of race and ethnicity in determining college admission continues to be fluid and volatile, with postsecondary education administrators in different states applying the most current court decisions differently. Certainly, some of the issues facing members of underrepresented minority groups attending college are the same as or similar to the issues facing first-generation students, but much of the usefulness of this idea will hinge on just how many first-generation students are in fact members of ethnic minority groups. Here the numbers are encouraging. According to one study (Saenz, Hurtado, Barrera, Wolf, & Yeung, 2007), 86.8% of first-generation freshmen who entered four-year institutions in fall 2005 were students of color, so the notion that the first-generation student category can serve as a proxy for ethnic minority status has its proponents. Somers et al. (2004), for example, recommend that certain areas of the country could benefit greatly from such a calculus, writing that in "the Mississippi Delta, the Missouri boot heel, and areas with large immigrant and refugee populations—certain institutions will serve large numbers of the F-gen [first-generation] students who are minorities. For these colleges, efforts aimed at improving the attendance and persistence of F-gens will also help minority students" (p. 431).

Even elite private universities are beginning to realize they can position themselves advantageously in the context of the diversity debate by adding first-generation student status to the mix. Stanford University, for example, began counting first-generation students in 2007 and is reporting to the public gains in this area. Stanford's Department of Admissions announced that the enrollment of first-generation students increased from 347 students in 2007 to 431 students in 2008, from 14% of the admitted freshman class of 2007 to 17% of the admitted freshman class of 2008 (Brown, 2008). Minority enrollment at Stanford has remained relatively constant in recent years, so one wonders if this new focus on socioeconomic diversity will come at the expense of minority enrollment (Hardin, 2007). Whatever the strategy for addressing diversity at Stanford may be, it is clear that first-generation students are becoming part of that strategy and are providing a different set of life experiences from those of the more privileged students Stanford has become famous for admitting, rightly or wrongly.

Although few public universities are counting first-generation students yet, some have begun recruiting them as a way of addressing the diversity question, especially to increase diversity in graduate school enrollment. For example, many graduate school applications now include a box applicants can check if they have "McNair Scholar" status. The McNair Scholars Program, a federal TRIO grant program hosted by the undergraduate divisions of four-year colleges and universities, assists high-achieving, nontraditional students in applying to and enrolling in graduate schools. There are currently more than 300 individual McNair Scholars projects located on campuses across the country. Two-thirds of any host institution's McNair Scholars must have both first-generation and low-income status; the other third may have ethnic minority status. Many graduate schools waive application fees for McNair Scholars and sometimes offer other incentives to encourage these students to enroll (Raymond & Black, 2008; Seburn, Chan, & Kirshstein, 2005). There are several reasons why graduate schools might want to know whether an applicant has McNair Scholar status, but the most obvious one is that, when a graduate school admits a McNair Scholar, there is a very good chance it is addressing the diversity of its postbaccalaureate programs. Although Stanford University does not yet have a box applicants can check on its graduate school application, according to Graduate Division Admissions Director Judith Haccou, it is the policy of Stanford academic departments with graduate programs to waive application fees for any applicants who make their McNair Scholar status known to them, and this is the policy of many other graduate schools across the county as well. It is important to include that box on the application, however, and one hopes that Stanford will make the change and join the movement to identify McNair Scholar status, because the box provides an official record that can lead the way for the rest of the institution to follow suit and begin counting first-generation students.

COUNTING THE INSTITUTIONS THAT WILL BE COUNTING FIRST-GENERATION STUDENTS

All of these new first-generation students are going to affect some postsecondary institutions dramatically and others to a lesser degree, but very few such institutions will be able to operate unchanged in the upcoming years. The higher-education establishment is becoming more interested in counting these students, and I predict that it won't be too long before we start counting those institutions that get it right and those that don't. The types of institution these students elect to attend—their structure and mission—will also have some bearing on these matters.

Many community colleges are already at the bursting point, but the community college system will continue to serve more and more students. In fact, enrollment is predicted to increase so much in some areas of the country that access to the community college system may become a problem for certain groups of students (Phelan, 2000). Some institutions may have to restrict enrollments by instituting performance-based criteria for staying enrolled and by limiting the enrollment of students who already hold degrees, among other measures (Phelan, 2000). Many of these institutions are already pulled in multiple directions by varied and complicated missions, and they may have to reorganize services and rethink basic functions to accommodate "the influx of traditional-age students into the system" (Bryant, 2001, p. 77), most of whom will be first-generation students. Although community colleges have always kept the needs of first-generation students in mind, the rush of traditional-age first-generation students may require them to bolster their preparation function, just one of many functions they provide, as a starting point for traditional-age students planning on transferring to four-year colleges and universities to earn a bachelor's degree.

The most populous state in the country, California, with the largest public postsecondary education system, has had ample time to prepare for the large influx of first-generation students, although the jury is still out on whether the system actually has done so. The California postsecondary system has three clearly demarcated tiers similar to those in many other states (which do not, however, always label them as clearly), so the California situation regarding first-generation student enrollment serves as a good model for other states and the country as a whole: These tiers are called the California Community College system (CCC), the California State University system (CSU), and the University of California system (UC). The CSU system comprises 23 teaching-oriented campuses that do not offer doctoral-level programs. The UC system comprises 10 large research-oriented campuses that do offer doctoral-level programs. In 1995, the California Postsecondary Education Commission published a document that has come to be known as Tidal Wave II, which predicted many of the conditions concerning enrollment described earlier. Tidal Wave II warned of a significant increase in enrollment in the CSU and UC systems in 2005, but it described a potentially dire situation for the CCC system, which was going to have to absorb as much as 78.5% of the total 488,030 student increase (California Postsecondary Education Commission, 1995). (Remember that the national percentage of the undergraduate population served by community colleges relative to public four-year institutions is roughly half this 78.5% figure, which is close to the California figure when private four-year institutions are included.) This lopsided distribution was going to come about, the Commission predicted, due to certain actions by the CSU and UC systems, including tightening admissions standards, the decision on the part of the CSU system to limit and eventually curtail delivery of remedial education, and the need to increase fees. All three of these predicted actions increase the likelihood that younger first-generation students will choose the CCC system in California, and all three of them have come to pass (although the CSU system has been unable to stop providing remedial courses completely).

Community colleges all over the nation are experiencing enrollment pressures similar to those at the CCC system, and for the most part, they are going to have to make changes similar to the ones being initiated in California. They have accommodated and will continue to have to accommodate many more traditional-age first-generation students, many of whom will be taking classes offered by community colleges to transfer to four-year institutions.

How are first-generation students distributed among the various postsecondary institution types? First-generation students are more likely to be enrolled in two-year community colleges and private, for-profit professional schools, for example, than are their non-first-generation counterparts (Nuñez & Cuccaro-Alamin, 1998; Phillippe & Patton, 2000). Nuñez and Cuccaro-Alamin (1998) established that 37.2% of non-first-generation students attend public four-year institutions, while 29.4% of first-generation students do; 22.1% of non-first-generation students attend private four-year institutions, while 11.6% of first-generation students do; 34.8% of non-first-generation students attend public two-year institutions, while 44.0% of first-generation students do; and only 3.4% of non-first-generation students attend private for-profit institutions, while 10.7% of first-generation students do.

The kind of institution—how it is structured, how the faculty who teach there see themselves, and how the students who study there see themselves—can determine what kind of student is most likely to succeed there and, by the same token, can determine the intensity of the first-generation student experience. It is important to note, however, that the basic blueprint for the first-generation student experience, described here and in ensuing chapters, is the same for all first-generation students, regardless of the type of institution they attend (Nuñez & Cuccaro-Alamin, 1998; Pascarella, Wolniak, Pierson, & Terenzini, 2003; Pike & Kuh, 2005). Although the blueprint is the same, the *intensity* of the experience—the intensity of both the negative and positive effects of this status—can vary dramatically by type of institution.

The intensity of the first-generation student experience can be lowest in a *community college* environment, for instance, if only because there is generally a higher percentage of first-generation students in the overall student population. Anytime one is attempting to become a member of a new, unfamiliar in-group, seeing a number of familiar faces, a number of people like oneself, can make the acclimation process easier. There are other reasons why the community college setting can be the most comfortable for first-generation students, as we shall see, but the constituency of the student population may be the most important. The intensity of the first-generation student experience can also be fairly low in many *for-profit professional schools*. The less the educational experience is like the traditional college experience, the more comfortable first-generation students may feel there. Some of the characteristics of for-profit professional schools, which often allow students to focus on a single, overarching objective, can be beneficial. If the professional school makes becoming a nurse or a paralegal, for example, the student's single objective, deemphasizing the many other objectives of a traditional college education, it can be the best place for some first-generation students. Because each of the several goals of a more traditional education can be unfamiliar to the first-generation student, not to mention the process of combining them to create a unified perspective, the focus provided by the professional school structure can reduce the psychological pressures that accompany being the first in one's family to attend college.

On the flip side, the first-generation student experience can be the most intense at four-year, degree-granting institutions, both public and private. Because students of all kinds are more likely to be allowed to stay passive about education and potentially become psychologically disaffected, or fall through the cracks, at large *public four-year institutions*, the common opinion is that having first-generation student status will likely cause the most trouble there. The "cafeteria" method of choosing classes and making other important decisions about the academic and cocurricular program can present a significant challenge for first-generation students who are often not sophisticated enough about higher education to make such decisions wisely. Because large public four-year institutions can make even non-first-generation students behave like first-generation students—their size and rigidly bureaucratic procedures causing students of all kinds to fall through the cracks—the typical challenges all first-generation students must face can become intensified, even multiplied there. But what about *private* four-year institutions? Some researchers suggest that smaller *private four-year institutions*—with their greater ability to acknowledge differences between student needs while still providing a more universal program of study—are better locations for first-generation college students (Pascarella, Pierson, Wolniak, & Terenzini, 2004). But not so fast. Sure, the focus on the individual may allow first-generation students to feel more like they matter, but it may also have the unintended effect of publicizing just how different the first-generation student experience is from the non-first-generation student experience. Instructors and researchers in today's political postsecondary environment who favor identity fragmentation theories over identity unification theories often overlook how comforting the normalization effect of going to college can be. They may not appreciate that many first-generation students prefer to blend into the landscape, at least at first, rather than feel like an alien feature of that landscape. So private four-year institutions can be problematic as well.

To sum up, the number of students entering the American system of higher education is growing at a rate that far outstrips the declining number of college-age Americans, not because of larger families but because of increased access to higher education for all American families (including recently immigrated families). For this and other reasons, it is fair to say that most of the recent increase in the number of college students has comprised first-generation college students, and that future increases also will be made up mostly of first-generation students for the next 10 to 15 years or more. This is a fair predication based on the literature cited in this chapter. The important thing to realize, however, is that these are only predictions for now because institutions do not count first-generation college students. When we do start counting them, the truth of these statements may change.

At some point, of course, enrollment of first-generation college students will level off as the daughters and sons of this bulge of first-generation students enter the system. When these sons and daughters begin their postsecondary education, they will not be first-generation students, of course, and the growth curve will begin to level off and, at some point, perhaps even begin a downward trend. Should this happen, it must be cause for celebration in both the education community and the wider American population, for it will mean that a higher proportion of new college graduates will have been first-generation students, and those graduates will be raising non-first-generation children who attend college. It will be a sign that we are finally making good on the promise that all Americans should have access to a quality education. But this will happen only if today's first-generation college students are retained at an acceptable rate and graduate at an acceptable rate, and they will be retained and graduate at acceptable rates only if they receive the specialized support they need to be successful.

Even if the retention and graduation rates of first-generation students do increase (and there is little sign of this happening yet, as we shall see shortly and again in chapter 2), the more competitive business environment in which American colleges and universities find themselves almost guarantees that institutional officials will soon become very interested in knowing how many first-generation students they have and, more important, very interested in knowing how to help them succeed. American colleges and universities will become interested because the ones that earn a reputation for knowing how best to assist first-generation students will likely be the most successful postsecondary institutions of the future.

NOW IS THE TIME FOR ACTION

The statistics show that now is the time for action. Although the term "first-generation college students" is used more today on American campuses than it was 20 years ago, first-generation students still need to make much more progress before their academic performance approaches the performance of their non-first-generation counterparts. The Nuñez and Cuccaro-Alamin study (1998) tracked the performance of beginning first-generation students entering the higher-education system in the fall 1989 semester. After five years, 55.0% of these students were still enrolled or had earned a college degree or professional certificate. This figure also represents, of course, a dropout rate of 45.0%. Non-first-generation students did significantly better: After five years, 71.3% were still enrolled in the institution or had earned a college degree or professional certificate (Nuñez & Cuccaro-Alamin, 1998). The dropout rate for non-first-generation students, then, was just 28.7%. Summing up, Nuñez and Cuccaro-Alamin reported that the first-generation students in their study were more than 40% more likely to drop out within five years of enrollment than were their more privileged counterparts.

A more recent NCES study (Chen & Carroll, 2005) described an even bleaker situation. This study examined the transcripts of students entering the American postsecondary system for the first time in 1992. The researchers were able to draw conclusions about the academic performance of first-generation students in a number of areas, including graduation rates. First-generation students enrolled in four-year-degree-granting colleges and universities in 1992 were only half as likely to earn a bachelor's degree *eight* years later than were their non-first-generation counterparts—34% and 68%, respectively (Chen & Carroll, 2005). This study did not examine the five- or six-year graduation rate.

Just as we should consider the kinds of institutions in which first-generation students are enrolling when we consider overall enrollment numbers, we should also consider the kinds of institutions students are staying in when we consider retention and graduation rates. As we have already seen, first-generation students are more likely to enroll in two-year community colleges and private for-profit professional institutions than are non-first-generation students, and this fact may have some bearing on the retention and graduation rates cited. Assuming that it is easier for first-generation students to remain in two-year institutions—for financial, academic, and other reasons—leads to the conclusion that the gap between the five-year retention rate of first-generation students and that of non-first-generation students *in four-year institutions* is even wider than the 16.3% difference noted.

As one might predict, first-generation students earn two- and four-year degrees at rates significantly lower than those of their non-first-generation counterparts. For instance, only 13.3% of the first-generation students who entered the postsecondary education system in the fall 1989 semester had earned a bachelor's degree five years later, while 32.5% of non-first-generation students had (Nuñez & Cuccaro-Alamin, 1998). This pattern holds less strongly for two-year degrees: 12.9% of the first-generation students entering in the fall semester of 1989 earned an associate degree, while 14.0% of non-first-generation students earned such a degree (Nuñez & Cuccaro-Alamin, 1998).

All of the state and national education statistics (California Postsecondary Education Commission, 1995; Chen & Carroll, 2005; Choy, 2001; Nuñez & Cuccaro-Alamin, 1998) indicate that the time is now for postsecondary institutions to get serious about addressing the needs of first-generation students. By putting together some of these statistics with their own experience, many educators are beginning to see the light, and one hopes the statistics quoted in this book can accelerate the process. To tie everything together at the end of this chapter, all we need is a close examination of a single institution. In this spirit of thoroughness, allow me to introduce Sonoma State University (SSU). As mentioned in the introduction, the material on SSU presented in this book, including the narratives written by SSU students that comprise chapter 4, allows the reader access to the first-generation student experience in the most personal way possible. The material on SSU balances the dichotomy between the lived experience of real, individual students and the necessarily more general discussion of the student group category, which is the main subject of this book. Knowing something about SSU will make reading the chapter 4 narratives more meaningful.

Describing, analyzing, and promoting the first-generation student category will directly affect all members of the category eventually, but this process occurs over a period of years. In the meantime, to keep the insights

into the first-generation student experience authentic and the recommendations on practice comprising chapter 6 relevant, we cannot lose sight of the
actual individual students who struggle against the odds to obtain a college
degree.

SONOMA STATE UNIVERSITY

Sonoma State University is a relatively small institution (7,000 to 8,000
students) dedicated to the liberal arts and sciences located 50 miles north of
San Francisco, near the wine-growing regions of Sonoma County. It qualifies
as a public Master's University by the Carnegie Foundation's description
standard and is one campus in the 23-campus CSU system. Sonoma State
possesses features that make it unique in the CSU system, but one feature it
has in common with all the other campuses (and most American universities
everywhere, for that matter) is that its officials do not know how many first-
generation college students are enrolled. Some SSU officials have a general
idea of how many first-generation students attend SSU, and most of them
know what the term *first-generation college student* means, although a
single definition is far from established there. SSU officials can tell you
exactly how many Latino and African American students are enrolled, and
they can tell you exactly how many students with disabilities are enrolled,
but they cannot tell you exactly how many first-generation students are
enrolled.

Like college and university officials everywhere, when it comes to first-
generation students, SSU officials have to estimate. One of the worst ways
to estimate how many first-generation students attend SSU is by using the
CSU Application for Undergraduate Admission. Question 38 on the
2008–09 application reads, "What are your parents' highest levels of formal
education?" This is followed by instructions to "Enter code in box for:
Mother and Father." There are seven possibilities (or "codes"): 1—No High
School; 2—Some High School; 3—High School Graduate; 4—Some College; 5—2-Year College Graduate; 6—4-Year College Graduate; and
7—Postgraduate. Assuming the data captured from the CSU application are
transferred accurately to the appropriate campus after student conversion,
the first problem SSU officials encounter in attempting to extract and communicate meaningful information from these data is that question 38 is

clearly marked "optional." More than one-third of prospective students simply do not answer it. The second problem has to do with the way prospective students perceive the application process. Most applicants see it, as they should, as part of the competitive process of being accepted for enrollment, which means there is considerable pressure on prospective students to represent themselves in as positive a light as possible. Even though having first-generation status or not having first-generation status has nothing to do with whether an individual is accepted into the CSU system, prospective students who would answer question 38 with a 1, 2, or 3 are more likely not to answer it at all. Thus, using the CSU application to ascertain the number of first-generation students attending SSU would likely skew the numbers downward, underestimating how many first-generation students attend SSU.

A better (and perhaps the only) way to estimate how many first-generation students attend SSU is through the CIRP freshman survey. The standardized CIRP survey is administered to the incoming freshman class at about 400 of the nation's baccalaureate colleges and universities every year (Saenz et al., 2007). At SSU, enrolled first-time freshmen attending orientation complete the survey before the start of the fall semester. Survey respondents, then, are actual enrolled students who have not yet taken an SSU course. When using the CIRP survey to determine how many first-time freshmen attend SSU, however, we should keep a number of factors in mind. Although a majority of first-time freshmen attend SSU orientations, not all of them do; the figure remains about 75% from year to year. Another thing to consider is that these students may not be exactly representative of all first-time freshmen; for instance, students attending orientations are likely to be more engaged in the education process than are their nonattending peers. Furthermore, first-time freshmen are not exactly representative of all SSU undergraduates—that is, they are not representative of juniors, seniors, or five-year seniors, etc. CIRP surveys from the fall 2004 semester to the fall 2007 semester show that an average of 34.5% of respondents were first-generation students. This is lower, it is worth noting, than the 43.4% figure reported in the Nuñez and Cuccaro-Alamin (1998) study for all American postsecondary institutions.

One could argue that the 34.5% figure is high for representing the first-generation student population for any given year by pointing out that this figure is generated by surveying students who have yet to attend a single class and by citing the research that shows first-generation students are more likely to drop out and "stop out" (an enrollment interruption for one semester or more) than are non-first-generation students. But characteristics of the SSU student population that might make the 34.5% figure *high* for representing the first-generation student population for any given year are more than compensated for by characteristics of the student population that might make the 34.5% figure *low* for representing the first-generation student population. First among these characteristics, perhaps, is the status of transfer students. At SSU, transfer students are mostly juniors. Transfer students, especially community college transfer students, are more likely to have first-generation status than are nontransfer students, and transfer students are not included in the CIRP survey.

When SSU officials talk about the number of first-generation students enrolled at their institution, they base what they say (if they base it on anything at all) on the data produced by the CIRP survey. It is not unusual to hear them say, for instance, that about 40% of the SSU student population is first-generation—and 40% probably is not too far off the mark. The point here, though, is that when SSU officials talk about the number of first-generation students enrolled at the university, they can only estimate this number; there is no way to know for sure.

Although SSU officials may have to estimate how many first-generation students they have in attendance, most—like college and university officials everywhere—are gradually beginning to understand how important first-generation students are to the institution. SSU is one of the campuses in the CSU system designated for fairly rapid growth in the next decade, and unlike the enrollment conditions at other institutions, the university has had to lower admissions standards slightly in past years to make target enrollment numbers. This means that students with slightly lower GPAs and slightly lower SAT scores are being admitted. This also means, as we shall see, that a high percentage of these slightly less able and slightly less prepared students will likely be first-generation students. All things being equal, growth is almost never a hardship for an institution like SSU in the long term. It is true that class sizes usually increase in the short term, and other undesirable outcomes can also result, but in the long term, growth means more opportunities for everyone—faculty, administrators, and students alike. And for institutions like SSU to grow, they need first-generation college students. Without them, there will be no growth.

Part of the reason that postsecondary institution officials have not paid enough attention to their first-generation student populations—in terms of their special needs and difficulties—is that they do not know exactly how many they have. More and more, they know first-generation students are there, but they do not know *exactly* how many are enrolled. And institutions are not likely to begin the time-consuming business of forming and transforming curriculum and policies to better serve first-generation students without knowing exactly how many such students they have enrolled. This is the first step and the most important and overriding recommendation of this volume: Officials and progressive institutions need to establish procedures for determining exactly how many first-generation students they have. The rest will follow.

NOTES

1. Not all students planning to attend or already attending a college or university fill out the FAFSA, even though many colleges and universities suggest they do. Although some students, even some low-income students, who could benefit from federal financial aid don't fill it out, most college and university officials assume the main reason some students don't fill out the FAFSA is because they don't need the money. Not filling out the FAFSA, in other words, is regarded in most cases as evidence that the student is not a low-income individual.

2. The Nuñez and Cuccaro-Alamin (1998) study uses a tripartite scheme for establishing first-generation status: (1) "first-generation students," (2) "students whose parent(s) had some college," and (3) "students whose parent(s) had bachelor's or higher degree." The point here is that the tripartite definition excludes "students whose parent(s) had some college" from belonging to the student category, whereas the definition advocated for and used in this book includes "students whose parent(s) had some college" in this category. This tripartite division was converted into the more familiar binary division to produce the 43.4% figure.

3. The CIRP report surveying incoming 2006 freshmen, *The American Freshman: National Norms for Fall 2006*, provides further evidence of the large number of first-generation college students in the American postsecondary education system. The report's findings "are based on the weighted responses of 271,441 students at 393 of the nation's baccalaureate colleges and universities. These data have been statistically adjusted to reflect the responses of the 1.3 million first-time, full-time students entering four-year colleges and universities as freshmen in 2006" (Pryor et al., 2007, p. 3). Respondents were asked for information about their parents' level of education, but because the report's methodology (common among many data-gathering organizations) does not compare the responses for "mother" with the

responses for "father," there is no way to determine the status of the child with regard to the *combined* level of education of the "mother" *and* "father." In other words, the report provides information on the level of education of each respondent's "mother" and each respondent's "father," but it does not provide information on whether each respondent's "mother" *or* "father" has a four-year degree, which is needed to determine how many of the respondents are first-generation students. With this methodology in mind, the CIRP report reveals that 47.2% of the respondents' mothers did not have a college degree, and that 47.1% of the respondents' fathers did not have a college degree (Pryor et al., 2007, p. 22). These figures do not include students attending community colleges; if the study did include such students, the figures would be much higher.

4. *The Chronicle of Higher Education* (Almanac Issue 2008–09, 2008), reports virtually the same projected numbers. *The Chronicle* projects 18.8 million students enrolled in American degree-granting institutions in 2010 and 20.1 million students in 2015 (p. 16).

2

The Observable Behaviors of First-Generation College Students

C HAPTER I ESTABLISHED ROUGHLY *how many* first-generation college students are enrolled in American postsecondary institutions and maintained that their numbers are increasing dramatically compared to their non-first-generation counterparts. In addition, these increasing numbers have largely escaped the notice of postsecondary education administrators, faculty, and staff members. Now that we have a sense of how many first-generation students are out there, the next step is to describe *what characteristics* they possess as postsecondary students: What life skills do they arrive with as freshmen, for example? How do their academic needs manifest themselves? How do they behave and perform as undergraduates? Chapter 2 illustrates that being a first-generation college student is no small thing. In fact, it is a very big thing . . . and it affects every dimension of being a college student.

First-generation college students have one main characteristic that separates them from students in other demographic categories and makes them recognizable to one another. Simply stated, first-generation college students are unfamiliar with the culture of college and, to one degree or another, unfamiliar with what it means to be a college student. By unfamiliar with the "culture" of college, I mean primarily that first-generation students are new to the insider knowledge, the special language, and the subtle verbal and nonverbal signals that, after one has mastered them, make one a member of any in-group, community, or subculture. Many people with only a passing knowledge of the first-generation student experience believe that this lack of familiarity can be addressed and overcome easily by showing students how to get around campus, where to pay fees, and what classes to take; however, becoming familiar with the culture of college is much more complicated than this. Although navigating the bureaucratic organization of postsecondary institutions is an important skill for all students to master, first-generation college students must also master a more profound set of skills and behaviors, the complicated and subtle ways of being that are required of contemporary college students everywhere. They must learn quickly how to fit in or learn quickly how to be comfortable despite not fitting in.

The first few weeks at college are stressful for all students. The transition from home culture to college culture can be traumatic, and all students usually need downtime to think through what they are doing and what is expected of them.

In their initial isolation, many first-generation students make the mistake of limiting themselves to one or two sources of information on the culture of college. At least in the beginning, they do not seek out the many different sources of information that are available to them. Even first-generation freshmen usually can locate *official* sources of information on the culture of college. They often make contact fairly quickly with academic advisors, financial aid officers, and even faculty members, people whom we might call *experts* on the culture of college, people who are so familiar with the culture of college that they have internalized much of their insider knowledge—of education jargon, for instance, and of the signals and rules that comprise so much of in-group behavior. Navigating on automatic pilot, experts know this stuff so well they do not have to think about it anymore. They are full of advice about annual events such as fee deadlines, class scheduling, and mandatory testing because this is the way they mark time in their work environment, but they often are less helpful when it comes to learning how to behave as a member of the culture of college and how to perform the role. And learning how to behave is crucial to learning how to be comfortable in the postsecondary environment. It can be difficult for some institution officials to put themselves in the shoes of first-generation students because they have internalized the rules of behavior so completely and, perhaps even more important, because they likely were not first-generation students themselves as undergraduates.

Not much information on the first-generation status of college faculty and administrators exists in the literature. Faculty members become faculty members for many different reasons and by many different means; some pursued their undergraduate and graduate education with very little assistance from their families, and some received lots of material and nonmaterial assistance from their families. However, when considering the backgrounds of college faculty, especially older faculty, do not forget the iron grip of privilege that has influenced academic achievement for so long in the United States. Because first-generation college students have only been attending American institutions of higher learning in significant numbers for a relatively short time, it stands to reason that many faculty members, holders of advanced degrees, let us remember, were not first-generation students when they were undergraduates. Realize that a family history of college attendance usually takes more than one generation to develop (National Center for Education Statistics, 1993; Seburn, Chan, & Kirshstein, 2005). At Sonoma State University, for example, this proves to be true. A survey administered in 2008 revealed that 44.0% of SSU faculty were first-generation students when they were undergraduates, but this is not the whole story.

There are a couple of reasons why students at SSU are even more likely than the 44%:56% ratio might indicate to have contact with faculty who were not first-generation students when they were undergraduates than with faculty who were. This same rationale applies to other institutions as well. One reason the 44%:56% ratio may swing even farther in the direction of non-first-generation faculty has to do with the survey itself. Although the survey was anonymous, nontenured or non-tenure-track faculty are less likely to respond to any question about their personal history than are tenured or tenure-track faculty, and at SSU, faculty who were first-generation students when they were undergraduates are less likely to be tenured or tenure track than are faculty who were not. Also, 80.3% of faculty participating in the survey who were not first-generation students when they were undergraduates reported having a full-time teaching load, while only 68.8% of faculty who were first-generation students when they were undergraduates reported having a full-time teaching load. Instructors with full-time teaching loads have contact with more students than do instructors who teach only part time.

The lack of understanding of the first-generation student experience these figures represent affects how first-generation students are received at SSU. Most SSU faculty know that first-generation students are sitting in their classes thinking first-generation thoughts, but too many of them do not know from experience what those first-generation thoughts might be. They do not know what it is like, for example, to be afraid to raise your hand in a college class, not because you are afraid of giving a wrong answer but because you are not sure college classrooms work that way, not sure raising your hand while a professor is speaking is something college students are supposed to do.

LEARNING THE CULTURE OF COLLEGE

Novices learning a new culture almost always benefit from having a variety of sources of information about that culture. It is possible, of course, to learn a lot about French culture by talking solely to experts on French culture—for example, French-language teachers or travel agents specializing in trips to Europe. It goes without saying that one can also learn a lot about French culture by talking to French citizens and observing their behavior, but for getting the most out of your Provence vacation, there is nothing quite like touring the Provençal region with someone from your own culture who has vacationed in Provence many times before, a person who has tried to fit in and who knows the culture from the outside in. Such a person likely has not internalized the rules of behavior completely, so he or she makes a perfect *guide*, one who can explain how to behave and show you what to expect.

The same is true for first-generation college students. Although it might seem counterintuitive, most first-generation students do not need an *expert* to introduce them to the culture of college; they need a *guide*. Experts are fairly easy to find; guides are not. Many non-first-generation students receive information about the culture of college from guides such as their parents, other family members, and family friends. These people are not experts, but they know the culture of college from the outside in. They tell stories about living in the residence halls and about butting heads with difficult professors. They pass on what is often called generational wisdom. Frequently, the transmission of this information from guides starts very early on, before the recipients are old enough to understand fully what they are hearing. Non-first-generation students grow up with guides to the culture of college by their side. First-generation students, of course, have a completely different experience. They are often encouraged by sympathetic family members to follow their dream of a college education, but first-generation students typically get precious little information from family members about how one actually goes about realizing this dream. If first-generation students need guides to help them learn the culture of college and guides are hard to come by, progressive institutions interested in improving the success of first-generation students will have to supply them. Institutions do this in a variety of ways, as we shall see, but there is no question that first-generation students do better when they have access to guide information. I like the term "guide information" to describe what first-generation students need, because it incorporates the notion that, for many first-generation students, becoming comfortable in the postsecondary education environment is an ongoing and sometimes lengthy process, a process they need to be guided through. In other words, it takes a long time (about 18 years, in most cases) to become *intuitively oriented toward college*, as most non-first-generation students are, by absorbing stories, opinions, and attitudes about college from parents, other family members, and friends. What progressive college and university administrators should do is construct an educational environment in which their first-generation charges can catch up, an environment in which these students can approximate being oriented intuitively toward college.

FIRST-GENERATION STATUS IS NOT THE SAME AS LOW-INCOME STATUS

By definition, then, the main, overarching characteristic of first-generation college students is their unfamiliarity with the culture of college. Before getting into their other more specific characteristics, it is important to address what many people, including many postsecondary educators, falsely believe is another of their main characteristics. Many people believe that first-generation students are also low-income individuals, but this simply is not true.

Some first-generation students are low-income individuals, of course, just as some African American students are low-income individuals, and some White students are. As every American schoolkid knows, earning power in the United States is correlated strongly with educational attainment. U.S. Census Bureau data (2006) show that workers with a bachelor's degree earn an average of $51,206 a year, while those with only a high school diploma earn an average of $27,915 (Longley, 2005). In addition, workers with a graduate degree make an average of $74,602, and those without a high school diploma make only $18,734 (Longley, 2005). It is because of this relationship between earning power and educational attainment, I believe, among other reasons, that many people just assume most first-generation college students come from low-income families. But let us look carefully at the figures; according to the National Center for Education Statistics (NCES) (Nuñez & Cuccaro-Alamin, 1998), 18.0% of first-generation students reported family income in the lowest quartile, while only 2.2% of non-first-generation students reported family income in the lowest quartile—a big difference, for sure, but this is hardly the end of the story, because 56.7% of first-generation students reported family income in the two middle quartiles, and 25.3% reported family income in the highest quartile. According to these statistics, then, less than one-quarter of first-generation students come from low-income families reporting income in the lowest quartile. Given such a reality, it is not safe at all to assume that first-generation students are also low-income individuals compared with the overall U.S. population. Their families do report less family income than non-first-generation student families, but the difference is less than you might imagine. The percentage of income to poverty rate of first-generation student families, for example, is only 22% less than the percentage of income to poverty rate of non-first-generation student families (Hahs-Vaughn, 2004). First-generation student families do report less income, but they should not be compared with non-first-generation student families when considering socioeconomic status. When considering such status, first-generation student families should be compared with the set of all American families. When compared with the set of all American families, first-generation student families represent the whole range of income levels, as we have seen, and are more likely to report incomes in the highest quartile than the lowest.

This misidentification with low-income status is one important reason why the first-generation student category has not crystallized in the same way that some other student demographic categories have. There are other reasons, too, among them confusion over the term "first-generation," for this same language is applied in the discourse on immigration and ethnicity status and in other contexts as well. For many people, including many post-secondary educators, the terms "first-generation student" and "low-income student" are synonymous. The two groups of students have the same needs and concerns, these people believe, and higher-education institutions should enact the same policies and programs to help both groups. And because there has been much more research on low-income students, and many more studies and papers published on the performance and academic difficulties of low-income students, it is very easy for uninformed people to make the mistake of thinking the two categories are interchangeable (Hahs-Vaughn, 2004). Another goal of this book, then, is to differentiate the concerns of first-generation students from those of low-income students, and even when they do have similar concerns, to suggest that a low-income background causes individuals to address those concerns differently from the way those with a first-generation-*only* background address them. Of course, when first-generation students are also low-income—18.0% of them do report family income in the lowest quartile—they do get a double whammy. The message of this volume is informed by researchers such as Lohfink and Paulsen (2005), who found that low-income status in the first-generation student population affected persistence in a dramatically negative way, suggesting that the barriers and challenges of first-generation student status are separate from the barriers and challenges of low-income status. "First generation students come from diverse social class backgrounds, have different amounts and types of cultural and financial capital, and access and manipulate capital and financial resource differently in their persistence decisions" (p. 418). Engle and Tinto (2008) found that first-generation students who are also low-income individuals were nearly four times as likely (26% to 7%) as their non-first-generation, non-low-income counterparts to drop out after one year of study. The double whammy should be understood, therefore, as having the characteristic difficulties of being a low-income individual added to the characteristic difficulties of being a first-generation student.

The First-Generation Student Experience: Implications for Campus Practice, and Strategies for Improving Persistence and Success is intended as a guide for developing better understanding of the first-generation student experience. Although it is necessary to refer to the precollege experience of first-generation students from time to time (especially at the beginning of the next section of this chapter), this book is not intended to be a critique of the American K–12 school system. The academic performance and psychological well-being of any college students, no doubt, will have something to do with the training they received during their K–12 schooling, as expert in the retention of college students Tinto (1993) and other researchers have shown (Choy, 2001; Horn & Bobbitt, 2000), but the precollege experience of first-generation students for the most part is outside the scope of this book.

What follows is a detailed description of what we know about the behaviors and performance of first-generation college students derived from both the author's many years teaching, advising, and counseling them and a survey of scholarly literature on the subject. These behaviors are divided into two major sections: (1) Learning at College and (2) Campus Presence. Section One describes where first-generation students come from, academically speaking, and how where they come from affects the way they learn at college. It is divided into six subsections: Precollege Preparation, Being Underprepared at College, Learning How to Study, Different Way of Learning, New Way of Perceiving the World, and Learning About Majors. Section Two, which describes how first-generation students make their presence known on college campuses, is divided into four subsections: The Imposter Phenomenon, Differences in the Classroom, Alternative Ways of Support, and Validating the Presence of First-Generation Students.

SECTION ONE: LEARNING AT COLLEGE

Precollege Preparation

It has been known for some years that good academic performance in mathematics in middle and high school is strongly correlated, not only with good performance in mathematics in college, but also with good academic performance in college in general. Students with a strong background in math and a high self-estimate of their math skills are more likely to enroll in four-year institutions more quickly after high school, more likely to stay enrolled in four-year institutions, and more likely to graduate with a bachelor's degree in a timely manner than are students with a weak background in math and low self-estimate of their math skills (Horn & Bobbitt, 2000; Oakes, 1989; Pascarella & Terenzini, 2005). Planning for college and patterns in course taking are established as early as the seventh and eighth grades, where algebra rather than general math is widely considered a gateway course needed to progress to advanced math courses in high school (Cabrera & La Nasa, 2001). Taking advanced math courses (any course beyond algebra 2, such as precalculus, calculus, trigonometry, algebra 3) in high school "more than doubled" the chances of a first-generation student enrolling in a four-year institution (Horn & Bobbit, 2000, p. viii). Oakes (1989) reported in her groundbreaking study that students in underrepresented groups are more likely to take courses outside of what she calls the "scientific pipeline . . . a critical sequence of precollege and college events that provide[s] students with the prerequisites for adult participation [in science and math]" (p. 12). Taking courses outside of the "scientific pipeline" is not only an indicator that the student might have difficulty in college science and math courses but also an indicator that the student might have difficulty in college in general.

Because the delivery of math instruction is so rigidly linear (understanding new concepts in math depends on understanding old concepts taught the year before) in most American middle and high schools, students can fall behind quickly. Further, because keeping a child on track depends at least in part on understanding the highly bureaucratic advancement structure of American middle and high schools, children of parents who did not go to college—whose parents, therefore, are likely to be less skilled at navigating this bureaucratic structure—are more likely to fall behind than are children whose parents did go to college, regardless of the individual student's ability to perform well in math courses. Sometimes ensuring your middle or high school child's success in math or science is simply a matter of getting the child into the class that is right for him or her. Some parents who have not gone to college do not fully grasp this fact of life in the public schools, nor do they fully grasp how choices concerning education made when children are in middle school can have a large impact on college preparedness and even on getting into college. Currently, there are countless college students in this country who say, "I can't do math" or "I have math anxiety," when asked to do a task that requires even average math competency. The parents of non-first-generation students are more likely than are the parents of first-generation students to nip this kind of thinking in the bud when they hear it, not just because they know math is important, but because they know having adequate preparation in math is part of having the proper orientation toward college.

What this precollege reality means, among other things, is that first-generation college students are more likely to arrive at four-year institutions with a weak background in math and are more likely to be enrolled in remedial math classes during their first year of study (Strayhorn, 2006). Although first-generation students are more likely to need remedial courses than are their non-first-generation counterparts, research shows some of them can catch up (Horn & Bobbitt, 2000). That is to say, they *can* catch up, but it often takes extra attention from the institution in the form of tutoring or supplemental instruction to make this happen.

Not always but certainly often enough, first-generation college students do arrive at postsecondary institutions less prepared, academically and in other ways, than their non-first-generation counterparts. Sometimes this is because they attended low-performing high schools, and sometimes it is because they chose a less than rigorous course of study at average or high-performing high schools (Harrell & Forney, 2003; Martinez, Sher, Krull, & Wood, 2009; Pascarella, Pierson, Wolniak, & Terenzini, 2004). Parents of first-generation students can be less aware of how poor 7th- through 12th-grade preparation can negatively affect their child in college and how certain of their actions, such as moving a child from school to school, can negatively affect academic performance (Horn & Carroll, 1997). College professors and administrators should recognize that first-generation college students' special lack of preparedness can be a significant barrier to success, but they should also recognize that it can be addressed successfully.

Being Underprepared at College

McConnell (2000) and others (Fenske, Porter, & DuBrock, 2000; Ishitani, 2005; Pascarella et al., 2004) reported that first-generation and other nontraditional students enter college with lower reading, math, and critical-thinking skills. First-generation students have lower SAT scores and lower high school GPAs (Warburton et al. 2001). Especially during their first year of attendance, first-generation students often demonstrate significantly lower academic performance than do their non-first-generation counterparts (Martinez et al., 2009; Pascarella et al., 2004). The 2001 National Center for Education Statistics study (Warburton et al., 2001) on the preparation and postsecondary success of first-generation students reported that the average first-year GPA of non-first-generation students beginning in the fall 1995 semester was 2.7, and the first-year GPA for first-generation students was only 2.4. In addition, first-generation students often find managing complicated financial affairs a burden, especially if the financial aid office is involved, and that managing hectic daily schedules can be a hindrance to academic performance. McConnell (2000) reported that, in comparison with non-first-generation students, first-generation students predict they will make lower grades in college, so self-efficacy and self-esteem appear to be issues as well.

If first-generation students recognize deficits in their preparedness for college like those just described, they start their postsecondary careers knowing they have some catching up to do. Many of them begin with the idea that they will have to study harder than do their non-first-generation counterparts. It has been my experience that they do tend to study harder, at least at first. Generally, they begin their first semester like a house on fire but then become bewildered and maybe even disillusioned about halfway through when their extra efforts do not appear to be paying off. There are probably many reasons for this pattern, which is familiar to all academic advisors, but the most important reason, the research suggests, is that first-generation college students often do not know *how* to study very well (Filkins & Doyle, 2002; Terenzini, Springer, Yaeger, Pascarella, & Nora, 1996; Treisman, 1992). They know they have to do the homework, and they have to put in the hours, but they may not know how to study *for performance* during those hours, so they may not be able to perform what they have learned. First-generation students may not know how to read for data attainment, or conversely, they may read *only* for data attainment when it is not appropriate. The result is that first-generation students spend less time studying overall than do their non-first-generation counterparts (Pascarella et al., 2004; Terenzini et al., 1996). Filkins and Doyle (2002) and Duggan (2001) report that one of the best ways to rectify this situation is by enrolling first-generation college students in study groups: "Not participating in a study group with other students decreases the odds of persistence to the second year" (Duggan, 2001, p. 9). Duggan does not offer an explanation for why this is the case, but these findings and others suggest that a lack of study skills is at the heart of the matter. It could be that first-generation students need the example of other students when they are struggling with new ideas, or it could be that studying alone is more formidable than educators have realized. Most likely, it is a combination of these and other factors. Duggan goes on to suggest that administrators and schedulers can have a big impact on the success of first-generation students by "actively promoting student participation in study groups" (p. 9). Other researchers have delved more deeply into the question. Filkins and Doyle (2002), for example, found that first-generation students embraced the concept of "learning effectively on your own" (p. 15) if they perceived the campus environment to be welcoming and supportive. Findings such as these might lead us to believe that when first-generation students begin their postsecondary careers, they must overcome the nagging suspicion that they will have trouble being a college student if left to their own devices. Being a college student is simply too much for them to do all by themselves.

Learning How to Study

Study skills is one area where private four-year institutions and community colleges may be able to make life a little easier for first-generation students. Larger public four-year institutions are more likely to expect all of their students to know how to study already, or simply to ignore the topic of study skills altogether. Ignoring the topic is surprisingly easy for institutions to do, and it is very widespread (Weinstein, & Mayer, 1983; Wingate, 2006). This is because study skills as a topic suffers from a double bind; on the one hand, most faculty consider such skills as subacademic, and on the other, study skills are difficult to teach. With their focus on the individual student rather than on a generalized student ideal, private four-year institutions are more likely to address what are often regarded as personal gaps in a student's preparation. And community colleges, for their part, may simply regard teaching study skills as part of the curriculum; this is not to suggest they always do it well, just that it is more likely to be on a community college instructor's list of areas to cover.

Complicating the matter, many postsecondary faculty are not inclined to regard learning on one's own as a skill they can address directly during classroom discussion and improve through guidance and practice. Learning, studying, and preparing on their own is one of the things faculty are paid to do, and they do it very well, but many of them do it without examining the process very closely. And too many of them do not teach it. For many first-generation college students, on the other hand, the various abstract mental processes that go into effective solitary study are unfamiliar and difficult to master. Their parents are unlikely to have modeled these processes for them, and if they have not received better-than-average training in grades 7–12, they are not likely to have learned them from precollege teachers. Being able to learn on your own, mind you, has nothing to do with scores on the Stanford-Binet test or any other so-called test of intelligence. Like most other skills required of college students, learning on your own is a skill that can be learned, but many first-generation students will need the steps clearly delineated for them to fully grasp certain concepts, abstract connections, and other mental processes for which they have little or no context. After they are introduced to such concepts, given the opportunity to practice them and get better, they will perform in this area just as well as their non-first-generation counterparts.

It bears repeating that first-generation college students need to be introduced directly to the methods and procedures of efficient study. If they are not introduced to them, they will continue to study by their own methods, not knowing that they need help in learning how to study. This was one of the findings of University of California at Berkeley mathematics professor Uri Treisman, who wanted to find out why his nontraditional calculus students did so poorly in his classes. These were nontraditional students, he knew, but they were also very able and motivated students—accepted at one of the most prestigious universities in the country, after all—yet still they failed. Treisman (1992) eventually found out that one reason nontraditional students did poorly was that they tended to study *only* by themselves. Only 10% studied with other classmates, while traditional students were much more likely to do so. Treisman goes further with his famous prescription for helping nontraditional students excel at math, but exposing them to the benefits of studying with other students is at the heart of the process. "We were able to convince the students in our orientation that success in college would require them to work with their peers to create for themselves a community based on shared intellectual interests and common professional aims" (p. 370). The conclusion we should draw from Treisman's work is that first-generation students not only need to be introduced to the methods and procedures of solitary study, they need to be shown the virtues of studying with peers as well.

Different Way of Learning

It goes without saying, of course, that first-generation students are as intelligent as their non-first-generation counterparts. What may not be as obvious, however, is that first-generation students think and learn *differently* from their non-first-generation counterparts. By administering the Collegiate Assessment of Academic Proficiency (CAAP) test to some 3,840 college students, Terenzini and others (1996) determined that the cognitive skills of first-generation college students were "weaker" than the cognitive skills of non-first-generation students. The CAAP test for precollege students consists of five 40-minute multiple-choice modules, but only three—reading, math, and critical thinking—were used in the 1996 Terenzini et al. study. Other studies (Filkins & Doyle, 2002; Pascarella & Terenzini, 2005) also have found that first-generation students have weaker cognitive skills, especially at the beginning of their college careers.

Possessing weak cognitive skills can be difficult to overcome for some first-generation students, who always feel as if they are one step behind their non-first-generation peers anyway and who often try harder than their peers with fewer positive results. Although overcoming weak cognitive skills is not easy, many first-generation students make great strides in this area before they graduate. It is interesting to note that Terenzini, Springer, Taeger, Pascarella, and Nora (1995) found that the campus environment played a big role in how quickly students made up their cognitive skills deficits. At least in the area of critical thinking, colleges and universities might maximize the gains students make, Terenzini et al. wrote, "by finding ways to promote their campus environment as one that values critical thinking, evaluative, and analytical skills" (p. 14).

This linking of academic performance to the academic environment comes up repeatedly in the research literature on first-generation college students (Chaffee, 1992; Clauss-Ehlers & Wibrowski, 2007; Rendón, 1995). The message is obvious: First-generation students do better when they feel aligned with the general purposes and goals of the institution and when they are confident their behavior conforms to the way they believe non-first-generation students behave. In other words, the more institutions make the academic life visible and accessible to everyone, the more comfortable first-generation students become trying out a way of being that is unfamiliar to them. The more institution officials put themselves forward as models for students to follow, Terenzini et al. (1995) concluded, and the more they emphasize "the academic and intellectual life of the institution" (p. 14) as a way of being that they want all students to emulate, the more first-generation students will adopt that way of being.

Some of these conclusions could hardly be more abstract, I know, but what could be more abstract than the life of the mind? Although some contemporary education theorists may regard this as an honorable but quaint concept, getting a college education, when you come right down to it, is still learning to live the life of the mind. The transformative power of postsecondary study is just this: finding out that there is a whole new way of thinking about the world. Because "an academic culture that prizes the life of the mind and the development of the individual into a reflective, mature thinker is foreign to many first-generation students," wrote Chaffee (1992, p. 83), director of critical-thinking studies at LaGuardia Community College, they can be positively giddy when the light finally does go on. Later in his article, Chaffee quoted one of his own students, who put it this way: "The words *critical thinking* [emphasis in the original] will never leave my vocabulary because by learning how to organize my ideas, support my point of view with reasons, and solve my problems rationally, I have learned more effective ways of dealing with my life, my children, and my schoolwork" (p. 83). Educators who work at LaGuardia, one of the largest community colleges in the nation and one with a very diverse student population, make sure that being a role model is at the top of their work priorities, and they get results. According to Chaffee (1992), the LaGuardia population is as nontraditional as it gets: 18% are Caucasian; 50% are foreign-born; almost half are over age 21; and, according to their test scores, 83% are in need of remediation in writing, reading, math, oral skills, or some combination of those areas. As mentioned earlier, course selection in the context of staying on the so-called academic track in high school can have a big impact on the academic performance of first-generation college students, including whether they need remediation. Just as important, though, is the fundamental rigor of the courses they have taken and the expectations of their middle and high school teachers. The 2001 National Center for Education Statistics study (Warburton et al., 2001) examined the performance of first-generation college students compared to non-first-generation students in terms of the fundamental rigor of the courses they took in high school. According to this study, the likelihood of dropping out for academic reasons was significantly higher for first-generation students than it was for non-first-generation students. Only 55.0% of first-generation students who did not take rigorous courses in high school were still enrolled or had graduated after three years, for example, while 67.0% of non-first-generation students who did not take rigorous courses in high school were still enrolled or had graduated after three years (Warburton et al., 2001).

New Way of Perceiving the World

For most first-generation students, acquiring a whole new way of perceiving the world through a college education also means acquiring a whole new way of perceiving the future, economic and otherwise. Although just about every American knows that getting a bachelor's degree means getting a better job and making more money, many first-generation students know little more about the benefits of a college education. They have not been shown the full range of benefits that a degree can produce, and even the relationship between college performance and landing a place in the workforce is often murky to them. As a result, they are more present-oriented while in college than are other kinds of students, who can be more future–oriented, interested primarily in what a college education is going to mean for them after college. Clarifying the link between the present of being in college and a future of having been in college is the great benefit of the for-profit, professional school, so for some first-generation students who really are not interested in the benefits of the more well-rounded, traditional education, professional schools can be the answer. Keep in mind that, for many first-generation students and their families, simply enrolling in a postsecondary institution is the main goal, the pot of gold at the end of rainbow; after all, few others in the family have gotten that far. Whereas non-first-generation students and their families often see enrollment, graduation, and employment as a continuous, interconnected process, many first-generation students and their families have a different, more disjointed view. They understand some elements of the college experience well, some elements not very well, and some elements not at all, which does not afford them the fluid view of their more privileged counterparts and their families. A superficial understanding of many elements of the college experience is characteristic of first-generation students, which makes it imperative that college officials, especially academic advisors, treat first-generation students differently from their non-first-generation counterparts, and from low-income students as well, when it comes to academic advising and planning.

Although both first-generation students and low-income students can focus on work after graduation during their matriculation, first-generation students have a different view of the relationship between education and work than do low-income students. Academic advisors and other college personnel must be quick to recognize the differences among all three categories of students: first-generation-only students, low-income students, and non-first-generation students. First-generation students, for example, often do gravitate toward majors that have the reputation of delivering high salaries after graduation, similar to low-income students, but they arrive at this choice by a different process. They are more likely to decide to declare as a business major, for example, after they have been exposed to the whole variety of majors and disciplines, and they are at least more open to supposedly less lucrative majors than are low-income students (Chen & Carroll, 2005). In contrast, it is not that low-income students are interested in "big money" only; it is more that they are averse to taking a chance on a lower-paying job because taking a lower-paying job does not change their life circumstances quickly enough. Plainly stated, declaring as a major in the humanities, low-income students likely feel, requires that they continue to struggle. Many low-income students have struggled financially and in other ways all their lives, so it should come as no surprise that they want to make sure their struggles end after graduation (Lynch, Kaplan, & Shema, 1997). It has been my experience from years of working with both first-generation-only students and low-income students that the latter are more likely than are the former to educate themselves fully on the connection between college and the world of work, and more likely, obviously, to begin making money as soon as possible after their college careers are over. Low-income students often regard making money right after graduation as a matter of survival, sometimes figuratively, but too often literally (Delpit, 1995; Payne, R. K., 2005). The college degree means a better life for them, but it also often means a better life for family members back in the home culture. For this reason and others, low-income students are focused on making that college degree pay off.

Learning About Majors

If first-generation students do not flesh out their superficial, incomplete understanding of the relationship between college performance and the world of work, they make decisions, the research shows, based on their superficial understanding. No surprise there. For instance, Terenzini et al. (1995) found that "first generation students . . . were likely to take fewer courses in the humanities and fine arts and social sciences" (p. 8). The assumption I will make here is that first-generation students are more likely to have been told that studying the humanities and fine arts, especially, is a waste of time because there are few jobs for people with degrees in these disciplines. It is also possible they have been told that although jobs for graduates with degrees in the social sciences are available they do not pay very well. For the same reasons that many first-generation students lack a sophisticated understanding of the general purposes and goals of a college education, the choice of academic major can be problematic. The most recent National Center for Education Statistics study (Chen & Carroll, 2005) on the progress of first-generation students confirms Terenzini's findings, reporting, among other things, that first-generation students take much longer to choose a major than do their non-first-generation counterparts. This is significant because students who take longer to choose a major also often take longer to graduate and are, therefore, at greater risk of dropping out. The Chen and Carroll study (2005) showed that 30.5% of the first-generation students surveyed had not chosen a major, compared with 13.1% of non-first-generation students at a comparable stage in their program of study.

The Chen and Carroll study (2005) also confirmed Terenzini et al.'s findings about the kinds of majors first-generation students typically choose. For example, only 4.5% of the first-generation students surveyed chose a major in the sciences, compared with 8.4% for non-first-generation students. Only 4.0% chose an engineering or architecture major, compared with 6.9% among non-first-generation students (Chen & Carroll, 2005). While first-generation students are underrepresented in some majors, they appear to be overrepresented in others, and, again, the cause for such asymmetrical data appears to have something to do with whether a major has the reputation of generating high-paying jobs. For example, 14.0% of the first-generation students surveyed chose a business major, compared with 11.9% of non-first-generation students (Chen & Carroll, 2005). And first-generation students are almost twice as likely as non-first-generation students to choose a major in vocational or technical fields: 4.5% and 2.4%, respectively (Chen & Carroll, 2005). The NCES study also confirmed that first-generation students are much less likely to choose a major in the humanities or the arts than are non-first-generation students. Only 2.1% of first-generation students chose a major in the humanities, compared with 6.6% for non-first-generation students, and only 3.1% of first-generation students chose a major in the arts, compared with 6.0% for non-first-generation students (Chen & Carroll, 2005). Although first-generation students often take longer to choose a major, the research shows that, once they've made the choice, they stick with it and resist further deliberation (Hahs-Vaughn, 2004). This may have to do with their lack of familiarity with postsecondary education in general—there being more incentive to stick with a difficult decision than an easy one—or it may have to do with the kinds of majors they tend to choose.

Finally, where first-generation students are concerned, it is always a good idea to consider the influence that complicated family dynamics might have on making an important college plan decision such as the choice of a major. London (1992) wrote that first-generation students "sometimes find a psychological resonance between their quest for individuation and autonomy and their choice of a major or career. For example, a student may receive pleasure from majoring in a subject that is remote from his or her parents' imagination" (p. 6). Whether the student gives a reason for the choice of major or not, a prudent academic advisor will plumb the depths of that choice and make sure the major fits the actual student, not some imaginary student created by her family or by the student herself.

SECTION TWO: CAMPUS PRESENCE

Whenever I hear my instructor colleagues at Sonoma State University complain about a particularly "dead" class they have been assigned, I always wonder how many first-generation students are enrolled in that class. "They never raise their hands, even if they've read the material," these instructors say. "They don't speak their mind, and I can't get them to dialogue with me." There are many reasons, of course, why a classroom of postsecondary students might be reticent about engaging with an instructor. Sometimes it has more to do with the instructor, and sometimes it has more to do with the students. Sometimes it might even have to do with the physical characteristics of the room itself or the time of day. Although all individual students and all classrooms of students have their own unique character, any informed observer should be able to tell a classroom of first-generation students from a classroom of non-first-generation students. The two kinds of students behave very differently in the same postsecondary school environment, and not only in the classroom.

It would probably be hard to find an adult who does not know that when polled about their greatest fears, most Americans place public speaking at the top of the list. Right up there with "dying" and "losing all my money," the idea of speaking in public makes even the most confident among us squirm. Since going broke generally implies much more severe consequences than being embarrassed in public, and dying implies . . . well, being dead, the extreme fear of public speaking expressed in polls seems to be an overreaction. Maybe. Although any rational person would choose public speaking over losing all of his or her money or dying, there are good reasons why so many people fear speaking in public. For one thing, people perceive public speaking as a threat to their identity. They believe that it has the potential to demonstrate to the world that they do not know as much as they claim to know, that they are not as smart as they say they are . . . that they are, in short, something of a fraud. If you can imagine the intensity of most people's discomfort at the thought of speaking in public, you have a pretty good idea how most first-generation college students feel about speaking in front of professors and peers in a college classroom. They are afraid the instructor and the other students in class—many of whom, ironically, are likely to be first-generation students themselves or non-first-generation students who dislike speaking in class just as much as they do—will find out that they do not know as much as they think they should know. The research shows that first-generation students speak in class less frequently than their non-first-generation counterparts (Rendón, 1995; Terenzini et al., 1996), and they volunteer for classroom presentations less frequently. They feel that other students, individuals whom they regard as the "real" students, should be answering the instructor's questions. Past president of the American College Counseling Association Bob Mattox, quoted in an article for *Counseling Today*, described this familiar behavior as being part of what he calls the "imposter phenomenon" (Hayes, 1997, p. 2).

The Imposter Phenomenon

Many first-generation students suffer from the imposter phenomenon, not only in the classroom when discussing a reading assignment, but also outside the classroom when passing a professor in the hall or chatting with a group of new friends outside a residence hall. They suffer from the imposter phenomenon when things are going badly *and* when things are going well. If they receive a high grade, for example, they cannot believe their good fortune. If an instructor makes a positive comment on a paper about a particularly cogent insight, they think the instructor is just being kind or is disingenuously practicing positive reinforcement as a strategy for managing the class. When they are sitting in a classroom full of students and the instructor asks for comments, they feel their comments are too obvious or that no one could possibly want to hear what they have to say. Performance anxiety affects just about everyone to one degree or another, but try telling that to a first-generation college student. Non-first-generation students (especially first-year students)—not to mention faculty and other college personnel—experience the imposter phenomenon as well, but research shows that negative feelings associated with anxiety about academic success are more frequent and more acute for first-generation students (Martinez et al., 2009; Terenzini et al., 1996).

Suffering from the imposter phenomenon is more serious than the typical vague feelings of not fitting in that many students experience on beginning their college education. It can include very destructive habits of mind, such as believing you are taking a place at the institution that should have gone to a more worthy individual, who somehow was overlooked during the application process, to your benefit. This is one reason why highly selective, high-reputation institutions—even private four-year institutions that claim to covet students for their individual characteristics—can be a difficult destination for many first-generation students. It is not just that students believe such institutions are being disingenuous with their personal approach, it is that first-generation students think the highly selective institution was wrong for accepting them or, more to the point, made a mistake (even a clerical mistake) by accepting them. For students suffering from the imposter phenomenon, then, a community college may be a better destination, at least until the student becomes more comfortable in his or her academic abilities. Most community colleges make no bones about their mission and publicize the fact that they will accept anyone for enrollment who has a high school diploma, so taking someone else's place is not an issue.

To put all of this in perspective and to help those who use the terms "first-generation student" and "low-income student" synonymously understand why they should stop this practice, let us use the concept of the imposter phenomenon to contrast these two different kinds of students. In contrast to first-generation-only students, low-income students are less likely to suffer from the imposter phenomenon, or, that is, they are less likely to have anxiety about not fitting in. It has been my experience that low-income individuals have a much more monolithic view of college. They suffer from the imposter syndrome less, not necessarily because their own sense of identity as a low-income individual is so well formed and stable (although this some-times is the case), but because they are less likely to prioritize the personal development dimension of a traditional education. Instead, they prioritize preparing themselves for the world of work. Developing as a person is some-thing you do "in" college, low-income students reason, and they are more focused on what they are going to do after achieving the degree. In this way low-income students are more *future-oriented* than are first-generation-only students, who are more likely to be *present-oriented*. Because there is so little research that discusses first-generation-*only* students, let alone research that compares the academic performance of first-generation-only students to low-income students, the conclusions I draw about the imposter phenomenon are based primarily on anecdotal evidence. Based on such evidence, however, I predict that first-generation-only students are more likely to be six- or even seven-year graduates, and low-income individuals are more likely to fit the following profile: They either burn out quickly and drop out during the first two years of college attendance, or they graduate fairly quickly, within five, or even four years.

Differences in the Classroom

Hayes (1997) and other observers of the postsecondary school environment (McConnell, 2000; Strayhorn, 2006) note that not speaking in class, whether or not it is a sign of the imposter phenomenon, is both a marker for first-generation status and a potential impediment to being an engaged learner. The recommendation that emerges out of this observation is that speech anxiety should be one of the main focuses of the so-called University 101 courses that are showing up more and more often on freshman class schedules these days. University 101 courses "provide students an in-depth orientation to college life, including help with study skills, test and speech anxiety, as well as career counseling and a general overview of the university structure" (Hayes, 1997, p. 1). With speech anxiety likely to be more of a problem for first-generation students than for their non-first-generation counterparts, you might think first-generation students would find large, impersonal lecture courses preferable to smaller, more intimate classes. In fact, the opposite might be true. Richardson and Skinner (1992) found that first-generation students "complained of large, impersonal lecture courses with little student participation and little interaction with faculty who might have 'five office hours for several hundred students'" (p. 33). Although this may appear contradictory, it conforms to most of what we know about the first-generation student experience. Although they do not always seek it out, first-generation college students definitely need personal attention from staff and faculty, and although they may hesitate to draw attention to themselves by speaking in class and may be weak in the cognitive skills associated with success in college, they are often willing to force themselves to do what they have to. For example, even though the thought of speaking to a professor face-to-face during office hours freezes many first-generation students with fear, they will make the attempt if they get the right advice. So the large, impersonal lecture courses characteristic of many public four-year institutions amount to something of a double-edged sword to many first-generation students; on the one hand, they can blend into the crowd and become acclimated to the college culture at their own pace, but on the other hand, they know that to succeed they need individual attention that will identify them as not "part of the crowd."

All of this is not to say that first-generation students are *always* averse to raising their hands. Although they may be very averse to expressing opinions about course content in the public forum of the classroom (but may force themselves to comment from time to time anyway), they often are the students in class who ask the instructor to confirm class rules and procedures, such as essay specifications and assignment deadlines. These are often perceived as safe questions by first-generation students, not to mention important, especially for those who often are a bit unclear on class rules and procedures. Richardson and Skinner (1992) surveyed recent first-generation graduates and concluded that instructors who make things such as classroom procedures and learning outcomes as transparent as possible receive the highest marks on teacher evaluations. "Graduates emphasized the importance of developing accurate expectations about course content and about necessary academic skills as well as readiness for the more general cognitive development usually associated with a college education" (p. 31). Instructors who leave such details unspoken make it difficult for first-generation students, who often take a little longer to get the lay of the land. Because instructor behavior in this area varies dramatically, and for other reasons, first-generation students must develop a support network that includes guides to the college culture early in their college career.

Alternative Ways of Support

Several researchers go one step further than study groups and workshops, suggesting that learning communities supply the best kind of support (both academic and other) for first-generation college students. Thayer (2000), citing the research of Tinto (1993) and others (Duggan, 2001; Richardson & Skinner, 1992), suggests that the recent data on college retention point to learning communities as the best way to help first-generation college students stay enrolled and achieve a timely graduation. "Within the learning community concept, there is room for a wide variety of implementation alternatives. For that reason, programs can tailor learning community activities to the particular characteristics of their institutions and student populations" (Thayer, 2000, p. 4).

Learning communities can benefit first-generation college students in other ways as well. As mentioned in chapter 1, first-generation students often must play multiple roles during their college careers, spending significant amounts of time in employee and family member roles in addition to the student role. The most recent Cooperative Institutional Research Program (CIRP) report (Pryor, Hurtado, Saenz, Santos, Korn, 2007) revealed that first-generation students are more likely than are their non-first-generation counterparts to work full-time during their college careers. A significant number of incoming first-generation freshmen, 36.7%, reported that "there is some or a very good chance that they will work full-time while attending college," while only 24.7% of incoming non-first-generation freshmen reported this (p. 11). Terenzini et al. (1995) concluded that having to play multiple roles is the most likely reason that first-generation students report they have less time to study than do non-first-generation students. "The two groups . . . [have] different curricular, instruction, and out-of-class experiences," they wrote (p. 13). These different experiences have much to do with very different schedules; there simply is not enough time in the day for some first-generation students. Many learning communities at least partially tear down the walls that separate class time, study time, and leisure time, which can make managing bursting-at-the-seams schedules a little easier. The nontraditional environment of the learning community, then, can support the traditional classroom if the learning community provides more time for preparing for class, including preparing for tests and doing homework. "Any endeavor to improve the classroom experience has great merit. If improved teaching methods and strategies can be used to optimize the learning that transpires in the classroom, students might need less time outside of the classroom to master the course content" (McConnell, 2000, p. 8).

Terenzini et al. (1995) concluded, "One clear implication of this evidence [that describes the first-generation experience] is the need to smooth first-generation students' transitions from work or high school to college and to extend active targeted support throughout their first year, if not beyond" (p. 12). "Active targeted support"—that is, specific study groups, mandatory tutoring, and specialized advising—certainly do improve academic achievement in first-generation students, but Terenzini et al. (1995) suggest that more "subtle forms of support" (p. 13) having to do with instructor and institutional attitudes toward first-generation college students might be just as important.

Validating the Presence of First-Generation Students

Other researchers have also recommended more subtle forms of support. Rendón (1995), for example, describes the process of validation as one of the single most effective ways of keeping first-generation college students enrolled and on track toward graduating: "Validation is an enabling, confirming supportive process initiated by in- and out-of-class agents that fosters academic and personal development" (p. 7). Although it may seem like a very abstract concept, first-generation students need to be made to feel like they belong at institutions of higher learning, to feel like their attendance is not an accident. Although establishing validation at an institution is time-consuming, it is well worth the effort. It requires serious introspection, and it requires that some institutions change their traditional approach to student development. Institutions that want to attract and serve first-generation students will have to devote resources to do so, but not every part of establishing validation at an institution needs to be arduous or costly. Some of Rendón's (1995) practical suggestions take very few resources—for example, practices such as calling students by name and encouraging faculty to praise students in class. Other practices, such as peer editing of academic writing, which Rendón also recommends, take more time and money. As any instructor who has seriously attempted to make peer editing work in the classroom environment knows, "providing mechanisms by which students support and praise each other" (p. 7) can be much more difficult and time-consuming than one might think, but if peer editing, for example, is identified as particularly important to the success of first-generation students, the institution should make it happen. In addition, progressive institutions will recognize that not every officer of the school must bear the same level of responsibility for ensuring that first-generation students succeed; they adjust instructor workloads so that initiatives such as peer editing of academic writing can be effective. Although it is true that all students benefit from validation, this is not a case of raising the water level to raise all the boats. First-generation students are always watching their non-first-generation counterparts; it is often necessary for them to see their counterparts responding positively to a campus wide initiative such as validation for them to respond positively to it. This dynamic that places first-generation students in the position of following the lead of non-first-generation students is sometimes hard to discern because the former can be sensitive about being "found out," but keeping the dynamic in mind is important to understanding how campus wide initiatives meant to affect all students often can affect first-generation students differently.

The classroom is obviously one place in which validation can make a difference, but Terenzini et al. (1996) and Rendón (1995) suggest that this change in orientation should be affected not only by faculty delivering instruction but by everyone who has a stake in the institution's being the best it can be. In other words, although faculty working one-on-one with first-generation students may have the greatest impact, everyone at the institution should have some knowledge of the first-generation experience and treat students accordingly (Yorke & Thomas, 2003). Validation occurs, Terenzini et al. (1995) wrote:

> when administrators, faculty, and other students all send important signals that they [first-generation students] are competent learners, that they can succeed, that they have a rightful place in the academic community, and that their background and past experiences are sources of knowledge and pride, not something to be demeaned or devalued. (p. 13)

Institution officials must recognize that the sometimes subtle barriers to success that first-generation students face are real and often difficult to address. They must recognize that first-generation students really do bring vitality and new ideas to the college environment, that they bring a different set of needs and expectations, and that the coming together of the privileged and the nonprivileged can be a positive, transformative experience for both first-generation students and institutions. Students can tell in a second if institution officials are being disingenuous about the value of different points of view, for example, including the different points of view of first-generation students. Officials should make clear that real value is gained by modeling behavior concomitant with the general goals and purposes of the institution. Sometimes these rewards are not as clear as they ought to be or, worse, clear that they are available only to certain kinds of students. Smart and Umback (2007) advocated that the reward system built into the institutional structure must be transparent, and, what is more, that every institution contains multiple environments that reward students for success in slightly different ways. "Our findings contribute to a growing body of literature suggesting that higher education researchers who study 'how college affects students' should focus more attention on distinctive academic environments *within* [emphasis in original] institutions that have been shown to have very disparate goals and structures" (p. 191). Smaller private four-year institutions often get high praise for attempting to make institutional goals and purposes more transparent to their students. They get credit for attempting to make every student feel like he or she matters, for paying attention to the individual life experience that every student brings to the classroom table. Although they deserve praise for these characteristics, institution officials must realize they have to penetrate much skepticism if they are going to be effective with many first-generation students. Helping them feel comfortable is not easy. Even though Stanford University now acknowledges the presence of first-generation students in the overall student population and claims to value this presence, some Stanford students are not so sure. One recent Stanford graduate put it this way:

> Sometimes, the university across the board has a tendency to say, 'If we can announce this number, we can announce this policy, then we've done our job.' . . . The thing that I would really like to see is a commitment made by the admissions office to make sure that there is some structure, some substance. If you admit more [first-generation students], but never make them feel welcome, how does that benefit? (Fuller, 2007, p. 3)

Studies indicate that first-generation students are more tuned in to the programs and services that do the actual work of helping them than they are to

the official statements of an institution's administrators about those programs or about what the institution is going to do for them in the future
(Rendón, 1995; Terenzini et al., 1996; Yorke & Thomas, 2003). Another
Stanford first-generation student said that he felt Stanford failed him when
he received a C− on a paper he thought was one of his best ever: "I was
scared. I worried that I would have to fly back to south Texas" (Johnston,
2004). Then he discovered he was entitled to tutoring and other support
services, which made the difference. If the private four-year institution does
not deliver on pledges of support, such statements indicate, first-generation
students might be better off choosing a different kind of school.

It is always important to keep in mind that the college campus really is a
better place because of the presence of first-generation students. Chaffee
(1992) reminds us, "As outsiders to the culture of higher education, first-
generation students often challenge the passive 'information transfer' model
of education, in which material presented in lectures is re-presented on
examinations" (p. 85). As he points out, first-generation college students are
more likely than are traditional students to ask, "Why is it important to
master this information?" (p. 85). Just as first-generation students are more
likely to ask this question, the institutions that educate them should be
asking, "Why should we make it easier on first-generation students?" The
answer very well may be, "It makes us a better, more effective institution—
for all students."

It is touching to see how badly some first-generation students want to fit
in. Although they can appear to be distracted or even apathetic, this is often
only because they are in an observation mode, watching what is going on
around them and soaking up information they can use later so as not to
appear to be a first-generation student. Having first-generation-student
status often produces a polarized way of being, that is, a disengaged stance
when in the presence of unfamiliar authority figures and activities and an
intensely engaged stance when there is not as much to lose by appearing to
be a novice.

In a sense, then, this chapter can be read as instructions for how to spot
first-generation students on your campus, but faculty, staff, and administrators cannot be satisfied with simply identifying these students. To help their
institutions be all they can be, institution officers have to figure out what is
going on inside the heads of their first-generation students, what they are

thinking about, and how those thoughts are helping them to become, or preventing them from becoming, successful contemporary college students. To this end, therefore, to understand the not-so-visible characteristics of being a first-generation college student, chapter 3 addresses their internal psychology.

3

The Internal Psychology of First-Generation College Students

A S MUCH AS MANY FIRST-GENERATION STUDENTS would like to believe they can hide their status from faculty and other institution officials, their characteristic behaviors, as illustrated in chapter 2, make them very visible on campuses. The kinds of questions they ask in class, the way they linger in the hall in front of a professor's office during office hours, and their solitary presence in the library gives them away.

Although academic advisors can observe these behaviors and make recommendations for better performance based on their observations, it is also important for them and all other institution officials to understand the complicated psychology of first-generation students to help them succeed. This psychology has many dimensions, certain of which make adapting to the routines of college-going more difficult than it has to be. The best course of action for advising first-generation students in many cases is to address negative habits of mind that often impede developing confidence and self-esteem. This is especially true of first-generation students early in their matriculation; when they find out that fitting in is going to take more time and effort than they imagined, they can become psychologically closed off and even depressed. Students who drop out in their first or second year often do so because they simply cannot wrap their minds around the idea of being a college student (Tinto, 1993).

What follows in chapter 3 is a detailed description of what we know about the psychology and performance of first-generation college students.

Again, the material is divided into two major sections: (1) An Extended Campus Acclimation Process, (2) and The Importance and Impact of Personal Relationships. Section One describes what first-generation students go through internally to compensate for their lack of familiarity with postsecondary education. It is divided into six subsections: The Existential Question About College Attendance, The Existential Question and Low-Income Status, Developing a College-Student Identity, Engagement With Physical Space, Campus Size, and Blending In. Section Two, which describes how personal relationships can both help and hinder the process of earning a four-year degree, is divided into five subsections: Family Relationships, Family Mythologies About College, Faculty Relationships, Nonfaculty Professional Relationships, and Peer Relationships and Role Models.

SECTION ONE: AN EXTENDED CAMPUS ACCLIMATION PROCESS

Most first-time college students—first-time first-generation students as well as other kinds of first-time students—experience some anxiety and sense of disorientation during their initial few months of enrollment. For many of these first-timers, these feelings of discomfort can linger longer than a few months. What with the unfamiliar behaviors to master and unique physical surroundings to navigate, the typical college campus and college culture can take some getting used to. Even for non-first-generation students, becoming comfortable as a member of the college culture is very different from being comfortable in the home culture.

Difficulties produced by having to straddle two cultures—having to occupy that ever-so-treacherous middle position between the college culture and the home culture—are well documented in the literature on first-generation students:

> Particularly as they begin to take on the symbols of the college culture—be it style of dress, taste in music, or range of vocabulary—first-generation students often sense displeasure on the part of [home] acquaintances and feel an uncomfortable separation from the culture in which they grew up. (Hsiao, 1992, p. 1)

The fallout from separation anxiety, though, can cut in both directions, sometimes in favor of the college culture, sometimes in favor of the home culture. Attending college can even require that first-generation students take sides against their family and friends, something almost every child is reluctant to do, and something almost guaranteed to produce anxiety and discomfort. Questions such as, "Why am I here?" "What am I doing?" and even "Who am I?" are repeated again and again during those first few months away from the home culture. Even first-generation students who live at home while attending college ask such questions.

The Existential Question About College Attendance

In their essay on the first-generation student experience and other lives in transition, sociologists Ochberg and Comeau (as cited in McAdams & Josselson, 2001) remind us that most people explain important life decisions to others and justify them to themselves—career choices, marriage choices, and decisions about education, to name only a few—by describing them as *personal choices*. "I became a social worker because I always wanted to help people," the social worker says. "I am a paleontologist because dinosaurs are all I ever wanted to study," the paleontologist says. Listeners accept these explanations that suggest control and individual agency as viable and valid. Explanations for career choices that are based on *sociological forces* beyond the subject's control or based on circumstance, on the other hand, listeners often consider as inadequate or even disingenuous. Statements such as, "I became a social worker because I had to" usually require further explanation. Considering that most people believe that career choice should be linked to identity, Ochberg and Comeau's logic seems reasonable enough, but it is not as if we cannot imagine exceptions to it.

> Psychosocial theorists routinely point out that the "self" each of us has come to be was shaped by our milieu and might conceivably seem no less precious to us for this influence. What makes our upwardly mobile students interesting is that they illustrate—if only in a tentative, preliminary way—how psychosocial understanding might help in ordinary life. . . . [First-generation students] have developed hybrid accounts in which sociology and personality are woven together. Both of these threads seem essential to their motivation. (p. 141)

Non-first-generation students are less likely to develop hybrid accounts, as Ochberg and Comeau call them, where personality and sociology are woven together to explain why they are going to college. It is all the same to them, we might say. In fact, advisors and counselors are quite familiar with tradi-tional students who do not consider the decision to attend college a decision at all. "Going to college is simply what a person like myself does," such traditional students think if they pause to think about these existential ques-tions at all. Sometimes they are confronted with the dilemma of which col-lege to attend, but they usually have not had to develop a reason for why they decided to attend college in the first place. If they are forced to give an answer to the question, "Why are you going to college?" non-first-genera-tion students often give what appears to be a *sociological* answer, in the lan-guage of Ochberg and Comeau, and say, "Everyone in my family goes to college" or "All my friends are going to college." As I say, this *appears* to be a strict, uncomplicated *sociological* answer, but this is because the link to choice and identity that expresses itself so often in first-generation students is absent in many non-first-generation students, who have sublimated this link so deeply that it rarely is expressed. In other words, what appears to be a *sociological* answer from non-first-generation students is often the only pos-sible answer. Simple enough . . . for them.

The Existential Question and Low-Income Status

The insights of Ochberg and Comeau (as cited in McAdams & Josselson, 2001) can also be useful in making a distinction between first-generation and low-income students and between first-generation and low-income concerns. One of the ways low-income individuals escape an impoverished home cul-ture and enroll in a college or university is by identifying going to college as a nonchoice. Perhaps a parent, an aunt, or an uncle has repeatedly told the child, "You are going to college. Do not even think about it. You *are* going." Even if role models who have gone to college are hard for such a child to find, this sort of repeated declaration can be effective. "And don't even think about dropping out," the mantra goes on. Further, many low-income indi-viduals with a low-income orientation toward the world regard education as the *only* way to a better life. They see it in binary terms. Growing up they have observed that many individuals who do not attempt to improve their lives through education stay in the home culture and continue living impov-erished lives. Those individuals who seek education, they have observed, often do not return. Depending on the severity of the poverty, that is, staying in the home culture is no choice at all. Who would *choose* a life of poverty?

So low-income individuals are more likely to give an answer to the existential question such as: "I want to get a good job. I want to make money." Unlike the hybrid accounts of first-generation students, this is a strict *sociological* answer. This is not to suggest that low-income individuals do not or cannot appreciate the personal growth dimension of going to college, or the many other nonmonetary opportunities provided by going to college, it is just that they are focused like a laser beam on what they regard as the primary outcome of a college education. They have what I call a *survivalist orientation* toward college attendance, and personal growth will have to be put on the back burner for now, they reason, while they figure out how to create a more livable life for themselves.

Baxter Magolda's (2001) description of "self-authorship" in the context of becoming acclimated to the college culture provides another lens for how to distinguish between first-generation student concerns and low-income student concerns. The term "self-authorship" refers to the process by which young adults in the college setting gradually become the authors of their own actions and choices, or, to put it another way, become fully aware of their own agency and ability to construct both a college and postcollege life for themselves (Baxter Magolda, 2001). Research by Pizzolato (2003) indicated that evidence of self-authoring behavior is very high among low-income college students, and, in fact, in some cases begins even before post-secondary enrollment. Self-authorship is very evident, the study goes on to show, unless these same low-income students are made to feel that they have some kind of privileged status at the college or university. One kind of privileged low-income student, of course, is the star high school athlete who is given a full ride to attend the university of his or her choice.

> High privilege [low-income] students had excessive support that crossed the line into protection. These students were protected from having to figure out how to apply to or pay for college, and from considering the implications of their going to college on their sense of self. Consequently, high privilege [low-income] students were kept from opportunities where they could have more fully developed self-authoring ways of knowing. (Pizzolato, 2003, p. 808)

The harmful effects of privilege in this context should inform our understanding of the first-generation student experience. Most first-generation-only students do not have the same kind of intense, personal relationship with the concept of privilege or lack of it that most low-income students have. Particularly if they consider themselves members of the dominant American culture, first-generation-only students can be unsure about their status, unsure whether they are privileged or not privileged. For them this sometimes ambiguous relationship to privilege neither increases, as it did in the low-income students Pizzolato (2003) studied, nor decreases the likelihood of developing self-authoring behavior. As a result of occupying this middle ground, many first-generation students must spend a lot of time examining and understanding their own agency in the process of becoming comfortable in the college culture.

Developing a College-Student Identity

Student affairs professionals have many identity theories at their disposal that can be useful in understanding the nexus where self-actualization, personal development, and slow progress to graduation meet for first-generation college students (Alessandria & Nelson, 2005; Baxter Magolda, 2003; Boyd, Hunt, Kandell, & Lucas, 2003). I would not expect any one of these theories to be much more effective than any other in facilitating a positive college experience for first-generation students. What is perhaps more important than recommending any single theory is simply to take note of how many of them appear to describe so *easily* the first-generation student experience. Academic advisors and other student affairs professionals beware. Let us remember that improving the graduation rates of first-generation students will not be affected by theory but by practice. There are real solutions to the problems these students face. What has been absent is for college and university officials to generate the will necessary to enact these solutions on their campuses.

Considering the college acclimation process in the context of the existential question, "Why are you going to college . . . why do you want to be a college student?" sheds some light on why so many first-generation students find their first semester so difficult. They find it difficult, in part, because college attendance in the United States, for those lucky enough to have it as an option, has always been seen as a rite of passage in American culture. Going to college is often figured in the popular media as an important stage in the development of an adult identity. For many non-first-generation students, that is, the question, "Why am I going to college?" is inextricably bound together with the question, "Who am I?" even if they do not consciously recognize this to be the case, even if they don't identify going to college as a choice they have made. Traditional, non-first-generation students pondering their first semester of postsecondary education think about who they are: "I am an eighteen-year-old American who goes to college." For many first-generation students, we know this is not necessarily the case. This is not necessarily how they think about themselves. The question, "Why am I going to college?" is very separate from the question, "Who am I?" Many of them have been raised to consider these two questions as belonging on two separate planes of inquiry. After all, their own parents have not defined themselves that way, have not developed their identities in terms of college attendance; it is unlikely they have heard many other family members or friends define themselves in terms of college attendance. Yet they know, because they have absorbed the messages and images produced by the greater American culture, that college attendance is a rite of passage that is very likely to change who they are.

Someone asking a first-generation student, "Why are you going to college?" should expect a complicated answer. Not that the actual utterance will necessarily be that complicated—18-year-olds generally are not capable of perfectly articulating these kinds of thoughts yet—but that the answer in the context of the very complicated first-generation experience cannot be anything but complicated. The point here is not that first-generation students always give well-considered, complex answers to the existential question, "Why are you going to college?" Their answers can sound just as superficial as the answers given by their non-first-generation peers. The point here is that if they do give superficial-sounding answers, they do so for entirely different reasons, and, more important, if they do give superficial answers, they are likely to change their tune at some time in the near future.

In most cases, having thought deeply about what I have termed the existential question concerning college attendance before actually having attended college is good for first-generation students. Yes, thinking about themselves in the larger context of everyone who attends college, in the context of all those privileged students with a family history of attending college, can lead to feelings of inferiority and crises of confidence, but at least they will have exorcised some of the demons during the process. They benefit from having a clear head to start the first semester, or at least the second semester.

Postsecondary institutions that have intensive and individualized preregistration orientation programs are often a good choice for first-generation students. Again, the kinds of orientations that are typical of larger public four-year institutions often will not do the job; the people who run these orientations simply cannot spend enough time describing and addressing the unique concerns of individual students—concerns involving identity development, for instance—and they probably only recently have begun using the term "first-generation college student" when disseminating information to orientation participants.

It is always better if first-generation students can begin identity development right from the start. Students who delay the process of considering the existential question can be in for a rude awakening, according to London (1992), for upward mobility is not without potential pitfalls.

> In the innocent belief that mobility is unproblematic, students are often unaware, at least initially, of its potential costs in personal and social dislocation. It soon becomes apparent, however, that old relations are changing and that new ones must be forged. It is only when we see that negotiating cultural obstacles involves not just gain but loss—most of all the loss of a familiar past, including a past self—that we can begin to understand the attendant periods of confusion, conflict, isolation, and even anguish reported by first-generation students. (p. 10)

As much as we would like some of the challenges of being a first-generation student to be dealt with early on and disposed of early, London reminds us that becoming intuitively oriented toward college takes a long time. The truth is, even if students have seriously contemplated what it means to have first-generation status and how college attendance will affect every relationship they have made and will make in the future, and even if they believe they have exorcised the demons, the chances are good that these kinds of issues will continue to come up, and there is always the potential that they will derail a timely graduation.

Engagement With Physical Space

The human geography associated with the postsecondary campus often is overlooked in discussions of how students acclimate to college life. The physical space can make the acclimation process more difficult for first-generation college students, even exacerbating feelings of confusion and isolation. Campuses with lots of open public space can remind first-generation students how psychically alone they are. Campuses with poorly demarcated rooms

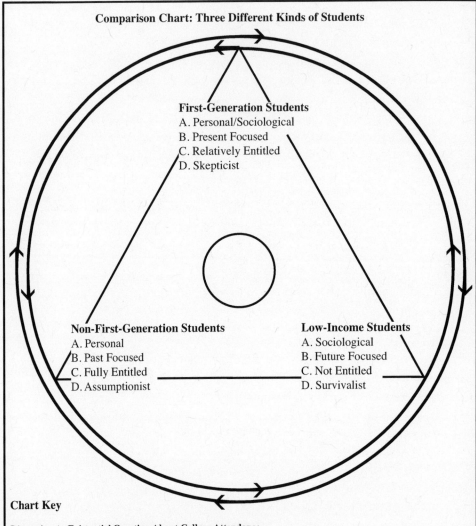

Comparison Chart: Three Different Kinds of Students

First-Generation Students
A. Personal/Sociological
B. Present Focused
C. Relatively Entitled
D. Skepticist

Non-First-Generation Students
A. Personal
B. Past Focused
C. Fully Entitled
D. Assumptionist

Low-Income Students
A. Sociological
B. Future Focused
C. Not Entitled
D. Survivalist

Chart Key

Dimension A: Existential Question About College Attendance

First-Generation Students. Hybrid *personal/sociological* answer to the existential question about college attendance, according to sociologists Richard Ochberg and William Comeau's theory of important life decision making. (The existential question is, "Why are you going to college . . . why do you want to be a college student?")

Non-First-Generation Students. *Personal* answer to the existential question about college attendance, according to Ochberg and Comeau's theory of important life decision making.

Low-Income Students. *Sociological* answer to the existential question about college attendance, according to Ochberg and Comeau's theory of important life decision making.

Chart Key continued on next page.

Chart Key (continued from previous page)

Dimension B: Temporal Orientation to College Attendance

First-Generation Students. Temporal orientation relative to college attendance that is *present focused*. When first-generation students ponder the idea of college attendance, the general purposes and goals of college attendance, they think about it in terms of what is happening during the current semester, what is going on in the present.

Non-First-Generation Students. Temporal orientation relative to college attendance that is *past focused*. When non-first-generation students ponder the idea of college attendance, the general purposes and goals of college attendance, they think about it in terms of what they have grown up understanding about it, what they have heard in the past from family members and friends.

Low-Income Students. Temporal orientation relative to college attendance that is *future focused*. When low-income students ponder the idea of college attendance, the general purposes and goals of college attendance, they think about it in terms of what it is going to provide for them in the future after attendance is over, after they get the degree.

Dimension C: Level of Entitlement

First-Generation Students. Feel that they are *relatively entitled* to a college education. They tend to believe that they are entitled to a college education relative to the effort they have put into preparing themselves for a college education.

Non-First-Generation Students. Feel that they are *fully entitled* to a college education. They believe they are entitled to a college education whether or not they have prepared themselves for one.

Low-Income Students. Feel that they are *not entitled* to a college education.

Dimension D: Attitude Toward Developing a College-Student Identity

First-Generation Students. *Skepticist* attitude toward developing a college-student identity. First-generation students are skeptical they will be absent a natural stage in life development if they don't attend college. They don't assume they will be different people when they finish college. They are not closed off to the possibility they will be different people when they finish college, but they are more likely to think they will be the same people they were at the start of college after they have finished college. In other words, they are more likely to think they will be the same people, only now with a college degree.

Non-First-Generation Students. *Assumptionist* attitude toward developing a college-student identity. Non-first-generation students figure attending college in their imagination as a natural stage in life development. In other words, not only do they assume they are going to college, they assume they will be different people when they finish college.

Low-Income Students. *Survivalist* attitude toward developing a college-student identity. Low-income students see college as a matter of survival, as a means of making the money necessary to elevate themselves out of a life of poverty. They don't associate attending college with identity development. In a sense, they defer identity development to that time in the future when they have their degrees and can begin making money.

and buildings can remind students just how much they have to learn. Non-first-generation students, on the other hand, have often been prepared for what to expect. In the case of legacy students whose parents talk about the quad, campanile, and other physical landmarks, this is especially true, but even non-first-generation students who attend campuses different from the ones their parents and family members attended have heard stories about college libraries, study rooms, and large lecture halls, which dilutes the sense of foreignness anyone would experience when first coming to the typical college campus. Campus space is as different from home space as it can be. It can be helpful for first-generation students who live at home to develop a "piece" of the campus space in their home environment, in the form of a study area in a bedroom, for instance, so the back-and-forth between the campus space and the home space is not as abrupt and jarring.

For these reasons and others, non-first-generation college students, are able to bring the campus space and the home space into some degree of psychic correspondence without too much effort. Homesickness will strike some, for sure, but they usually can manage the effects of being away from home for the first time easily enough. For first-generation college students, however, even a fuzzy correspondence between the campus space and the home space is difficult to achieve, and some will never achieve it. The degree of separateness of the campus space from the home space can be represented by phone bills, bus tickets, and many other hard data, including the statistics on who lives on campus and who does not. Duggan (2001) reported in his small study—small compared to the massive NCES studies, for example—that non-first-generation students are more likely to live on campus than are first-generation students: 70.0% versus 50.0%, respectively. Nuñez and Cuccaro-Alamin (1998) confirm this finding, reporting that 45.3% of non-first-generation students (when considering all postsecondary students nationally) live on campus, while only 26.5% of first-generation students do. First-generation students are also significantly more likely to attend a college close to home, whether or not they actually live on the campus, which means they are less likely to appropriate the campus space fully as their own (Duggan, 2001). In addition to these findings, we should consider the types of colleges and universities students choose to attend, because the type of institution contributes greatly to the level of physical foreignness students feel. For instance, attending a private for-profit institution may feel less foreign to a first-generation student because the physical environment is often reminiscent of business office space, a kind of space with which most students are likely to be somewhat familiar. Urban institutions, public and private, can feel less foreign, too, because the common images of college space produced by the American mass media exaggerate the importance of the classroom and, perhaps, the laboratory to college life, neglecting what goes on outside the classroom, and more to the point, neglecting what *is* outside the classroom. It helps in this case, of course, if the student comes from an urban environment.

Campus Size

Campus size can have a significant impact on the psychology of first-generation college students. Regardless of institution type, a large, complicated bureaucracy necessary for accommodating a large number of students can have the effect of depersonalizing the individual student. The literature on nontraditional students, though, is divided on whether large campus size is positive or negative. It could be that some first-generation students gravitate toward and thrive at large institutions because they give students more time for learning how to blend in. On the other hand, some first-generation students attending large institutions might never get the individual attention they need to overcome their lack of familiarity with college-going.

Although smaller institutions appear to offer some benefits for first-generation students, the gains may be short-lived or even superficial when considering their long-term development; first-generation students have a lot more to learn during their five or six years in college than the curriculum of their discipline or major. Lohfink and Paulsen (2005) found, for example, that first-generation students were less likely to persist at smaller private institutions, and perhaps paradoxically, the smaller size of the campus may have had something to do with this: Smaller size overall may mean fewer public spaces, and fewer public spaces may prevent first-generation students from finding a place they can call their own. Their study found that "institutional size was positively related to persistence" (p. 419). More places to hang out on campus may mean a smoother and quicker acclimation process.

The above paragraphs suggest that administrators at progressive institutions should be asking themselves, "How well are our first-generation students physically integrated into campus life?" If students are not physically present, of course, as is the case in many so-called commuter schools, it is hard for them to be fully integrated. But let us not forget that being physically present on the college campus is only part of the story. Sometimes *being there* only serves to show how out of place you are. Think about your first trip to a foreign country and how different the people and the place seemed. Non-first-generation students can be perceived by some first-generation students as practically citizens of a foreign country.

If the physical space is foreign to first-generation students—and it is—so are the ways of the foreigners occupying that physical space. The two groups of students often do not frequent the same places on campus. It is surprising, perhaps, that a large percentage of first-generation college students do not frequent the financial aid office, and many report dismay when they find out for the first time how many of their non-first-generation counterparts fill out the Free Application for Federal Student Aid (FAFSA) form and apply for financial aid, even if they come from relatively affluent families. First-generation students often do not understand that a student does not have to have low-income status to apply for and benefit from financial aid. "F-gens [*sic*] are debt averse, avoiding accumulated debt load even at the lowest level. This may be a reflection of their limited knowledge of and family history with student loans" (Somers, Woodhouse, & Cofer, 2004, p. 429). They are less likely to have credit cards and less likely to ask for financial help from their families, for fear of causing the family to shoulder debt (Somers et al., 2004). Having credit cards, and the freedom and bondage represented by financial aid, are also related to the way first-generation students imagine the physical space of an institution. Quick access to money has the effect of increasing the amount of physical space a student must manage, which can be particularly difficult during the first two years of study. Expanding the human geography of education to include retail stores, coffee shops, and other off-campus hangouts can become a time management issue. A campus space small enough to manage easily is a virtue for first-generation college students: Keep it small to know it all is a good rule of thumb. Reporting on a program designed to enroll more nontraditional students in college, Burd (2002) agrees with Somers et al. The key appears to be knowledge about financial aid, not access to the money itself, so if first-generation students who need financial aid help can master the ramifications of receiving the money, including the increase in the amount of physical space the money represents, they do better than when the money is just handed to them. The success of the program Burd profiles "resulted from better counseling, not more aid money. Students in the program are attending college with aid that they didn't know existed, and it was learning of that aid—not an increase in its size—that made the difference" (p. 22).

If you speak with first-generation students at length, you will discover that they often regard the financial aid office as a place on campus to avoid. Understanding and analyzing all the issues and details involved in determining whether you should apply for financial aid (and how to do so) is difficult enough by itself; finding out that your whole orientation toward borrowing money needs to be adjusted as well just adds to the overall confusion and disorientation. "Where's the stigma?" many first-generation students ask. "You mean everyone applies for financial aid?" Issues like this can make getting acclimated to the campus environment difficult, indeed.

Blending In

Becoming fully integrated into the campus culture means paying attention to a long list of symbols that determine in-group membership. "Taste in clothing, food, grooming, and hairdo" are some of the things first-generation students know they will have to deal with, according to London (1992, p. 7). Not appearing to fit in is one of the biggest worries first-generation students say they have the summer before college classes begin (Clauss-Ehlers & Wibrowski, 2007). They know they should not be so concerned with such things, but they imagine the pressure to fit in will be so intense that they just cannot drive the worry out of their mind. Added to the preceding list are the areas that catch them by surprise once they actually begin classes. "Tastes in music, sports, cars, and recreation" (London, 1992, p. 7) and other areas of concern turn out to be so nuanced and so specific to the college experience that no amount of information can prepare them for what is to come. The symbols and activities that characterize college life outside the classroom will be much different from what first-generation college students have been accustomed to back in the home culture. For some first-generation students, the game will be to avoid appearing to give in to such symbols and activities, even if they *are* giving in to them. Other students will work hard to keep the campus culture and the home culture separate in terms of space and ways of thinking. "Many first-generation graduates remained somewhat skeptical about the opportunities associated with college. Some came from communities where a college education was not an important element in becoming an adult and were discouraged by the stories of college graduates who returned home to find no employment" (Richardson & Skinner, 1992, p. 31). In the end, however, much of the research points to a high level of integration as being a good indicator for the success of first-generation college students (Lohfink & Paulsen, 2005; Terenzini et al., 1996). The more they are involved in the life of the campus, the more likely these students are to persist and achieve a timely graduation. Commenting on the 2001 National Center for Education Statistics study (Warburton et al., 2001), "Bridging the Gap," which described the academic performance of first-generation students in American institutions, McConnell wrote (2000), "First-generation students were less likely to attend racial or cultural awareness workshops, were less likely to see faculty as being concerned with student development and teaching, and were less likely to receive encouragement from friends" (p. 5).

As mentioned, integration into the life of the campus can be greatly facilitated by faculty, administrators, and other institution officials who invite first-generation students to take part in campus activities and events and who validate the presence of first-generation students on their campus. Faculty and administrators have to be the example: They cannot just be heard talking the talk; they also must be seen walking the walk. Depending on their degree of alienation from the student population in general, many first-generation students will not take part in extracurricular activities and events unless they see faculty and administrators doing the same. First-generation students are not likely to persist, write Somers et al. (2004), "unless they are engaged in the life of the campus through living on campus, doing well in specific courses, finding support from a faculty member, or finding a 'social niche'" (p. 429). In the end, then, the idea is for first-generation students to be comfortable in both the physical and social realms of the college campus and to understand that the two come together to form a single reality. More than anything else, first-generation students need a place to go, a place to be themselves, when they begin their college career. Finding a place to go, to study, to hang out with friends, accelerates the acclimation process by directly addressing the transition from the home space to the college space. According to Richardson and Skinner (1992) many first-generation students report that it was:

> important for them to reduce or "scale down" the physical dimensions of
> college attendance—that is, to find places where they could study, meet

friends, or seek support, spaces that provided some measure of "comfortability." These spaces could be almost anywhere on campus, for example, a study lounge or cafeteria, the office of student support services, or a specific academic department. (p. 37)

The movement on many American college campuses to reduce the square footage of public space—usually fueled by a corporate business model that regards any inconsistently used space as a hit to the economic bottom line—can be bad for all students, but it can be especially damaging to the success of first-generation students. Chapter 6 discusses the corporatization of American colleges and universities and the deleterious effect this phenomenon can have on the success of first-generation students.

SECTION TWO: THE IMPORTANCE AND IMPACT OF PERSONAL RELATIONSHIPS

Although some first-generation students will never be able to bring the campus space and the home space into any degree of correspondence, with the passage of time, most will become reasonably comfortable living in the campus space. Managing personal relationships with the people who populate these two discrete spaces, however, is another matter. For many first-generation college students, home culture relationships can make or break a college career, so it behooves academic advisors and support faculty to know something about the psychology of the students' home culture relationships and the newer campus culture relationships during the process of advising them.

Family Relationships

Many first-generation students get ill-defined and ambiguous (if often enthusiastic) support for pursuing postsecondary study from family and friends; parents often encourage children to apply for admission, for instance, but then become more and more detached as acceptance leads to enrollment, which leads to orientation, and so on. Not having been to college themselves, they usually cannot provide much help with the details; for example, they often do not distinguish between two-year and four-year institutions, between public and private institutions, or between nonprofit and for-profit institutions. Although many first-generation students receive this significant but ill-defined support, many others are completely on their own. "While some come from homes that value postsecondary education, many F-gens [*sic*] lack this kind of support. The difference between the values and expectations of their two worlds is likely to cause significant dissonance" (Somers et al., 2004, p. 429). Being on your own is one thing, and many first-generation students do fine making important decisions without much help from friends and family, but some must confront more than a detached attitude or the absence of advice from the home front. In his article on the challenges many first-generation students face in Florida, Padron (1992) referred to the dean of students at Miami-Dade Community College, who reported dismay at the

> increasing numbers of first-generation students whose parents are indifferent or even antagonistic toward the educational system. Almost always . . . the school system failed these parents when they were students, and they dropped out in the tenth or eleventh grade with the actual skills at a fifth- or sixth-grade level. These parents are most difficult to reach and can diminish their children's educational aspirations and opportunities. (p. 74)

Nonsupportive family and friends behave in different ways and exert different kinds of influence. The out-and-out antagonistic ones rarely have a positive effect on the student, obviously enough. Others do not intend to make things more difficult, but they cause difficulties all the same; for example, they draw students away from their studies and back to the home culture when it is not appropriate. Many times these people do not fully appreciate the demands of attending college and do not attempt to understand them; they simply miss the student and want to have more contact with him or her. First-generation college students often need advice on how to handle this kind of pressure, and many times they have to decide what and whom they must leave behind. Students sometimes have to learn how to create distance between themselves and home culture friends who want personal relationships to remain as they were before college.

Some of the retention models student affairs professionals favor account for the kind of family backgrounds associated with nontraditional students, and others do not. Tinto's model (1975) that emphasizes both academic and social integration as keys to retention has been criticized as being too oriented toward traditional student profiles (Braxton, 2000; McCubbin, 2003).

To the degree that Tinto's model is too oriented toward traditional students, it has limited value for predicting the success of first-generation college students. In response to this perceived inadequacy, Bean and Metzner's model (1985) emphasizes family background and financial issues, which may or may not be more appropriate for conceptualizing activities and policies that address the retention of nontraditional students. As far as first-generation students go, however, we know family background is especially important.

Family dynamics are complicated, needless to say. Sometimes parents can put aside their private anxieties to give their children usable advice, and sometimes they cannot. Although it is common practice for American families to play some role in the college attendance of their younger members—and current trends indicate that families will play larger roles in the future—the participation (or interference, as we shall see) of families of first-generation students can sometimes take on an exaggerated importance in the student's mind when juxtaposed with the multiple other issues that he or she must address. Institution advisors and counselors can do their institutions a favor by learning to recognize certain psychological patterns in their first-generation charges. In his analysis of the reports describing first-generation students' college attendance, London (1989), using language developed by the German psychiatrist Helm Stierlin, explains how first-generation students can be "bound" by their relationships with their parents, "delegated" by their relationships with their parents, and sometimes "bound and delegated" (p. 148) at the same time. London explains that, according to Stierlin's definition, it would be unlikely to find a fully bound child attending college; however, because of the closeness of many first-generation student families and because sending a child away to college is such a great unknown for them, first-generation students often do suffer from being partially bound to their parents in a way that is nonproductive for the child. That is, some first-generation students have parents who describe themselves as "dependent, and [imply] that unless the child provides essential satisfactions and securities the parents will suffer. . . . Enjoying autonomy becomes virtually impossible, for any experimentation with independence raises the specter of treason against the parents" (London, 1989, p. 149). It is not unusual for first-generation college students to think about their parents from this point of view, to understand that their parents see their leaving for college as a movement against family unity. Although having feelings of being bound does not necessarily lead to poor academic performance, it is easy to see how such demands on a child could get out of control. Being figured as a "dele-gate," on the other hand, moving on to Stierlin's second category, can have a more subtle, if no less pernicious, effect on first-generation students. Dele-gated children may not be as tied to their parents' emotional ups and downs as bound children, but that is not to say they do not feel a strong connection to the home culture. "What distinguishes the delegated from the bound child, however, is that the former demonstrates loyalty by leaving the family, not by staying in it. Leaving, or more accurately, leaving as a delegate, para-doxically becomes a proof of allegiance and even of love" (London, 1989, p. 154). Although "delegation is by no means always enslaving or exploitative" (p. 154), London continues, first-generation students can suffer from the imagined burden that they are a family's only hope. They may feel as if they must represent the family at all times and in every capacity. Although any student can wilt from too much responsibility for carrying the family name into the world of college and of work, these feelings can be especially strong in first-generation students. Finally, London reports that some first-genera-tion college students can be both bound and delegated at the same time in their relationships with their parents; this is truly being caught between a rock and a hard place. Believing they must return home to help the family and stay at school to represent the family simultaneously, bound and dele-gated first-generation students hardly have time to be students at all. In severe cases, the contradictory psychological forces can become intolerable, and interventionist counseling becomes the only hope for keeping such stu-dents enrolled.

For students who tend to be a "delegate" in their relationship dynamics with their parents, tasks such as choosing an institution to attend can become problematic. Parents who think of their children as delegates may become very interested in the status of the college or university their children plan to attend. This would not necessarily be a problem if it were not that first-generation students' parents often do not know much about the post-secondary institution pecking order. First-generation students' parents who delegate their children may be more interested in the way the college or university their children plan to attend is represented in the popular media; for example, they may express the opinion that an institution without a football team, and a nationally recognized team at that, is not good enough. And even when a community college is obviously the right choice for stu-dents, such parents may advise their children in other less appropriate direc-tions. One common pattern familiar to academic advisors everywhere describes the first-generation student who enrolls in a large public four-year university at his or her parents' urging without being committed to the institution or to a specific program of study. The student may not be ready to start a four-year program at all and may need a couple of semesters of a less rigid course of study before enrolling. A community college could be the right destination for such a student, one who is not quite ready to carry the family banner all the way to a four-year degree.

Family Mythologies About College

Many first-generation student families see college attendance as a place where a child leaves the family behind, for good or bad, whereas non-first-generation student families see college attendance in a different light. Non-first-generation students leave their families, too, of course, but because leaving for college has become incorporated into the family mythology, part of becoming a full member of the family, separation anxiety does not hit them nearly as hard. The family mythology predicts certain steps in the process, and parents and other family members have guided the student to expect them. Although the size of first-generation families tends to be larger than that of non-first-generation families, leaving a large family does not appear to be any easier than leaving a smaller one; in fact, just the opposite appears to be true (Duggan, 2001). Although his results obviously could have been produced by factors other than separation anxiety, Duggan (2001) found that "first-generation students from families with three to four members were 12 percent more likely to persist than [were] ones from families of seven or more people" (p. 9).

Unlike the helpful family mythologies that support the college attendance of non-first-generation students, some first-generation students have unhelpful family mythologies to deal with. Without consciously helping or hindering, parents can pass on unproductive beliefs about college and the world of work.

> First-generation students may be more likely to believe in the myth that they can work long hours at college and a job and succeed in college. Their parents, unaware of the general education requirements of college, may even offer counterproductive advice regarding choices about which courses are necessary, thinking accountants do not need to take English. (Inman & Mayes, 1999, p. 2)

When considering the success of first-generation students, it is important to acknowledge how little some parents know about higher education, and advisors and counselors must be prepared to address this lack of knowledge with respect. Parents' inaccurate views about higher education can come from Hollywood movies, TV, and other popular media sources—the seminal classroom environment itself is wildly distorted in most popular culture depictions—and, of course, parents will not be up on the latest movements and trends in postsecondary pedagogy. Although new insights into student development have helped many institutions examine their concept of the classroom as the main (if not only) place student learning takes place, for instance, contemporary postsecondary pedagogy that broadens learning to include service learning and other kinds of activities carries with it, paradoxically, the potential to hinder the progress of many first-generation students. Many first-generation students and their families identify classroom learning as the quintessential college experience. When first-generation students get to college and find out that this is not necessarily the case anymore, questions about authority can arise. Suddenly, roles are reversed and the child is telling the parents what the world is like, surely the stuff of cultural confusion. Parents of first-generation students who hear reports of community service and other nonclassroom learning activities may react with suspicion at first. "Just what am I paying for?" we can imagine a parent asking.

Everyone at a college or university who works with first-generation students should understand that there are some things the parents of these students can do, and some things they cannot do. Student affairs professionals need to make sure their expectations concerning parent support and engagement are realistic. The research shows, for example, that parents do have a strong positive effect on college aspirations (Dennis, Phinney, & Chuateco, 2005; McCarron & Inkelas, 2006). It may be, however, that once their children realize these aspirations and reach the gates of academe, the parents' ability to affect their child's academic success positively is severely limited or maybe even nonexistent.

As mentioned, most colleges and universities today provide postenrollment preregistration orientations for parents and students. Although there is virtually no research analyzing orientations in the context of parent participation and, more important, the effect of parent participation on the college acclimation process of their children, we can imagine the potential difficulties. To communicate the kind of complicated information that would allow the parents of first-generation students to be of help to their children, some institutions are even contemplating separate orientations for first-generation student families. But what would an orientation expressly designed for the parents of first-generation students look like? It is hard to understand how the general orientation most public four-year institutions provide parents and students, for example, would even begin to do the job. If the premise of this book is correct, and the absence of the intuitive orientation toward college is a very big deal, how can a one- or two-day orientation hope to fill in the gaps? Training first-generation parents to become useful advisors to their children seems too big a task.

London (1989) used the term "breakaway guilt" (p. 153) to represent the vague sense that descends on many first-generation students that they are doing something wrong when they leave the home culture for college. Other researchers who have focused on this state of mind as well, including Somers et al. (2004), call it "survivor guilt" (p. 431). According to them, first-generation students from areas where few of their peers have had the chance to attend college can suffer from survivor guilt when considering the plight of their friends, especially if those friends run into bad luck or fail to thrive while the student is away at college. If survival or breakaway guilt is likely to be a problem for first-generation students, and it is for many of them, the best choice of postsecondary institution for them may have nothing to do with whether the school is public or private, two-year or four-year; the best choice may have to do with geography and distance between home culture and campus. In some cases the less information about what is going on at home the better. First-generation college students who are likely to be drawn back to the home culture by guilt may benefit themselves, their families, and their friends in the long run if they distance themselves from home culture issues as much as possible.

Faculty Relationships

Of course, first-generation college students not only must learn how to manage potentially complicated home-culture relationships, but also learn how to create and manage new campus-culture relationships as well. No one should be surprised that achieving a personal relationship with a faculty member is one of the strongest markers for academic success for students who are the first in their families to attend college. Astin's (1984, 1993) retention model suggests that faculty/student relationships may be the single most important variable in keeping students enrolled. As is the case with so much of the student affairs literature addressing all students, the findings on retention for all students go double for first-generation students.

We have all heard the seemingly apocryphal stories of the highly esteemed woman or man of letters who mentors the needy, unsophisticated student from the wrong side of the tracks and changes that student's life for the better. The Pygmalion narrative is as strong as ever in American culture, and this is one case where the research bears out the myth. Although few contemporary students need or want the kind of attention that Henry Higgins confers on Eliza Doolittle, first-generation college students do exhibit a higher degree of success if they are able to develop a personal relationship with a faculty member. What's more, the kind of personal relationship they develop appears to make a significant difference. The research of Filkins and Doyle (2002), for example, suggests that "the frequency and nature of student-faculty interactions have the greatest impact when they focus on topics that engage students on an intellectual level in contrast to an exclusively social level" (p. 3). The converse of this statement, of course, is that non-first-generation students are more likely to establish social contacts with faculty members rather than "intellectual" ones, compared with first-generation students. Although I know of no research to confirm it, I suspect this might be the case, not because non-first-generation students avoid intellectual, academic-oriented relationships with faculty, but because many first-generation students *do* avoid social relationships with faculty members. Because first-generation students are sometimes hyper aware of their deficiencies and try hard to keep them hidden, they can be very quick to feel patronized. Whereas many non-first-generation students may be delighted when a faculty member attends a campus club event or happy when they run into a faculty member at a friend's graduation party, first-generation students are more likely to regard these kinds of contacts as external to their reasons for being at the institution (Smart & Umback, 2007). Filkins and Doyle (2002) go on to say that not only does academic performance improve when first-generation students have "active . . . involvement with faculty," but "personal growth" (p. 14) improves as well, demonstrating that achieving personal relationships with faculty is connected to the student's development of self-esteem.

The accessibility of faculty is always an important issue to investigate when determining the kind of institution to attend. Although just about every postsecondary institution brags about the accessibility of its faculty on Web pages and brochures, there are some structural differences inherent to the kind of institution a student attends that make these dynamics particularly important to first-generation college students. It is not as simple as saying the smaller the institution and the smaller the class size, the better things are for first-generation students. Although it is true that smaller liberal arts colleges may provide the greatest potential for contact with faculty, especially compared to larger public four-year institutions where the professor may only be a voice at the front of a huge lecture hall containing 200 students, the precise kind of contact is also important. First-generation students appear to do better in an environment rich in academic content such as one might receive in a large lecture hall at a large public four-year institution, while needing the intense faculty contact in the smaller classrooms of the private liberal arts college. This conflict is hard to resolve, but some institutions can manage it, or at least have managed it in the past.

When it comes to assisting first-generation college students become more successful, it sometimes can be helpful to pass over the woeful statistics of the present for a moment or two and look backward. Some practices that were designed before our age of massive specialization in both academic study and student support theory have application for today's student. Some past practices that were created to appeal to all students have fallen by the wayside as education theorists have scrambled to come up with new practices with particular students in mind. It used to be, for example, that institutions encouraged student participation in academic senate meetings, and some still do. Of course, discussion at academic senate meetings and other formal institution functions can revolve around fairly arcane matters that might seem of little interest to students, but remember, research shows first-generation students do best when they align themselves with the general goals and purposes of the institution. If institutions are constructed so discussions of broad goals and purposes are held only among individuals of like rank and function, to the exclusion of others, when are the goals and purposes made public? First-generation students cannot align themselves with their institution and reach their potential as learners if they do not know what the institution has done to service them better and what it is seeking to do.

Nonfaculty Professional Relationships

Although the most important campus-culture relationships that first-generation students can establish, especially in terms of academic success, may be
with faculty members, personal relationships with other institution officials
can be very helpful as well. Any professional staff member can have a positive
effect if he or she is willing to take on a mentoring role with a first-generation
student, especially if the staff member comes from a similar background.
Research shows that relationships with academic advisors are especially
important to the academic development and personal growth of first-generation students (Sickles, 2004; Varney, 2007). Duggan (2001) reports that
"first-generation students who never met with their advisor to discuss plans
had a 58.0-percent persistence rate compared to 87.0 percent for those who
often met with their advisor" (p. 8). Harrell and Forney (2003) also reported
that the quality of a relationship with a professional staff member is significant to the success of first-generation students: "It is essential that advising
be an ongoing proactive process that is coupled with a strong mentoring
program" (p. 151). The mandatory, once-a-year meeting where the advisor
is mainly interested in clearing time for his or her next appointment will not
cut it for many first-generation college students, who can always tell when
an institution's procedure is superficial or perfunctory. What they need more
than anything else is a real invitation to take part in the campus culture, in
the general concerns of the institution.

Students, especially first-generation students, should know the function
of all relevant institution units. Students should learn about these units by
attending to and witnessing decisions actually being made, not by means of
a single-page flier. Again, it is not unusual for staff members to say students
can attend meetings, but a lackadaisical invitation, if there is any kind of
invitation at all, is not good enough, nor is the bromide that students should
have some say in the decisions that affect them. Of course, students should
have some say, but more to the point, they should have the opportunity to
learn. To be successful at being college students, first-generation students
have to learn the philosophy, institutional parameters, and personal concerns
of institution officers who make decisions. Students can agree or disagree,
but the important thing is that they attend and witness, so they can align
themselves with the goals and purposes of both the campus unit and the
larger institution.

Peer Relationships and Role Models

One way to generalize about the subject matter of chapters 2 and 3—the characteristics of first-generation college students—is to recognize that such students are usually considered to be outsiders. The observation that they need to be encouraged to become more engaged in the life of the campus confirms this status. First-generation students carry with them to college the effects of a lack of sophistication about primary and secondary school education. They must operate from the outside in, managing a lengthy process to become sophisticated about postsecondary education, and the postsecondary school establishment has all but ignored their needs, even though they make up a large portion of the college and university student population. Because of the slow development of the demographic category, first-generation students may even feel like outsiders to their own student group.

Not much has been published about the peer relationships of first-generation students, and what little has been is a mixed bag, at best. Certainly, first-generation college students—especially those students, and there are many, who have never considered what it means to be a first-generation student—benefit from meeting students like them when they begin their college careers. They meet, they recognize similarities in the kinds of difficulties they are experiencing, and they move on. Whether the students they meet will become a source of support is likely to hinge on the details of their backgrounds, which can be extremely variable as we have seen and will see again in chapter 4. Although the details of the backgrounds of first-generation college students vary greatly, this does not mean there is not a core, even universal, first-generation student experience—as we will see in chapters 4 and 5—but it does mean that the support these students can expect from each other may be random and hard to predict, as evidenced by the lack of discussion of this issue in the literature.

We can infer certain information about the peer relationships of first-generation students, however, by examining reports in related studies. Some published accounts of the first-generation student experience have shown that such students do not consider non-first-generation students to be their peers, even though both groups, of course, are college students (Johnston, 2004; Lohfink & Paulsen, 2005). In fact, the more obvious the presence of non-first-generation students and the degree to which the institution orients student activities and services toward traditional students, the lower the persistence rates of first-generation students (Lohfink & Paulsen, 2005). The

Lohfink and Paulsen study went so far as to link the persistence of first-generation students to the opportunity to stand on the sidelines at large public institutions for a period of time to blend in gradually, a profile that perhaps undermines the value of peer support.

> Larger institutions may have more diverse student populations thereby providing increased opportunities for FGS [first-generation students] to find meaningful affiliations with fellow students from similar backgrounds, whereas on smaller, private college campuses the characteristics of FGS [they] bring with them to college may cause them to stand out—as outsiders perhaps—in ways that might hinder persistence. (Lohfink & Paulsen, 2005, p. 420)

Baxter Magolda (2003) offers another clue to the peer support puzzle when she points out that peer relationships on college campuses often center on nonacademic, outwardly oriented activities and interests, which may be less valued by first-generation students, similar to what we see with faculty relationships.

> College students already face hard choices about relationships, interactions with diverse others, and life decisions. These often happened outside of partnerships with educators and are processed instead within the peer culture. The peer culture, however, often exerts a press toward confirming to external approval rather than toward defining an internal compass. (p. 246)

First-generation students appear to gravitate toward relationships with peers that revolve around new (for them) academic concerns, which places them swimming against the current of the general flow of peer relationships as Baxter Magolda describes them. Pascarella and Terenzini (2005) confirm this thinking: "First-generation students also appear to derive greater benefits than other students in internal locus of attribution for academic success from several college experiences over the first three years of college, including coursework in various areas, academic effort, and extracurricular involvement" (p. 625). First-generation college students, it would seem, do better when they perceive the successes they have achieved as coming from their own hard work, rather than from the kind of collective effort a peer support network would suggest.

Related to the issue of peer support, of course, is the need for and effectiveness of role models for first-generation college students. No one really suggests that role models are unimportant because of the "internal locus of attribution for academic success" reported by Pascarella and Terenzini (2005, p. 625) or because of anything else, but the outsider persona that appears to be an important dimension of the first-generation student presence on campus may require a somewhat different attitude toward role models than what student affairs professionals are used to. Certainly, faculty and other figures representing academic success need to be in the picture, but what we know about first-generation students suggests another kind of role model, perhaps a second kind, is necessary as well. Because faculty are often kept at a distance, especially when it comes to nonacademic contact, perhaps first-generation students also need role models who are in the process of becoming, not just ones who have already become. This has been the experience of many of the TRIO McNair Scholars projects across the country (Hahs-Vaughn, 2004; Raymond & Black, 2008; Seburn, Chan, & Kirshstein, 2005). Described in chapter 1, the national McNair Scholars Program seeks to assist nontraditional students, especially first-generation students, in applying to and enrolling in American graduate schools. Many McNair Scholars projects have reported that role models in the form of McNair program graduates enrolled in and attending graduate school are very effective motivational tools. Because these graduate school students have not finished their graduate degrees yet and represent where the protégés would like to be in a few years, they appear to be better able to model behavior than is the faculty role model who has already completed the act of becoming a scholar.

To conclude, let us turn one last time to the seminal 1998 National Center for Education Statistics study (Nuñez & Cuccaro-Alamin) on the experience of first-generation college students. In particular, let us turn to the section titled "What Mattered to First-Generation Students" (p. 43) because it highlights and completes the profile of the people just described here and in chapter 2. The 1998 study (Nuñez & Cuccaro-Alamin) asked first-generation students and non-first-generation students to describe what mattered most to them in the context of going to college. In effect, it asked them the existential question concerning college attendance: "Why are you going to college . . . why do you want to be a college student?" Students were asked to rate which of several possible responses fit them the best. The three responses that had the biggest percentage differentials between first-generation students and non-first-generation students were: "Be well off financially" (61.4% and 48.7%, respectively), "Give own children a better opportunity" (85.3% and 77.4%), and "Live close to parents and relatives" (20.7% and 14.2%). These numbers are instructive, and to a great extent, they speak for themselves. They certainly do not imply that non-first-generation students do not care about these important issues, but they do demonstrate, through comparison, what first-generation students are like. Chapters 2 and 3 are devoted to what first-generation students, as differentiated from their non-first-generation counterparts, are like. I hope they will be useful to postsecondary educators as they prepare to serve the college student of the future. The postsecondary institution that knows these things about its first-generation student population, I believe, will be among the successful postsecondary institutions of the future. With regard to the second response above—indicating that first-generation graduates are likely to make sure their own children go to college—look out. Enrollments are going up. The success progressive institutions achieve in the future probably will go hand in hand with the success of their first-generation student populations. And if the numbers quoted in chapter 1 prove to be even fairly accurate, enrollments of first-generation students will be going up for some time to come.

4

In Their Own Words

C HAPTER 4 CONSISTS OF 14 NARRATIVES written by first-generation college students attending Sonoma State University during the
last decade. The student writers were gathered as part of an activity
initiated by the TRIO Student Support Services project, called Learning
Skills Services, on the SSU campus. TRIO Student Support Services projects
are federally funded to assist low-income students, first-generation students,
and students with disabilities to earn their bachelor's degrees. Learning Skills
Services staff posted and distributed solicitations around the campus, calling
on those with first-generation student status to write for a "first-generation
student publication." (This publication was created and distributed to all
Sonoma State University faculty and staff in an effort to raise campus awareness about the issues facing first-generation college students.) Some respondents were Learning Skills Services participants; others were not. Some 25
of the students who answered the solicitation were chosen to begin writing,
but only the 14 whose pieces are included here completed the writing process. After the narratives were finished, the student writers each received a
$150 payment for their time and effort.

Each of the students began the writing process by meeting with the narratives editor, Ivy Stocks, herself a first-generation graduate student in Sonoma
State's English Department. At this initial meeting, Stocks explained the
purposes of the activity and gave each student writer a package of documents
that included an article describing the first-generation student experience,
which they were asked to read; a timeline for completing the writing; and a
set of instructions. The instructions described the preferred form of the narrative: (1) "Every first-generation student narrative must have a recognizable

beginning, middle, and end"; (2) "The first part of the 'beginning' should
be an 'introduction'"; and (3) "Part of the 'end' should be a 'conclusion.'"

The instructions also included suggestions for the content of the narratives. Students were not required to follow the content suggestions, but most
of them did. It was suggested that they write about their family background;
their nonfamily background, including descriptions of people important to
them and of their high school experiences; and their Sonoma State University experience, including observations before the first day of classes, observations after the first day of classes, and observations after one year of
attendance (if applicable).

Stocks met with the student writers as many times as necessary to enable
them to complete the narrative. Some writers required several meetings to
complete the narrative; others needed fewer meetings. Because some narrative writers were graduate students and others were first-year students (and
everything in between), we expected that writing skills would vary, which
proved to be the case. Some students came to the project as skilled writers
of academic prose; others were in earlier stages of development as writers.
Stocks attempted to preserve the voice of the individual writers as much as
possible during the writing process and did not make editing suggestions
that would alter individual style. All students participating in the project
were instructed to write as they "typically wrote" and to avoid adopting a
"writing persona" in an attempt to please some imagined audience. Some
light editing was done after Stocks and the student writers were satisfied with
the final product, mainly to provide consistency from narrative to narrative
in terms of titles, institution names, abbreviations, etc. Finally, the names of
the student writers were changed; they are referred to by pseudonyms to
protect their privacy.

The narratives are not meant to be read as "case histories" in the strict
social science sense of that term. For one thing, the writers are not social
scientists. They wrote not to represent facts as accurately as they can be
represented, nor to represent themselves as examples of certain kinds of
behavior that might be called "first-generation student behavior." Like so
many first-generation students, several of the writers did not even know they
were first-generation students before reading our solicitation and studying
the brief material on the subject we gave them. Although they all were told
what the term "first-generation student" meant before they began writing,
for the most part, they simply wrote about their experiences at SSU. If

certain repeated themes do emerge (and they do)—themes that are labeled first-generation student themes in chapter 5—they emerge as a result of these students writing as college students who just happen to be first-generation college students, not as first-generation college students writing about the first-generation student experience.

I recommend reading all 14 of these narratives in one sitting, if possible. This is the best way to recognize patterns and note similarities and differences. Although every narrative is unique, the first-generation student experience is something that all of these writers would recognize easily in the narratives of their fellow writers. In addition, reading all 14 narratives in one sitting provides the greatest insight into the significance and intensity of the first-generation experience. As mentioned in chapter 2, some postsecondary educators still regard first-generation student status as something of a nonissue, something that can be addressed in a one-day orientation by showing students how to get around campus, where to pay fees, and so forth. And some postsecondary educators still regard first-generation status as synonymous with low-income status. Reading all 14 narratives in one sitting is the best way I know to deconstruct these assumptions. Reading them this way makes it impossible to miss the common difficulties and challenges that all first-generation students face. It is impossible to miss, that is, how the absence of an intuitive orientation toward college affects every aspect of becoming educated at an American college or university as a first-generation student.

NARRATIVE ONE: ROSA AVILA

I was born on December 14, 1983, in San Diego, California. My parents, Roseanna and Richard, divorced three months later. My mother was left to raise me and my two older sisters, then nine and twelve, on her own. She struggled, working double shifts to raise us and to keep our house, without ever receiving child support from my father; we struggled each month just to make ends meet. While my mother worked, my maternal grandmother and my sister Katrina took care of me.

I do not have too many early childhood memories of my oldest sister Gina, now thirty-two. By the time I was five and had entered kindergarten, she had dropped out of high school and moved out of the house. My other sister Katrina, now twenty-nine, was like a second mother to me growing up, always there for me and always encouraging. Like a typical girl, I idolized my big sister and wanted to be just like her, until she was about nineteen, when she did something I would never want to copy.

Around third or fourth grade, when I was about eight years old, Katrina came home and announced she was pregnant. A month later, Gina admitted she was pregnant too. At that time Katrina had just graduated high school and was still living at home with me and my mother. Watching what Katrina went through during that pregnancy and the early years of her being a mother was a sad yet positive thing for me to experience. It made me have more discipline and dedication with my own life, and started me thinking early on about my future.

At that time, most of Katrina's friends went away to college while she attended the local junior college full time and had a full-time job. I watched her get up in the morning, get herself and her baby dressed for the day, go to school, come home exhausted from work or school, do homework, try and spend as much time with her little girl as she could squeeze in, and then endure sleep-deprived nights. And then she had to listen to the stories of the kids her age out and about late at night, going away to college, partying, seemingly having the time of their lives—it made me so sad for her, but also made me want to avoid her experience. I still admire her for the way her life turned out and what she has done for that little girl, but I wanted to make sure I didn't have that struggle.

Three months after Katrina had Briana, Gina gave birth to Richard. Gina is three years older than Katrina, but their maturity levels are quite different. Gina was not quite as ready as Katrina to have a child. Because Richard was diagnosed with ADHD [attention deficit-hyperactivity disorder] and other emotional problems, it was very difficult for her to cope with her own growing up while raising him. While Katrina was at school and work, my mom baby-sat Briana, and after about a year or two, my mom took over full custody of Richard. The house was full at that time, and with all of Richard's problems, it was complete chaos. There were kids crying all the time and, of course, since I was the aunt and was still young myself, I was expected to baby-sit all the time and to play with the kids.

A few months after Richard was born, my father's second wife found out that after five years of trying, she was finally pregnant. While growing up, I'd had little contact with my dad, but once the baby was born all contact was cut off. Since that day I have spoken to my father only once, and he knows nothing about me. It wasn't until my sophomore year of high school that he knew I was attending private school, and I can honestly say I have no idea if he even knows or cares that I am in college. It hurts to think about that, not knowing whether or not he even thinks about me, or if he wonders what his little girl is doing with her life at the age of twenty. I have heard that his life isn't going as well as it once was. The next time I see him I want to be done with college and have my law degree and show up at his door and say, "Look at what I did with my life." I want to tell him, "Look at what you decided you wanted nothing to do with," and I hope he regrets it when he's old and has no one left.

As you can see, in a span of about two years my family situation had become chaotic; both my sisters had just had kids. Emotionally, I was in a state I don't think any child should have to be in. It is the norm in my family to not graduate from high school or to go to a junior college for a while then drop out or to get a minimum-wage job. Most of the kids in my family didn't have plans to go on to universities. It was too hard or too expensive or they just ended up with kids. I had a lot of older cousins and aunts and uncles asking me when it was my turn or talking about when I was going to graduate and have kids; some would talk to me about college but not really expect it to happen. They all thought it was just talk. Well, I was out to prove them wrong, to prove to everyone, myself included, that I could be different, that I could be, well, better than all of them. It may appear shallow, I know, but that mentality is what got me to SSU.

When I was in junior high, Katrina transferred to the University of San Diego. While she was there, she started toying with the idea that maybe I should attend a private high school, even though it was a luxury we definitely could not afford. Her biggest issue was that I would not agree to leave my friends in public school and go to a private school for my last four years. Well, I shocked her and myself when I agreed to look at the applications she brought home and considered not attending the public school. I took the brochures and looked through them, not allowing my mom or my sister to give any input on the different schools; I wanted to make the decision myself. I found one school that appealed to me, and it was, ironically, the University of San Diego High School. I took a tour of the campus and thought about the decision a lot. Was I ready to leave the friends I had known since kindergarten and go to a school clear across town, where I would have to work three times as hard to get scholarships to be able to pay tuition? Could I go to the public school and excel and still go on to college?

I decided that, yes, I possibly could go on to college from the regular high school, but why have it a possibility when I could be almost 100 percent positive that it would be a reality from the private school. Leaving my friends was hard, but I knew I would still live in the same neighborhood and would still have contact with them, and I knew also that my education was far more important than whether or not I could still eat lunch with them. So I applied to the University of San Diego High School, got my recommendations from teachers, took the placement test, and went through the interview process. This was a stressful time for a thirteen-year-old, and you can bet I was relieved when the mail came with my acceptance letter. I think I was probably happier than any other kid who got her letter that year, because I wasn't being forced to go like most others. Though it wasn't originally my idea, in the end I had made the decision my own.

In high school, I had the same guidance counselor all four years. I admired him; he was so sweet and seemed to care about me. It wasn't until my junior year that I started to change my mind about him. At that time we started looking at the different colleges that interested me. I really wanted to attend the University of California at Santa Barbara, for several reasons. Even though I had maintained a 3.0 average in high school, however, he basically told me, in so many words, not to bother with applying there because I wouldn't get in. I was crushed. This was my dream school. I had known it was a long shot, but I still think he should have encouraged me to try. I was told by other students and teachers to apply anyway, but I figured since he was the counselor he would know better than anyone. My counselor then pulled out the list of California state colleges and circled the ones he felt would be easiest for me to get into. I didn't exactly pick all of those to apply to. I mostly just picked the ones that looked appealing and applied to ten of the campuses off the California State University list.

The first response I received was from SSU, congratulating me on my acceptance. I was shocked that my first communication from a university was an acceptance letter, as I had been expecting the worst: to be rejected. I then looked at the list of other colleges that I had applied to, in order to see how they compared to SSU. After a few hours, without knowing what other schools would accept me or how much financial aid I would receive, I decided to attend SSU. The small population, in the small town of Rohnert

Park in beautiful Northern California, made the school seem appealing to me. To be honest, one of the attractive aspects of the school was that I would have to share a bathroom with only four other girls, as opposed to sharing with a whole dorm floor of students. So without even viewing the campus in person, I was preparing myself to leave my hometown of San Diego and the same house I had been raised in, to move ten hours away to a place where I had never been and knew virtually no one.

At first, my family was very supportive, congratulating me and telling me that they knew I could do it. My sister went out and bought me a congratulations card, very excited that her investment in my high school education had paid off. My mother, although proud of me for my accomplishment, preferred that I stay local or at least not go quite so far away from San Diego. When I received acceptance letters from Fullerton, Northridge, and San Diego State, she tried as hard as she could to convince me to change my mind. Today she is more supportive of my decision, realizing how happy I am with the decision I made, although she sometimes makes little comments about wishing I were closer to home.

I was very eager to start school, excited and ready to pack days before it was time to leave for Northern California. I don't know if it was because I was so eager or because I am a fairly outgoing person, but right away I met awesome people and made amazing friendships, which helped my first year of college fly by. Living in the dorms is something I am so glad I did. I made so many more friends in the dorms than just in class. Classes were, for the most part, what I expected at the college level: some were a little more difficult than others, but because of my training at a college preparatory high school I was able to handle it. Sometimes, though, it was difficult to manage my new-found freedom along with school, work, and maintaining my social life.

Because I was so excited to meet new people and to hang out with my friends, I did not look forward to getting a job. College was not something my mother could afford, so with the help of financial aid and the job I got at the SSU library, I was able to pay tuition. The job was a very good one; I was paid well and could only work twenty hours a week. Even though this was part time, it seemed like I was always working. Most of my friends didn't have to get jobs their freshman year, or at least not the first semester, and I felt like they could frolic as they pleased and go have fun, while I was stuck in the library. I hated it at times, but I realized that if it were not for my job, I would not be able to continue at SSU. Today the job doesn't seem quite so much a chore, although like many college students, some days I just want to call in sick. The job has helped me pay for so much—necessities for school, books, groceries, and so on.

I don't exactly dread going home for vacations, but I actually prefer staying at school. I love San Diego. It will always be my home, my hometown. However, SSU is, for the time being, home. I love my family very much; my mom and my sister mean the world to me, but I would much rather stay in Rohnert Park while in school than to have the long summer and winter vacations in San Diego. The longer I am at SSU, the more I enjoy it.

NARRATIVE TWO: CRYSTAL HALVERSON

I was born in Inglewood, California, in 1964. My parents were both twenty and had been married for only a short time. My brother, Paul, was born three years and one day after me. Because of the young age of my parents, my maternal grandparents and my paternal grandmother and aunt played vital roles in my upbringing. My parents divorced when I was five years old, and my brother and I remained with my mother. We had been living by the beach in a beautiful three-bedroom house in Manhattan Beach, California. My father moved to an apartment near the ocean, but my brother, mom, and I moved to a duplex by the railroad tracks. This was the beginning of my struggles with limited financial resources, class discrimination, educational disadvantages, gender bias, and loneliness.

All my family members have worked extremely hard. My paternal grandmother, who had only received an eighth-grade Catholic school education, raised nine children. As a daughter of German and Polish immigrants, she did not speak English until she started school. Unfortunately, having been discouraged from speaking her native Polish as a child, she is no longer fluent in that language. She worked as a housekeeper at the local hospital where my brother was born. Her family had to endure the alcoholism and violence of my paternal grandfather. Even at the age of ninety-four years old, she continues to support me emotionally.

My maternal grandparents received little formal education as well, but they both graduated high school, as did my parents. They loved to read and did not own a television. My mom did not believe in watching television either, so I spent much of my childhood reading at home, school, and the many public libraries I encountered (after having moved over twenty-two times in twenty years).

My maternal grandparents owned encyclopedias and had twelve book-shelves in their house. They always took me on vacations, and to museums, parks, plays, cultural events, and book discussion groups; when I turned eighteen, they encouraged me to vote. My maternal grandfather was a self-taught mechanic and an award-winning marathon runner. My grandmother was a master seamstress, cook, homemaker, and a member of the PTA and League of Women Voters in San Luis Obispo, California. They encouraged me to always try my best and attempt to go to college. As a teenager, how-ever, I lacked financial support and needed a better educational foundation in order to succeed in college. Initially, my grandparents supported me while I attended Cuesta Junior College for a year in 1983. The stress overwhelmed me after I attempted seventeen units and held three part-time jobs. I needed tutorial support and time management skills but because I did not qualify for independent status under financial aid guidelines, no academic support or resources were offered to me as a nineteen-year-old community college student.

Eventually, both my parents attended community colleges after their divorce. I remember my mom attended five years of night school while working full time as a secretary. My mother now needs only four units for an associate of arts degree. My father says he has recently received a master's degree. [Because Crystal's father earned his degrees—if he does in fact pos-sess them—after she began her own postsecondary education, she still quali-fies as a first-generation college student.] He rarely contacted me during my childhood and did not nurture a close relationship with me. He never encouraged me to strive for an education either and once told me he didn't think I would become the scholar of the family, but that my brother would. When my brother turned twelve, he decided to go live with my father. My brother actually completed his university education before I did. He is now making a good living and owns his own home. My brother feels that I was not given equal treatment and has tried in his own manner to make amends. He was instrumental in getting my father and relatives to attend my Sonoma State graduation and to participate in celebrating my achievements.

Moving constantly while growing up proved to be one of the greatest barriers to my education. By my senior year of high school, we had moved twelve times. I had attended ten different schools, each with different requirements, different socialization issues, and different expectations. Teachers often gave me the impression that since I was from a lower-middle-class background, nothing productive or successful was expected of me in general. Fortunately, a few teachers thought differently, and they went out of their way to provide access to community events, journalism, creative writing, and poetry. These mentors, however, were few and far between. Their assistance, because of my constant moving, was erratic and piecemeal.

I attended a total of five high schools, all located in the San Francisco Bay Area. I was on the spirit team at two different high schools, joined a gymnastic team, and was a journalist on a school newspaper. I enrolled in advanced placement English at a Daly City school and a Los Altos school. The two schools had radically different concepts of what "AP" meant. I completed high school with a 2.68 GPA. My grades went up and down with very little correlation to my true potential and abilities. In the low-income schools I attended, I never heard anyone discussing the possibility of a university education. Community college seemed an option. At the more affluent schools in Millbrae and Los Altos, though, postsecondary education was often the main focus, and many students talked about attending a university after high school. Many of these students had been enrolled in college prep classes since junior high. I did not even know what a formal essay was until I was a junior. By the time I became a senior I had only been in the two college prep classes, both of which entailed a lot of work to absorb the challenging material and to maintain and achieve some academic success. Additionally, I was constantly being tested. The high school proficiency tests that I was required to take and pass were the precursors to today's exit exams. I had to take them a total of twelve times! Mills High in Millbrae had ten proficiency tests of their own. I felt totally denigrated by the public school system. Two high school teachers actually told me I was not college material! However, I passed all the proficiency tests.

I wanted to take the SAT, but paying for it was a problem. I had been helping my mom pay bills and buy school supplies and clothes since the age of twelve. Paying for an expensive SAT test was not a priority—survival was.

And as it turned out, I survived for fourteen years without college. During the interval I experienced my own divorce, homelessness, and a two-year health issue that required me to be on state disability. I never forgot the positive influence of my grandparents, however, reminding me I could do it if I wanted it bad enough. My grandfather had worked three jobs at one time to support his family, learned auto body repair at night, and had been a radio talk show mechanic. He also won nineteen marathons in the senior class. My grandmother published articles in the *Los Angeles Times* and had been a protest marcher against the Diablo Canyon Nuclear Power Plant. They made me feel I was never too old to try for an education. They were very inspirational, and I attribute my current achievement and academic success to their positive examples.

I was so fortunate to be able to return to Santa Rosa Junior College, located right here in Sonoma County. With the assistance of Reentry Services and the Tutorial Center, my academic performance really improved. I started at SRJC in 1996. While I was there, I was finally diagnosed with a learning disability and was able to get tutoring and mathematics remediation. I worked hard every day. I often worked three and four part-time jobs to supplement my income in order to survive—as I continue to do to this day. However, I believe without SRJC's personal, professional, and academic support, I would never have made it to the university level, despite my high level of motivation and initiative. It takes a reliable support network to overcome so many personal, economic, and academic barriers. While at SRJC, I achieved a 3.6 overall GPA and a lifetime membership to the Alpha Gamma Sigma Honor Society. I received the Doyle Academic Scholarship for six semesters and twenty-four individual scholarships. I still am an active member of the SRJC Campus Alumni and am a Spanish-speaking GED proctor.

I initially chose SSU for economic reasons. It is located less than fifteen miles from my residence. I live in public housing and receive food stamps and medical assistance from the state of California. Financially, I thought it was the only realistic option open to me. I received two transferable scholarships while attending SRJC, but lost both of them when, due to my learning disability, I had to complete another semester of mathematics to meet the entrance qualifications required for my major. Before my first day of classes in the fall semester of 2000, I had only been on the SSU campus once, when I had attended an EOP (Educational Opportunity Program) orientation. I had wanted to go to Smith College, but I had no way of financing that dream. I had been told by students who went to SSU and returned to attend SRJC that SSU was expensive, that you did not get enough academic assistance or guidance counseling, and that the students were all in their twenties from middle- and upper-class backgrounds. I did attend an SSU orientation at SRJC, but I couldn't really get an accurate representation of the campus climate from that isolated experience.

My first impression of university life was that it was hard and not altogether friendly. I did not see many students in their thirties like I had at SRJC. I really enjoyed the Hutchins School of Liberal Studies (a school internal to SSU) seminars, but was not quite sure of the requirements. I was really frustrated in my math class and struggled because there was not enough university tutoring available.

I missed the support system of Reentry Services at SRJC and the intense one-on-one learning facilitators there. I also missed the tutorial center hours and the beautiful SRJC campus and surrounding environment. At SSU I felt like an outcast, very uncomfortable and out of place. I did not fit in. During the long transition process I became depressed and withdrawn. I had trouble completing my coursework and often felt inadequate, especially in a course that had an economics component, as I had never taken economics before.

I am now attending my third year at SSU, and finally I feel comfortable. It took at least a year to build a new support network, find good employment, get new scholarships, make new friends, and acquire new learning skills and strategies with the assistance of EOP [Educational Opportunity Program], Disabled Student Services, the Hutchins School, and the Education Department at SSU. Many of my friends are also first-generation college students, and therefore we easily relate to each other's issues on many different levels. Without the services provided by Learning Skills Services, I would not have been able to complete my university education. LSS has provided the educational tools I needed to excel. They helped me learn to comprehend academic material and jargon that may have been previously undecipherable to me.

I graduated from SSU in December 2002, with a bachelor's degree in the Hutchins School of Liberal Studies. I graduated just under honors due to my learning disability. I have maintained a 4.0 GPA for three semesters now and have been acknowledged and recognized a dozen times at SSU for merit and community service. My experiences at SSU helped me grow personally and intellectually. It is with the assistance of key people, mentors, professors, organizations—and my own tenacity—that I have had both a positive and successful experience here overall. I think all the mentor systems that do exist here encouraged me to continue. For me, it was during the year 2003, as a graduate student in the Multiple Subject Credential Program, and as a Sonoma State Scholarship recipient, that I finally felt I really belonged here. I have worked hard and have earned the right to be here.

I would recommend that all first-generation college students build a support network with tutoring, academic support classes, writing assistance, departmental assistance, clubs, and community organizations. Low-income students should apply for every single scholarship and financial aid grant available. I would suggest keeping a notebook with pertinent information, reading every email on the server, and checking every bulletin board notice on campus. Be an active observer, questioner, and participant—this will make all the difference in having a positive and successful experience at a four-year university. I am willing to meet with any student currently attending elementary school, junior high, high school, SRJC, SSU (or other universities) to offer my personal insights if this would help even one student attend a university and realize his or her true potential. Support is the key to success for all of us, and, as first-generation college students, we must work harder to both keep it and get it in the first place. Never give up on yourself or your dreams!

NARRATIVE THREE: CALVIN KNIGHT

One of my earliest memories is of the Christmas my parents bought and assembled a Big Wheel for me. Immediately after receiving the present I took the three-wheeler to the garage and carefully disassembled and then reassembled it using my father's tools. My family thought it was cute and a little strange, but I think of the episode as an example of how isolated I felt as a kid. I knew from an early age that other people, in particular my father, could not be counted on; as a result I was forced into self-reliance. I had to apply the do-it-yourself ethic, even when there was an easier way or, as in this case, when someone else had done it for me.

I was born in South San Francisco, and my family relocated to Rohnert Park in the early 1970s. My parents are from a working-class background. My mother was a skilled typist and secretary turned homemaker, and my father was a journeyman electrician who commanded high wages when he was sober enough to work. He went through Army Airborne training and later trade school in the electricians union. I believe my parents had a pride, a certain dignity, which came from growing up poor and knowing they had paid their dues. I have one older brother, and for many years I idolized him. My memories of when my parents were together are fuzzy—I remember a lot of fighting, my father being away for weeks at construction jobs, and a lot of fear. I remember my father seemed to have a new car every week, not because we were wealthy, but because he would get drunk and total cars, somehow escaping unharmed. Eventually my mother couldn't take it anymore, and my parents divorced. My brother went to live with my father, and I went to live with my mother in Santa Rosa. My mother and I went from having a typical middle-class lifestyle to being part of the working poor. I rarely saw my father after the divorce, but I heard about him often, such as the time when the police pulled him over on the Golden Gate Bridge and discovered a loaded deer rifle in the front seat. When asked about the gun, he replied that he was just going to pay a visit to my mother and me.

In elementary school I spent the majority of my time in the library (perhaps because I thought the cinder block walls could stop a bullet from a hunting rifle), and I read a lot of books. This escapism served me well, at the time, as I did well in classes and on tests. Immersing myself in learning always helped me forget about my problems. Most of my teachers at Montgomery High School in Santa Rosa were excellent, and they started directing me toward advanced placement classes. A couple of my teachers encouraged me and tried to help me see my potential. I even planned to go to summer session at UC Berkeley with some friends one year, but was unable to go, as I could not afford the fees. Even as I exhaustively prepared for and took the PSAT test, deep down I believed I would never go to college because my family was too poor. We ran into the catch-22 situation where we were too poor to pay for college yet made too much money to qualify for financial aid programs. I felt completely trapped by my circumstances: I could not afford college without getting a good job, which required a degree—a vicious cycle. I concluded that since I wasn't going to college, getting good grades really didn't matter anymore. I felt I had no future and therefore no hope of escaping from my life circumstances. My experiences thus far were that class barriers were insurmountable, so trying to fight them seemed pointless.

At school, there was an almost palpable caste system. Outside of school, I was friends with many kids from well-to-do families, but at school they would often join their friends in ridiculing me for having old clothes or not following the latest fashion trends. Most of my friends were from well-educated, upper-middle-class families and were discussing attending schools like UC Berkeley, Princeton, or Yale. My parents were born during the Great Depression, and I think this influenced how I felt about the baby boomer/yuppie parents of my friends. It was hellish to have affluence and the wide range of options it brings flaunted before me constantly. The more I hung out with my friends at their upper-middle-class houses, the more depressed I became, leading me to completely turn my back on these friends.

I began associating with outcasts of a different sort, the so-called stoners of our school. Most of them were from low-income, blue-collar families like me. I became caught up in a wave of depression, self-destruction, and drugs. I began getting high before, during, and after school. My GPA fell from a 3.83 to a 0.4. Eventually being high and going to school became irreconcilable, so against the protests of my school and parents, I dropped out of high school. I had no plan and no skills. I took and passed the high school proficiency exam and later the GED exam. I went to work as a dishwasher, a busboy, and a waiter. In my free time, I immersed myself in playing guitar, drinking, and doing drugs. I rapidly became unemployed and unemployable, spending all my time trying to get high so I could feel normal. During high school, I had been a very social person, but now people began to avoid me and I them. My vocabulary degenerated to the point where I only spoke a few drug-related words each day, and I consciously resigned myself to the fact that I was going to be the stereotypical Irish alcoholic, dead in the gutter.

I vividly remember the last time I drank or used drugs, which was May of 1990. I went to a friend's high school graduation party, and although it was a warm, sunny day, I wore two long-sleeved shirts and a leather jacket to hide how drug abuse had withered me down to ninety pounds. During this time I could drink massive quantities of alcohol with my friends, but I did not get drunk. One day I had an epiphany, a moment of clarity during which I admitted to myself that I was sick of living that way. I entered a seven-month residential drug and alcohol program. It took me a long time to feel normal without chemicals in my system. The treatment program was an educational experience about the science and psychology of addiction and alcoholism. I learned that although some people can use alcohol and drugs in a controlled manner, I was not one of them. It was also an opportunity to unlearn the subtle prejudices of my grandparents and the blatant racism of my father. My housemates in the treatment program were a diverse group of people from every race, culture, and social class. My assumptions and misconceptions about all these people were directly challenged and destroyed. I learned some of the skills that enable me today to live an honest life, and I decided that I did not have to go through life trying to live up to my father's outlaw ideals. Once I finished the treatment program, I returned to Santa Rosa Junior College (SRJC), but my mind was still a desolate wasteland, scarred and bombarded by drugs. I had to drop all my classes, but I resolved to return to school if my mind recovered.

Around this time my father encouraged me to go into the plumbing trade. My father had made empty promises for years to send me to school, but on this occasion he pulled some strings and helped me get into the apprenticeship program. It seemed like a good opportunity to learn a marketable trade. Nine months into this apprenticeship, I was seriously injured on the job (ironically, while working on the roof of one of the SRJC buildings) and was forced to go on disability. My prospects seemed grim, as I had thought that the plumbing apprenticeship was my last best chance at a good career and future. I became further isolated from clean and sober people when my best friend and role model from the treatment center returned to drug use and died soon after from a heroin overdose. He was like a big brother to me. The last time I saw him alive was on a respirator in the hospital. Every time the machine would force him to breathe, he would look like a person coming up for air from the bottom of a pool, but he never regained consciousness. Several other friends died from alcohol and drugs in the months that followed. Over time, my address book came to look like an obituary; the epitaphs for my friends were outdated addresses and disconnected phone numbers.

Thanks to rigorous physical therapy, my back injury stabilized and I returned to work. I began a string of unfulfilling menial jobs: waiter, plastic molder, ceramic molder, painter, landscaper, and warehouse worker. During my time in the plumbing apprenticeship and recovery from my accident, I had so abandoned myself that I had no idea what I wanted or who I was anymore. The extent of my dreams became being able to drive the forklift in the warehouse. Eventually my employer recognized that I had the skills and intelligence to go further, and I was promoted from warehouse worker to office worker. I began taking classes at SRJC, loosely following the California State University general education pattern. The first problem was scheduling. SRJC offered a decent selection of night classes, but many of the seminars and classes for reentry students were during my work hours. I might have progressed much faster if the seminars had been available at night. Also, the junior college counselors were not especially helpful, and, like my high school counselors, they gave the impression of people who did not really care. I know that many counselors, over time, tend to burn out on hearing other people's problems and that may be the case for university counselors as well. I was fortunate to meet one college counselor who helped me see my educational potential, who helped me broaden my horizons and clearly recognize my strong and weak points. That counselor saw more value in me than I saw in myself at the time.

I continued working full time while attending school full time. During the period I was on disability, I had built up a load of debt as well as back taxes, so I took on a part-time job to supplement my full-time job. I would work all day, then work every night I didn't have classes, then fall asleep while reading my schoolbooks nearly every night. In early 2001 I decided to take a full course load of sixteen units. Two weeks into this semester my grandmother died. She had been supportive of my return to school and, despite her fixed income, had sacrificed some funds to pay for my books and tuition. In the three years before her passing, we had been very close. I was overwhelmed with grief and was thankful that I had chosen to fill my schedule with classes. Between school and work I was able to move slowly through the mourning process instead of being drowned by it. In 2001 I achieved a lifelong goal when I graduated from SRJC with an associate of arts degree. It was very meaningful because not only was I the first in my family to earn any degree, but also because I had started something and seen it through to completion.

In 2001 my father also achieved a lifelong goal: drinking himself to death. Since most of the people I had hoped would be able to recognize my accomplishments had died, I became a bit lost. I had to rethink my education and accept that I had to do this for myself, that my family members' opinions didn't really matter anymore. To some extent, I was no longer constrained by my grandmother's practicality or my father's focus on having a marketable trade. I felt freer to focus on what I wanted to do. I had originally returned to school to gain greater earning power, but my father had shown by example that money cannot buy happiness. I noticed that gradually my goal had been supplemented by the awareness that now I was really attending school to become more of a whole person.

After I received my associate of arts degree, I took a few more general education courses to facilitate transfer to a four-year school. I considered the schools in the Marin and Sonoma County areas, as well as the University of Phoenix. I looked for schools that had good business programs tailored to working adults. Many schools in the area offered alternative degree programs, but most were very expensive. I quickly ruled out online education (although from a time perspective it still looks attractive) because it was cost prohibitive. Additionally, I don't know that employers value an online degree any more than they value a degree from a Sally Struthers correspondence course advertised by infomercial. Either way the cons outweighed the pros for me. Next, I looked at Heald Business College, Empire College, and Golden Gate University, all of which ended up being far too expensive for me. In addition, the business professionals I had met with degrees from these schools weren't much further along in their careers than I already was. I also researched the University of San Francisco. They focus on working professionals, but their tuition goes beyond what I can afford. I finally settled on SSU because I knew that a bachelor's degree from SSU would take me further than most of the other local schools, at a reasonable cost, and it was close to work and home. I knew also that SSU courses are easily transferable. If I chose to pursue a master's degree at another California State University campus, or possibly one of the University of California campuses, I would not have to take additional lower-division general education courses, which I likely would have to do coming from one of the other schools.

I applied to SSU and was accepted. I felt excited and nervous about this new phase of my education. At the start of the semester I was concerned that an influx of resident freshman students, arguably a greater source of income for SSU, would effectively shut me out of classes. I went to an orientation day and then went to the pre-business major orientation. I wanted to make sure I was on the right track from the starting gate. The number of seminars at SSU really impressed me.

Attending seminars and orientations made me feel less like a foreigner at SSU although I still had a lingering fear that something would go wrong. This fear did not abate until I had actually received my registration appointment. Then I was shocked that I would have to wait until the second round of registration. This made scheduling classes even more stressful because the few night classes available might be full by the time of my registration appointment. Juggling a full-time job and family commitments forces me to take night classes, but the selection of night classes is sub-par. I am sometimes envious of the students who take classes during the day while I am working. Eventually I will have to complete all the courses required for my degree, and some are offered only during the day. This likely means I will have to leave my job for a part-time job (or several part-time jobs). This wouldn't be distressing except for the fact that I currently make as much as some college graduates. In fact my current yearly salary is the same as what my mother earned at the time she retired. At present, I am running up against a brick wall in my career: no matter who I know, how many office skills I have, how many computer programs I master, or how well I interview, I cannot move past that brick wall without the degree. Once again, I am stuck in a catch-22: I can't make more than my current yearly salary without a bachelor's degree, but I can't get that degree without giving up my current salary.

As a first-generation student from a blue-collar family, I don't take education for granted. In my family, education is not viewed as an entitlement, and on some level maybe I feel I don't deserve it. I have met a lot of students at SSU who believe in doing the absolute bare minimum, that a "C" grade is sufficient, and for them perhaps it is, but I have worked so hard to get this far that I'm not going to slack off until I graduate. What may differentiate me from other students is that I don't pursue my education for the respect or acceptance of my family, just self-respect. I work as hard as I do because I want to be able to look at myself in the mirror and be able to say I did the best I could. I also want to wake up every day, and even if I don't exactly look forward to my job, at least I won't dread going there. Since I pay my own way at SSU, I take my classes seriously and try to make sure my class time is productive.

I often hear from other students that they have no idea what they will do when they graduate, or how or where they will look for work. This is another difference between my fellow students and me. I am in the business world every day, and I know that as soon as I graduate I will either move to a higher-paying position at the job I have or I will accept a position somewhere else. As a full-time worker, it is difficult for me to switch from the competitive work world to the semi-cooperative educational one. At SSU I bring some of the competitiveness of the business world into the classroom and I try to encourage that in other people; instead of coasting along and riding others' coattails, I challenge them to participate in their own educations.

When I first began attending SRJC and later SSU, I had hoped that I would be surrounded by students hungry for knowledge and teachers eager to share theirs. Although I have sometimes found this quality, I have found that college is a microcosm of the outside world, including bigotry, racism, ignorance, dishonesty, backstabbing, intimidation, and manipulation. I have also found that the Pareto efficiency discussed in economics is definitely at work in the group projects at SSU. Basically, the Pareto efficiency means 80 percent of the work is being done by 20 percent of the people. Every time the professors insist we work on a group project, I mentally prepare myself for the kind of parasitic manipulation, intimidation, and scam running that I would expect from the most hard-core street-hustling dope fiends. Those students who show kindness, interest, compassion, or enthusiasm are often perceived as easy marks, and others will take advantage of them. This standard is frustrating, especially in a time when EOP programs are being cut and the people who are actually willing to do the work are prevented from attending school due to financial or other class obstacles.

As I continue my education, I foresee many challenges. Once I complete my bachelor of science degree I will probably go on to get a master's degree, either at SSU or at another area college. When I began attending SSU, I had tunnel vision, thinking that I would have to take business classes and get a bachelor's degree to get a good, stable job. This ideal is still my primary goal, but now I am starting to change my focus. I am currently planning to major in business or economics, which will enable me to get a higher-paying job, which in turn will enable me to pursue a degree in ecology or other fields related to environmental studies. I do not see a bachelor's degree as the answer to all my problems; it is a tool, a means to an end. A bachelor's degree from SSU will be a ladder to the next plateau of opportunities and, for once in my life, I will have viable choices. My experience thus far illustrates this ladder: my associate of arts degree enabled me to get a higher-paying position at work, which paid for better-quality musical equipment, which in turn allowed me to play in two bands, and now I can afford quality snowboards and season passes. Ideally a bachelor's degree will have a similar positive effect upon my life, and will also further allow me to enjoy my free time with my family. The associate of arts degree has also enabled me to pay my own way through school, which has reinforced my deeply ingrained Irish pride of not taking handouts. Accepting gifts and kindness from others is one thing, but I know there are students who need scholarships and grants far more than I do. I am blessed in that now I am not alone in this journey, because my girlfriend of two and a half years has recently returned to school as well. My educational experience has already been of benefit to her as she takes steps toward a degree. No matter what, I know that I want to give our children the opportunity to attend school, to help them bypass the problems I created and dwelled on. While I never want my children to say they were first-generation students, I hope that I can foster in them compassion and understanding for those who are not so fortunate.

I am grateful for all the experiences that opened my eyes. I am grateful that, unlike most of my friends, I have lived a life of sobriety long enough to see my brain recover from the damage done by drugs and alcohol. I am grateful for my blue-collar background, which instilled in me the do-it-yourself ethic, and taught me right out of the starting gate that I had to do things for myself.

NARRATIVE FOUR: MARIA BRAVOS

My family immigrated to the United States over fifty years ago. My grand-father was the first to leave Mexico in the year 1948. He brought his family here in search of a better life while my father was sixteen years old. My mother and father worked in the grape fields when they first arrived in California, earning twenty-five cents for each bucket of picked grapes. My siblings and I were born in Sonoma, California, but soon after we moved to Mexico for the first five years of my life. Later we returned to the United States in time for my first year of elementary school.

I learned English fast, considering I was one of only a few Hispanic girls in my elementary school. I had to learn English in order to communicate with my classmates. I had Anglo friends all through elementary school and practiced my English with them daily when playing games. I have always been a very determined person, and I am willing to struggle, as long as I reach my final objective. School has not always been so easy for me. Neither of my parents had much of an education. They both finished elementary school in Mexico, where they learned basic reading and writing. They were never able to help my siblings and me in any of our homework, which meant I had many unanswered questions, starting at a young age. For my parents, learning the English language has been a struggle in itself and to this day is a barrier for my mother. My parents would have me—when I was still very young—write checks, translate letters, and make phone calls. I always did what was asked because I knew they could not do simple tasks like these. Attending a university as a first-generation student is very hard. My parents have been supportive, but financially they have not been able to help much, which puts extra pressure on me. My siblings and I grew up appreciating the importance of receiving an education, through my parents. Joel, my older brother, is currently in his first year of Marine Corps service, and my sister Sandra is a junior at Sonoma Valley High School. She wants to attend college. My brother received a college scholarship from the Marine Corps that he will use after he finishes his service. I am very proud of what we have accomplished together as a family.

In high school I was one of the few Hispanic girls to be in academic AP classes. School was a day-to-day challenge for me, especially since I was trying to balance it with work. I started working in my sophomore year in high school at a local restaurant, and I worked there until my senior year, when I found an office job at the Sonoma Valley Chamber of Commerce. My parents wish they could provide everything for me, but unfortunately they can't, and working was the only option. I was able to maintain good grades throughout high school and received many local scholarships. I received over $9,000 that I have used to help pay for my college education. For me, high school was a time for working hard, no matter what I had to do. Nothing came easily. I had a good relationship with all my teachers, asking them many questions about homework, attending study sessions in late evenings, and much more. My teachers always encouraged me to do well in school and were always interested in knowing my family background. They knew how hard I had to work to be at the same level as the other students who came from college-educated families.

Choosing a college is a difficult choice for most students, but I had only one option. I knew if I was going to attend a four-year college, it would be Sonoma State University. My culture is very family oriented, and girls are required by tradition to stay close to home. I don't mind this because I am very attached to my family and would not be comfortable far away from home. Sonoma State University is a thirty-minute drive from my hometown, Sonoma, which is perfect for me. I had only been on the college campus twice before enrolling, because I really wasn't concerned about how the campus looked. I decided to use the scholarship money to live on campus for the first year. This plan would save me from an early drive to school and a late drive home. My parents were not very convinced, at first, but they finally accepted the situation. They had never visited the campus until the second week of school, when my mother stopped by to drop off my sister. My father came later but has not toured the campus. I don't really mind that they did not tour the campus with me or help me move in because I know they have to work.

I attended Summer Bridge, which is a student orientation for EOP (Educational Opportunity Program) students, who are all first-generation and low-income students. It was a ten-day program, which was extremely helpful for me because I had many questions, especially since I'm the first person in my family to attend college. I made good friends and met SSU faculty members. We were able to register for classes with the help of our peer mentors during Summer Bridge. We did a library tour and took our picture ID before the rest of the students arrived. During my senior year in high school, I also received some information from an SSU representative, Eloisa Colin. She told me what applications to fill out and when they were due. There were many nights when I was on the phone speaking with Eloisa about the FAFSA because I had to fill out all these types of applications myself. Being a first-generation student means doing many tasks without the help of your parents.

Living on my own has been fun because I have time for studying, and I have my family close by for the days when I am feeling down. I enjoy living on campus because I can take advantage of all the tutorial programs offered and have my own space for studying. The hardest thing for me to get used to about college life has been the extensive amount of reading required. I have a daily schedule in which I have incorporated time for my reading. It has become part of my homework routine now. I also had a hard time taking a class in which you are graded solely on three tests (two midterms worth 25 percent each and the final worth 50 percent). I don't consider myself the best test-taker, so it was a bit scary my first semester. I keep good relationships with all my professors, and I feel comfortable going to their office hours if I need help. Good time management skills are required to survive the college atmosphere. After the first two weeks of college, I fell into a routine that became comfortable for me.

NARRATIVE FIVE: ERICA CAMACHO

I was born and raised in San Jose, California, the place where my parents bought their first home. Becoming home owners in Silicon Valley when they did was very fortunate because real estate prices have been increasing ever since. I attended my local elementary school, middle school, and high school with neighborhood friends. San Jose is a very diverse city, and my friends were of various ethnic backgrounds, something I now feel lucky to have experienced. I am the youngest of four children, with parents who encouraged me to attend a four-year college. Growing up I was the closest to my brother, who is only a year and a few months older than I am.

Neither of my parents attended a four-year college, and my father only attended school until the second grade. He was born and raised in Michoacan, Mexico. His parents needed help with the family income, so he had to start working in the fields at an early age along with his father and siblings. My mom was born and raised in San Jose, California, and was able to attain a high school diploma but did not receive a college degree. My maternal grandmother attended a four-year university. She was very successful and became an accountant for the Dole Corporation in San Francisco. She later went back to school in order to be promoted to a higher position. My grandmother was a great role model for me while I was planning my future.

While going to high school, I always made sure to keep my GPA at 3.0 or above. I worked very hard to receive good grades, so I could go on to college. Unfortunately, during my freshman year of high school, my mom was diagnosed with lupus, a disease that attacks the immune system. This became a financial hardship on my family due to medical expenses. It was hard to cope with the news and concentrate on my schoolwork at the same time, but I was able to pull through and keep my GPA high. I did not become fully involved in high school until my sophomore year when I was introduced to a program called Puente. My English teacher at the time told me to change my class schedule so I could join the program, which meant I needed to enroll in a different English class at a different time. It was hard to part from my friends in my regular English class, but I knew this opportunity would benefit me in the future. Puente is intended to give awareness and educate students about college and what steps to take to get to a four-year university. This program opened up my eyes to the opportunities offered to students like myself, students of Hispanic heritage.

During the second semester of my sophomore year, my parents decided to divorce. This was devastating to me, especially since I had lived in a two-parent home my entire life. I thought of myself as fortunate, compared to my other friends, to still have married parents. The divorce impacted my academic progress. My GPA slipped below 3.0, and I felt distant from my studies. I knew if I wanted to attend college I had to pull myself together and get my mind off the hardships and move into the future. During my junior year I became very involved in school. I was still in Puente, in the school choir, and had begun to get involved in a club called Project Earth, which was devoted to cleaning the environment. My friends had been in Project Earth in prior years and encouraged me to join. I enjoyed doing volunteer work, and I thought this work would benefit my community.

My senior year I was highly involved in school. I was the secretary of the California Scholarship Federation, a member of the National Honor Society, coordinator of community service for Puente, a member of the school choir, and I also played varsity badminton. My friend Vanessa had been in the California Scholarship Federation in prior semesters and told me anyone with a GPA of 3.0 or higher could join. So I filled out the paperwork to verify my GPA and was accepted. I had received a letter from the coordinator of the National Honor Society wanting me to apply based on GPA and community and school involvement. It was a nerve-wracking week waiting to find out if I was accepted, but in the end I was. I had applied previously my junior year but did not get in. These activities took up much of my time, but I still managed to keep up with my school work. I graduated with honors and a 3.4 GPA. The next step in my life would be college, a challenge I was waiting to take on.

I was introduced to the Educational Opportunity Program (EOP) by my high school counselor. I also received information about EOP from a representative from Sonoma State during a recruitment call. I chose to attend SSU because they offered me a lot of support and also a lot of financial aid. The Summer Bridge program really helped me understand living on campus and all the issues around succeeding at college. The week and a half of orientation gave me the opportunity to make new friends, which was great because when I started school I did not have to transition on my own. I also felt very comfortable with the students in EOP because they were diverse like me and the city I grew up in.

Before going to the EOP orientation, my mom and I visited the SSU campus to get a feel for where I would be living and attending school. I wanted to have awareness of the campus environment. Moving day came and there was something I noticed: the campus was not very diverse. Had something changed since the orientation? Something had. Outside of EOP, I was now a minority. This was very difficult for me to cope with because I had come from such a diverse school and city. During the first week of my college life I couldn't help but feel ostracized from the other students who were not of the same cultural background. I also felt people were being ethnocentric toward me. It was pretty obvious I was not White because of my physical features. And because of this I felt other students were staring at me in a way that suggested they might be thinking "How can she afford to come here?" or just thinking of stereotypes of my Hispanic ethnicity. A friend of mine who is of Hispanic ethnicity had a child's car seat in the back seat of her car because she had a godchild who often traveled with her. A group of female students, who were White, commented that she should be at home with her child. They assumed she was a mother because she was Hispanic and had a car seat in her car. My friend confronted them with their problem, and they again commented that they were surprised she had a kid at home while she went to school. It was an incident that made me think more about how people feel about my heritage, especially on the SSU campus.

During this pre-enrollment campus visit, it felt like the majority of SSU students assumed they were superior to minorities. The majority of SSU students I saw had blonde hair and blue eyes and most drove brand new cars. I have a 1988 Acura Legend; it's older but it gets me from point A to point B. EOP students helped me through this first transition because, out of all the students at SSU, they understood my situation the best. My roommate was also a member of an ethnic minority group, so that helped me a little bit too, although her financial situation was more secure than mine.

During my first semester at SSU, I noticed that members of different ethnic groups clustered together as if each other's company was like a safety blanket. African American students hung out with other African American students, Hispanics with Hispanics, and Asian students with Asian students. You can tell right away in the cafeteria the EOP students from the non-EOP students. I myself tended to hang out with EOP students, mostly because I had friendships with them from the orientation and also because they understood me better. We mix well together ethnically because back home we are used to highly diverse environments. I do notice some EOP students continue to stick with their own ethnic group. When comparing myself to non-EOP students, I find myself trying to keep up with their class.

When I say their "class," I mean their financial situations and gender ideals. Many students at SSU come from homes where their parents received college degrees and can pay cash for their children's education. It's very hard to say I can only afford so much while everyone else is dining out and shopping every day, while I struggle to keep my last dollar in my wallet. It is a struggle to try to mask my financial situation from the students who don't struggle like I do with money, because I feel I will be looked down on for not being at the same financial level as other students.

I am now in my second semester at SSU. I passed my first semester with a 4.0 GPA and hope to attain the same GPA this semester. I feel attaining this GPA means that I successfully put aside the difficulties of adapting. An interesting thing happened in my English class this semester. We were put in groups of four students each, and I happened to be one of two Hispanic students, and the other two students were White. I worried that the group would not take my voice into consideration, mostly because I am Hispanic, but I also felt my thoughts were inferior because I was not in the same social class as the majority of SSU students. To my surprise, however, as soon as the discussion started, one of the White students in my group listened to my comments and we worked together to get the task done. I feel more comfortable now than I did before. I am the first in my immediate family to attend a four-year university, and I don't want being a member of a minority group to hold me back from my dreams. My major is business, and I plan to minor in communications. I want to transfer to UC Berkeley or San Jose State my junior year to attend business school. I would like to work for a major corporation in marketing or maybe purchasing.

Being the first in my family to go to a four-year university means a great deal to me. I am able to be a great example to my younger cousins who, later in life, will take the next step in furthering their education. I believe first-generation students are looked upon with the most respect by their families because they have taken steps to improve themselves that their parents were not able to take. First-generation students may face difficulty attending college financially, but as long as they receive the necessary financial aid, they can manage the money difficulties. I receive financial aid and am enrolled in the EOP program, which also helped me out with grants. Anyone who feels she can't afford college should think twice; there is money out there being offered to students who really need it. It is just a matter of working hard to get it, but the hard work will pay off. It has for me.

NARRATIVE SIX: JESSICA GOMEZ

Enticed by the American Dream, my mother immigrated to the United States in 1981. She had to leave my sister, four years old at the time, behind in El Salvador. This was the toughest decision my mother ever had to make. She knew coming to the United States was the only way to earn American dollars, which would help her support her family in El Salvador.

Growing up, I wasn't part of a typical family. My sister lived in another country, and I didn't know who my father was. Ever since I was born my father denied me as his daughter, which was completely heartbreaking to me and my mother. Throughout my childhood years my mother struggled to put me through school. She has been both mother and father to me in my twenty years of living. She raised me the best way she could without ever giving up.

At the age of thirteen, I finally had the opportunity to meet my older sister. She was twenty-one at the time. This was a big moment and a big transition for me. I had been an only child for the previous thirteen years, and having someone else in my room was different. I remember my first meeting with my sister in October of 1996. She felt very awkward being in the United States and uncomfortable around me. In many ways I felt like she was a complete stranger and that I would never get to know her. As the years passed by we have grown together even though we did not grow up together.

Life was not always easy for the three of us. My mother would spend her weekdays cleaning houses for $8 an hour in order to put food on the table and pay the bills. Not having a male presence in the house was not the only problem. My mother did not speak English and finding a well-paying job was next to impossible. I began to work at the age of fifteen in order to have lunch and transportation money. This would help my mom a bit toward lessening her expenses.

Growing up in San Rafael, in the "Canal Area," was quite an experience. For years people have stereotyped my neighborhood as a ghetto. Indeed, it is probably not the cleanest place in San Rafael, and there has been a history of violence. It was not unusual to wake up at 3:00 a.m. to the sound of sirens. My mother would come into my room and make sure that my sister and I were OK. She was always worried about things outside our building complex, and it was my job to reassure her that everything was fine.

The residents of the Canal Area are predominantly Latino. Even to this day seeing someone who is not Latino walking down the street is rather surprising. Years ago many people (including myself) believed the Canal Area was not safe because of the heavy involvement of gangs. Luckily, times have changed and our community is getting stronger and less violent.

Attending college has been a goal of mine since middle school, but I had to face my high school years first. High school was quite an experience and gave me the chance to branch out as an individual. My freshman year I had to deal with self-esteem issues, and quite frankly I did not know how to fit in. During my sophomore year, I realized I had potential to do many things. Ever since I was a young girl, I had always wanted to play tennis. Finally, during my sophomore year in high school, I had the courage to try out. I became a member of the San Rafael High School tennis team and was the happiest teenager ever. Being on the tennis team for three years was one of the best experiences of my life, and it gave me the drive to get involved in many things in high school.

That same year I became a peer mentor for the Huckleberry Teen Health Program and part of a dance club, Corazon Latino. At that point I was not confident enough to call myself a "leader." I continued to become involved in things I knew would benefit me in the future, however. That summer I became part of XCEL (Cross-Cultural Environmental Leadership Program), which consisted of being at camp for two weeks and being a vegetarian. This program definitely opened my eyes in many areas. I learned what it means to be a leader in society and deal with issues from around the world. I continued in this program during my junior year in high school.

During my junior year the thought of college began to occur to me. I knew I wanted to attend college but did not have the resources to get started. My mother had only gone to the fourth grade, and my sister had only graduated high school in El Salvador. I honestly had no one to turn to and at some point became concerned that I would not be able to attend a university. I was always told that I was college material but was not given instructions on how to get there. Fortunately, I applied to the Summer Application Institute, a program sponsored by the Marin Education Fund in San Rafael. I never would have thought that such a program would help me get accepted to six state universities. This program consisted of living at Dominican University for a week and eating not-so-tasty cafeteria food. As part of this program, I was given a mentor who would help me apply for scholarships and admittance to universities during my senior year.

This was exactly what I had been looking for, someone to guide me through the challenging application processes. Now that I look back, I honestly did not think I would get accepted to a California State University campus. As it turned out I had the choice of going to my local junior college or going to a university. I knew that going to a junior college would be less expensive, but in the back of my mind a state university sounded more appealing to me. I decided to attend scholarship meetings during lunch time at school. I ended up applying for a couple of scholarships, hoping that I would get them. I interviewed for one of the biggest scholarships offered at the time. During senior awards night, I was given two big scholarships. By then I knew nothing was going to stop me.

Fall of 2001 was my first semester at Sonoma State University. For one reason or another I always felt motivated to do well in school. My good grades paid off because I was now attending such a recognized institution. I felt good inside. I remember move-in day so clearly because it was the first time moving away from home for me. I woke up that morning with butterflies in my stomach. Tears rolled down from my eyes as I loaded the car. This was the scariest thing I had ever attempted.

When we reached SSU, everyone was moving in. Looking at so many new faces intimidated me. The summer before fall semester began I took part in Summer Bridge, an Educational Opportunity Program (EOP) service that gave me the opportunity to meet first-generation students like myself. I began to search for familiar faces and saw a few. Now I was feeling a bit more comfortable and continued to move in my belongings. One of my roommates was a high school friend, but I did not know the third roommate. I realized this was the beginning of a whole new life for me and was anxious for it to begin.

I entered Sonoma State as a declared psychology major because ever since high school the subject had been engaging to me. During my first semester in college I made the decision to also major in Spanish. I knew that declaring as a Spanish major would give me the opportunity to apply and hopefully study overseas. Clearly, I had my hands full—juggling two majors and general education courses—but this didn't hold me back. I knew I was meant to be at this university, regardless of all the work I had to do.

Throughout the months I realized that living in a household with ten young women was going to be difficult. I remember being crammed in a room with two other people and adjusting to how they lived and vice versa. It was hard living with people who did not have the same lifestyles. Today I am fortunate to live in the newest apartments SSU has to offer. I now have my own room and a private bathroom, which is much more convenient.

The cafeteria was the ideal hang-out place my freshman year. All my friends and I would sit at a table and have conversations while eating our meals. Adjusting to cafeteria food was quite the experience for all of us who had to eat it. Second semester of freshman year I did not look forward to eating such food. After making a series of adjustments at the end of my freshman year, at the beginning of my sophomore year I was finally in my comfort zone. From then on I knew coming to Sonoma State was the right decision, and I was well on my way to becoming the independent woman I am today.

After being at SSU for three years, I have become a strong leader, which I never thought I could be. I rushed and pledged to a multi-cultural sorority called Lambda Sigma Gamma. This organization has made my college experience more enjoyable. The sorority is like my second family. After being a member for a semester, I was elected president for the following term. Being president was one of the most challenging things I have ever done. I learned to cope with different personalities and opinions that sometimes did not agree with me. Now that I look back I realize that being a leader for my sorority has opened many doors for me.

I continue to be an involved member of the campus community because I enjoy doing new and challenging things. I was a summer orientation leader for incoming freshmen during the summer of 2003. During fall of 2003, I also became a peer mentor for a classroom of first-time freshmen. I have also been involved in numerous other things, gaining new leadership skills in the process, and I have the confidence to say that I am a leader on this campus.

My number one goal was to attend college, and today I am here making a difference while getting educated. After graduating I will have enhanced my knowledge as an individual and be better prepared for the future. Students who are not first-generation have more knowledge of how an institution works. They have parents to turn to when they have questions or concerns. Potential first-generation college students in high school may underestimate themselves. They may honestly believe that they will not be accepted to any university, which is exactly what I once thought, and as a result they might not apply at all. Some of them may believe they have to attend a junior college because of lack of money. I view this as giving up too soon. Everything is possible in life; you must have the desire to excel and be determined. I highly encourage seniors in high school to apply for colleges and scholarships with an open mind. You never know what life may give you unless you try. This is definitely the mentality that kept me going while applying to college, and I have not lost it since. Resources are out there, but you must look for them because they will not just come to you.

I have always been admired for the determination I carry within myself. I look back at my life, and I am amazed at all I have accomplished. All the goals I set have been met, including studying abroad in Spain. I will be in Granada, Spain, for the 2004–2005 school year. It is a great opportunity to live in a country such as Spain and to fulfill my dream of studying overseas. Through the years, obstacles have presented themselves to me, but not once have I given up. I would like to inspire other students like myself to set goals for themselves so they may reach them, as I have done.

NARRATIVE SEVEN: JEFF PETERSON

"Oh stop that," said my father in a typical response to the intellectual conversation I was attempting to have with my aunt.

I often feel I can't speak freely with my folks or with anyone else in my family due to their lack of education. I think both my parents feel inferior when I speak at a college level. My mother especially feels inferior because all my life she has been the one who had to be in control and was full of advice to give. Now that I am in college and about to graduate, I have passed her educationally. Growing up in my household was tough on me. Trying to study with my parents around was almost impossible. My room was my sanctuary for studying, reading, or preparing for tests. Even though I removed myself from distractions, the noise in the house always broke my concentration, and trying to learn in that kind of environment hindered my progress. If I tried to be social while reading, it never worked out. My parents usually talked to me as if they didn't care I was studying, an indication they couldn't relate to what I was trying to accomplish. My parents have a high school education along with full life experiences, yet I have always felt completely alone in my attempt to pursue a higher education.

My parents both come from nonloving, nonsupportive households. They were born and raised in Sonoma County, and so was I. Their goal was to raise my brother and me with love and support and change the pattern set forth by their own parents. My parents definitely loved us and supported us in whatever we wanted to pursue. The problem with that approach, however, is that they were too passive in their support of education. They did not care whether or not we went to college; whatever made us happy was OK with them. In no way am I trying to bash my parents here, but their limited knowledge of what college can do for a child directly affected me in more ways than one. Most families prepare for their children's college expenses by saving money early on. My parents, being a working-class family, saved all they could to buy a house and have the things that we did have while I was growing up. My folks seem to feel college is just a way to make more money; they couldn't grasp the concept of going to school for learning purposes. So I was left to fund myself through school. I think it is a tremendous feeling of accomplishment to know you paid your own way through school without help. On the flip side, however, having that help does soften the bumpy road and can open your college experiences up to more than just going to class and working full time. With this in mind, I know I will make my children's experience much better than mine. Because I am aware of college expenses and the rewards that come from a college education, I will create a college fund for them and push them in the direction of education.

My extended family's opinions about education coincide with my parents' views. They too want to know what degree I am seeking, so they can forecast how much money I will be making. When you come from a working-class background, full of construction workers, dairy farmers, truck drivers, and other manual laborers, that seems to be the focal point of life. You live to make money to make ends meet, and wait for the weekends. Working-class people are often not concerned with global issues or even what's going on around them. If space aliens had observed my family while I was growing up, they would have returned to their planet to say that these people live for football, eating, and sleeping. So given all this, I definitely live two separate lives: the one at home and the one at school. At home I have to communicate differently from the way I normally speak in the company of college class-mates. I feel like I can never just be me. I have to play separate roles in order to survive in my two separate worlds.

My high school experience was different from most students'. For my first two years, I commuted two hours to and from school. At this point in my life, getting an average grade was all I cared about. My folks didn't care either, as long as I passed with a "C." Those years were full of adjustments to high school and figuring out how to survive. The only thing that kept me plugging away was baseball. As far as school went, I couldn't wait until class was over so I could go out to practice, where I felt like I fit in. Baseball was the only thing I seemed to be encouraged to do, so I stuck with it. When I was out on the field, I felt confident and sure of who I was. In the classroom I felt so sub-par that I actually dreaded class during these years. I was a failure at math, and no matter how hard I tried, I just couldn't grasp what was being taught to me. The only subject I cared about was English because there I could write about baseball. If I wasn't doing schoolwork or writing about baseball, I was drawing baseball diamonds while the teacher lectured. The teachers discouraged me from writing about the one thing I loved, so high school wasn't a positive experience. I switched schools before my junior year and had to make adjustments again. Baseball was still my number one focus because I was never encouraged to do anything different. Most guys I knew got a job after high school, and that was the last I heard of them. I had some baseball buddies who attended Santa Rosa Junior College to play sports. I attended for the same reason. High school did not prepare me for college because school officials refused to encourage students like me. My counselor in high school asked me what I wanted to do with my life after graduating, and I said I wanted to be a professional baseball player. She signed my evaluation, never encouraging me to focus on school or other life pursuits.

When I realized professional baseball was not an option for me, I went through the biggest life transition that I had yet experienced. Putting all my eggs into one basket, and making baseball my reason for school, was a mis-take from the beginning, and I was forced to deal with what was left over.

In my third year at the junior college, I had accumulated enough units to fulfill the A.A. requirements. At this point in my life, I met a very special person who nudged me in the right direction. Rachel, my girlfriend at the time, came from a long line of college graduates. She preached to me constantly about how much college was necessary for success in life and encouraged my talents in writing. During this same time I took an English course at the junior college from Professor Ryan Cooney. I enjoyed his class and for the first time I was told it was OK to write about baseball if I wanted to. He taught me that when people write about what they really want to write about, they usually create something better than when they try to write about something they have no interest in. I was evaluated at the end of the semester, and I remember Professor Cooney saying I had potential to write excellent UC-level work. With that boost of confidence and family and friends encouraging me to go for it, I was finally accepted at Sonoma State University in the fall semester of 2002.

My parents did not attend orientation with me; my college experience seems to be mine only, mine and no one else's. I have never asked my parents to come with me to any school event and have never shared my papers with them because they don't ask. I don't feel I have to approach them; I mean, I am the only Peterson on the family tree to attempt what I am doing, and so shouldn't they approach me? I have support from my peers in class and my teachers at Sonoma State have honestly been the best I have had thus far. I live off campus and have been on my own since my second year at Santa Rosa Junior College. After attending the junior college, SSU was not a huge transition for me. The biggest obstacle for me personally was finding out what kinds of help were available to someone in my situation and where to go for that help.

I am a liberal studies major at Sonoma State enrolled in the Hutchins program. I can't think of a better atmosphere to learn than Hutchins. I have the freedom to express my views and have learned more about who I am above and beyond just an ex–baseball player. My Liberal Studies 302 class made me feel the most comfortable that I have ever felt in a college class. The feeling of acceptance and support is something I have never experienced in a school situation. After realizing in class that there were other people like me who were first-generation students, I began to feel at ease because I was not the only one. Looking at my grades, I have a "B" average for the first time in my life with some "A's" sprinkled in as well. I just wish I had more people to share this with. I have learned that sometimes we have to depend on ourselves for encouragement.

As a first-generation college student, I think I am representing my family's name very well. I never thought I would be able to say I am graduating in a year with a bachelor's degree in liberal studies and am pursuing a master's degree thereafter. Sonoma State has instilled so much confidence in me as a person, as a student, that I finally feel like I am where I belong. I know my parents are proud of me, yet I feel they still don't understand what it is like to work full time and carry a full-time school load at the same time. I hope more first-generation students are able to tell their stories as well. We are out there, and having someone reach out to us definitely will make a difference. In my situation, for instance, if I did not have excellent teachers, friends, and other supporters, I doubt that I would be writing this today. I hope more teachers are aware of these kinds of students and the struggles they face to meet the challenges of a college education.

NARRATIVE EIGHT: ANNA GUTIERREZ

I was born and raised in a third world country. So every academic step I have taken in my life has required enormous support from my family. I immigrated to the United States from Mexico seven years ago. When I started college, I not only became a student but also a wife and a stepmother. Although the path has been full of obstacles, I have not let my dreams disappear in the fog. Obtaining a bachelor's degree in chemistry with a minor in biology was necessary before taking the next step in my career, graduate school. Managing our financial situation and social pressure, I have demonstrated that success comes to those who work hard. I have been able to conquer many obstacles, and I have not lost my drive to continue studying.

Scholastic success and volunteer work in Mexico was a part of my life since I was a young girl. Even though I worked part time with my mother at her flower shop (which soon became the only source of income for a family of five) from the time I was eleven years old until I turned seventeen, I was able to succeed at everything I put my mind to—thanks to my mother's encouragement. I remember her saying over and over, "Look at me! You do not want to end up like me! You have to go to school and study hard!" These words resounded in my head so that before I turned sixteen years old I had completed, with highest honors, a microcomputer specialist certificate, an English language intensive program, passed the TOEFL (Test of English as a Foreign Language), and participated with excellent results in regional and national contests regarding history, mathematics, and computer programming. I remember looking at my mother's worn clothes and then looking at my clothes. She would always get the best for me and my sisters without ever thinking about herself. Part of what gave me drive to continue school was that my mother had continued to try to get her junior high diploma while my sisters and I were teenagers. Her example showed me that anything can be done if you put your mind to it.

My mother always made sure I kept a good balance between extracurricular activities and school, so that by the end of junior high in Mexico I had won a scholarship to attend a highly regarded private high school. Still, my parents continued struggling to provide me with the best. My father had just lost his job and was unable to get another one due to age discrimination. As a result, my mother's job became the only income to maintain our whole family. The private high school student body consisted mostly of the children of upper-class families, one of whom was the president of Mexico's son. Of course, it was really hard to fit in there. For the first time since preschool, I was not required to wear a uniform to school. This was a problem because most students at this private high school could afford name-brand clothes and I could not. Fortunately, I made some very good friends who, interestingly enough, turned out to be other scholarship recipients in the school.

I am glad I found very good friends in high school. We shared the same goals in life. We were all highly involved in extracurricular activities. For instance, our science club set up permanent experiments around the school and provided tutoring to raise money. We used some of the club's money to visit exploratorium and science museums in Southern California. Most importantly, we all wanted to grow to become better people, and to attend college. We all took advantage of the opportunity to learn a foreign language and took challenging science classes. My high school friends provided moral support while my family went through a transition and helped me keep my drive to continue school. This support was to become even more important, since I got married right after high school and moved to the United States.

Right after high school I became reborn. Situations that would be routine for most people in Sonoma County would take me twice the effort to master.

Aside from the Spanish names of American cities (San Francisco, San Rafael, and Santa Rosa), nothing else reminded me of home. People acted and looked different. Even more important, I looked and sounded different than they did with my broken English. The drastically different educational system only added to my bafflement. Letters for grades? I still can't make sense of how they can average letters. Choosing your classes semester after semester, and keeping track of units, credits, full classes, and waiting lists: all of these events were unfamiliar concepts to me. Little by little I began to understand and feel comfortable with the system.

On the other hand, I have to say that there were some very well appreciated new features in this educational system: extended office hours, credit/no credit classes, tutorial services, English writing centers, top-of-the-line computer technology available twenty-four hours a day, PowerPoint presentations, etc. I could not believe most of the services were free. Altogether, this experience made me grow as a person and as a student. At Santa Rosa Junior College (SRJC) I found a quiet, comfortable place to study with all the things I needed, including free Internet access, inter-library services, reserved books, and a computer lab where I could do my homework. Soon, I obtained an associate degree in science (A.S.) with the dean's highest honors from SRJC in the fall of 2000, regardless of the fact that I did not own a car or a computer. This was my first accomplishment in the United States.

Now, the next problem was to choose a four-year college. I was on my own. My first thought was to go to the University of California because of its good reputation. Then I learned that the classrooms could be as big as an auditorium, and some of the professors would not even know your face or your name—definitely not the kind of experience I was looking for. I had attended SSU previously as a cross-enrollment student. The school had smaller class sizes and a great professor-student ratio. I also heard very good things about SSU from friends who had graduated from SRJC and transferred to SSU. Best of all, I would be able to commute there on the bus. Also, I would be able to obtain scholarships to be able to afford it. Overall, I had a smooth transition from SRJC to SSU. An orientation and many appointments with advisors and admissions and records specialists made things even easier.

While attending SRJC I joined the Mathematics, Engineering, and Science Achievement (MESA) program, a program established to increase the number of underrepresented students in the sciences. I became an active

MESA member by volunteering as a bilingual science and math tutor. It was through MESA that I was able to participate in a three-day leadership retreat in Mendocino County. During this leadership retreat I was introduced to leadership theories and to marine biology and chemistry research techniques. Participating in the leadership retreat not only helped me firm my resolve to pursue a career in chemistry with a minor in biology, but it also made me realize that chemistry can be one way to reach both motivated and unmotivated groups in the community. I believe that through chemistry one has a better understanding of the elements. As a result, one can better convey to the community the importance of appreciating and taking care of our natural resources. To create awareness in people is to help protect the continuation of a healthy biological system.

I have learned many valuable lessons from the volunteer positions I have held, thanks to the volunteer list available at SRJC. I volunteered at the Convalescent Hospital of Petaluma, the Commonwoman's Health Clinic, and at political offices. I was able to see, firsthand, how society is evolving, and I realized ways that I could make a difference. At the Convalescent Hospital of Petaluma I had the privilege to interact with people with Alzheimer's disease. This experience made me realize how I can touch peoples' lives by spending quality time with them, and that nobody should have to feel lonely in a convalescent hospital. At Commonwoman's Health Clinic, a clinic dedicated to family planning, I realized, among many other things, that I was able to positively influence these patients by giving appropriate guidance and education. Because of other community service I also got the opportunity to survey grants regarding the restoration of natural resources in the area. This helped me comprehend the arduous and often unsuccessful process of trying to protect our natural environment. Volunteering has made me realize that I can make a difference by reaching individuals early in life, and enlightening them with valuable knowledge to create awareness and responsibility for our natural resources as well as for each other.

Now at SSU, I find myself very busy but comfortable. My first impression of the school stands. People continue to be friendly and professors' main goals continue to be for us to learn. I feel welcome. The first couple of weeks at SSU went smoothly, although, to my surprise, classes filled up quickly. Fortunately, this changed as my classes became more and more specific to my major. Furthermore, classes continued to challenge me and push me to achieve my maximum potential.

At the same time, SSU has provided me with many opportunities to become involved in the community and research. Thanks to self-discipline, I have been able to continue to appear on the dean's honor list on more than one occasion since I transferred from SRJC. The academic excellence I have accomplished has earned me the SSU scholarship for the 2002 academic year and the SSU Department of Chemistry scholarship for the 2003 academic year. Academic success has not come easy for me. I had to confront social and economic obstacles. First of all, Mexican culture does not fully embrace women going to college, nor does it see the great advantages of planned parenthood. I am inundated with questions about when I am going to have a baby from family and friends. I even get warnings about how bad it is to wait for so long to have children. Then, I think about how bad it is to have them when you are not ready, and I wonder about how many really valid reasons people in my culture have to have kids. It took me a couple of months before I grew accustomed to these types of questions. Some people even told me I will never be a complete woman until I have a child of my own.

The hardest social obstacle I have encountered is becoming a stepmother. It has been, by far, the hardest and yet most rewarding thing I have encountered in my life. I have had the privilege of sharing my life with a beautiful boy for over six years. In him and through him, I have seen how unfair the world can be to children. Also, I have seen the results of lack of education in parenting. A great amount of my outside-of-school life has been devoted to counseling, caring for, tutoring, and providing guidance to this child, while my husband works a full-time job.

Economic obstacles are always there. Only because of my husband have I been able to continue studying. Thanks to self-discipline and academic excellence, my accomplishments have earned me the above-mentioned scholarships. Without these awards, my path as a student would have been finished much earlier. Almost the whole time I've been in school, I have gone without a car or a computer, but I have not let these obstacles stop me.

Looking toward graduation made me realize that going to school is group work, where the person who benefits the most is me. This group includes teachers, professors, parents, relatives, and friends. Each one of them helped me take a small but very important step toward my goals, in the forms of academic knowledge, strength, diligence, support, insight, and moral support. Close to the end, I have come to appreciate better what a degree is about, and what it is not about. As a first-generation student, I always thought it was about assuring a well-paying job after school. Now, I know it is more than money. Earning a degree is about evolving as a person, a human being, and being able to provide to the community and those who surround us. A degree is not about a specific skill that you earn. It is about learning what it takes to learn. Learning how to deal with different cultural and social aspects of everyday life is something that you learn in the process of college academics. It is learning how to make decisions about what is best for yourself. It is learning about *who I am*.

My next goal is to earn a Ph.D. in chemistry. I look forward to incorporating the best of the chemical and biological fields to study different areas. Lastly, but most importantly, I strongly feel that I should continue to volunteer. I hope to help educate minority and majority groups about our environment in the Bay Area, and the importance of staying in school. I have gained so much, and have experienced so many academic and personal opportunities in my life, that I wish to help those less fortunate, but who have the potential to become educated and strengthen the country. I believe obtaining an advanced degree will allow me to reach these goals.

NARRATIVE NINE: JOHN HUNTER

You have heard this story a million times. A family immigrates to the United States, starts a business, is prosperous, buys a house, cars, and a boat, takes vacations, and lives happily ever after. This is the promise of America. Hunter and Sons Electric Inc. is an all-American company. The name says it all. We are just an average working-class White family who, maybe because of our English heritage, practice a sort of nepotism. I am *a* Hunter, but not *the* Hunter. I am *a* son but not *the* son. If I joined the company, it would have to be Hunter and Sons and Grandsons.

My grandparents were immigrants. I don't know if I should use that term to describe them anymore; they did not arrive on a crowded boat, they never had to go over or under any fences, and they did not have to wait years for a visa. My family arrived by train to the Bay Area from Victoria, British Columbia, Canada, in 1959 with the promise of better work prospects. They had some humble possessions, command of the English language, and the support of the Murphy family with whom they were soon to share a home in Salinas. My grandfather first did electrical maintenance for the Firestone factory and later ran a small business out of the family's garage with increasing success. It seems the American entrepreneur spirit runs in our Canadian blood.

My father would often take me with him to side jobs when I was barely old enough to hold a hammer or screwdriver. While he was engaged in more complex activities and I could not be of any help, I would round up scrap pieces of two-by-fours, grab my dad's heavy hammer, a handful of nails, and practice driving them into wood. My dad made it look effortless, but no matter how hard I tried, I could rarely get them to go in straight. Next I would try to join these scraps of wood into a sturdy unit and actually construct something, just anything. I was obviously a flighty, unprofitable apprentice. When I was young, I thought he wanted my help because with my expertise he could finish a job twice as fast. As a teenager I thought he brought me along just to fetch parts and tools for him like a servant. Now, looking back, I realize I had no expertise, was of little help, and wasted his time when I went to search for parts. "Get me four strut straps," my father would say. "They are in the box with the compression couplings and one-hole straps." These requests meant little to me since I was clueless about the names of the electrical parts. He might as well have given me the directions in Russian. I was included for two reasons: to build a relationship with my father and to begin learning the basics of the electrical construction trade. When I learned the names of some of the tools and parts, I was pleased; my father and I finally spoke the same language, and we could work more closely.

My father, the oldest of the five children, did well academically and socially in high school. I'm sure when he was not speeding around town in his red Ford Mustang, bought with the income from his many jobs, he strutted around town in his letterman's sweater. He attended San Jose State University for a year; I don't know if he was motivated by a desire for a degree in civil engineering or by the attention he received from being on the wrestling team. His college experience was short-lived; he quit school and began working for Hunter Electric, making it Hunter and Sons. Under his care, the company grew in size and profitability. Shortly after my parents were married in 1975 they converted to what Leo Tolstoy called "the American religion"—the Church of Jesus Christ of Latter-day Saints. This faith is marked by its commitment to both industry (the motto of the state of Utah) and education (it owns and subsidizes four universities or colleges). This, I suspect, completed the Americanization process of my family. My father and mother work and live with an uncommon moral and financial discipline. Business successes have provided my family with many possessions and freedoms and have unyoked my brother, sisters, and me from the financial constraints that would have otherwise limited our options in life. But this narrative is not an ode to my parents.

My parents' philosophy of education is very typical—education is to provide the learner with a specific trade or skill that will function as a highly valued commodity in America's capitalist marketplace, ensuring continual employment and a large, steady income. Any schooling that does not contribute to this end is superfluous and impractical. Immediate job training and experience or getting a business degree would be most practical in the current economic climate. It is no surprise I am encouraged by my family, verbally and nonverbally, consciously and unconsciously, to join the business world.

This privileging of business occurs on many levels of American society, not just among my family members. The current administration in Washington, for instance, seems to believe that defending American business interests is always in our nation's best interests. President Bush has a master's degree in business administration, not a master's in arts. It is a sad fact, but universities are increasingly accepting similar philosophies. Since universities must be profitable to survive, it is no surprise they are enlarging business programs while slowly squeezing out less practical, which often means less lucrative, humanities programs. Colleges have learned the best way to make money is to teach *how* to make money. Hugh Nibley, a defender of the humanities in his book *Humanities Disciplines Rock the World*, explains, "Today we use the cares of the world, the imperatives of business, to neglect and condemn serious study." For me, the fastest way to a six-figure salary is through Hunter and Sons Electric, but I am after something more elusive—a profession I have daily excitement for, that adds to my enthusiasm for life, that puts me in a position to contribute to social improvement, and provides me with time for continued education. This is my pursuit of happiness, my American dream.

In the summer of 1996 I moved out of my family home and into the freshman dorms at Sonoma State. I planned to play on the soccer team, get to know every girl in the dorms, and maybe attend some courses. I came to learn that, in moving from Fremont to the dorms, I was not merely changing cities, but entering a whole new world—a world I was not sure I fit into. My four roommates were an eclectic bunch: a class clown whose father is an entrepreneur, an SSU baseball player whose parents are art teachers and sculptors, a musician and actor whose father is a professor at Chico State, and a so-called computer nerd whose father is a General Mills executive. Amazingly, we all became very close, very fast. My roommates became my new family. We would stay up late into the night, often with visitors from neighboring rooms, and talk about the past and present. In one of these discussions my roommate recommended a book, called *Amusing Ourselves to Death*, by sociologist Neil Postman. I was uninterested in my class work at that time, so I read this text instead. As I read Postman's critique of modern technology and Americans' obsession with amusement, I experienced an awakening and resolved to quit television. In the time gained from not watching television I read other equally interesting books. This triggered my slow transformation from a good soccer player masquerading as a mediocre student, into a good student who plays mediocre soccer.

In college, as both classes and new friends introduced me to countless fresh ideas, I was prodded to reevaluate my beliefs and future plans. Largely because of an anatomy lesson in elementary school and the example of a family friend, I had decided I wanted to be a chiropractor. My mom encouraged me; she thought I would give her free back adjustments and massages when she was older. Since I had contributed to her aching joints by making her chase me around the house when I was a kid and around the town when I was an adolescent, she thought of it as payback. One summer Saturday afternoon, however, while my mom and I were having burgers at a fast-food restaurant on our way home from my little sister's soccer match, I brought up new career plans. "Mom, I think I'm going to change my major from kinesiology to English and become a college professor instead of a chiropractor," I stated timidly. She subtly glanced over her shoulder like she was evaluating our level of privacy, slightly tilted her head to the left and said softly, "John . . . ," searching for the words, "professors are weird people." At that moment I realized two things: my college goals and career plans would not be easy for myself or my family, and, it was time to accept it, I was weird. After two years at SSU I transferred to the University of Utah and graduated with a degree in English. I immediately applied to the master's program in American literature at Sonoma State and am now just finishing my class work with the intention of teaching junior college composition, high school literature, or maybe pursuing a Ph.D.

These decisions have had consequences; I seem to have created a division between my family and myself. It is common in immigrant families for divisions to arise when children abandon the parents' language, profession, or traditions for those of the new society. Although the divisions between those who have experienced college and those who have not are subtle and not obvious, they exist and can be problematic for many first-generation college students. You can quickly feel like home is not home, when compared to the university community to which you have grown more accustomed. Each time I visit home, I am reminded I do not fully understand their world and they do not fully identify with mine. This is not a tragedy. Although I cannot discuss theological themes in nineteenth-century American Transcendentalist poetry or when to use a 2,000-amp MSB at 480/277 volt 3 phase 4 wire at 60,000 AIC rating electrical panel, the most valuable things we share and the things that make family bonds infinitely strong remain undiminished.

My family has not ostracized, disowned, or even criticized me. The worst treatment comes during good-natured teasing at holiday gatherings by uncles who, if you mentioned the work of Emerson, would likely think you are referring to the work of Emer and Son Electric. When I was young and accompanied my father on jobs, the feelings of unity were strong. We shared cups of hot chocolate before leaving, spent half a day in the same room working on the same project, and shared the satisfaction over what we built together. After I moved away to college, the number of weekend side jobs increasingly diminished. Now my parents and I live in different communities, work on drastically different projects, and have come to speak different languages. But we do share satisfaction. Despite new differences and divisions, shared satisfaction comes from knowing that through education and a career in the liberal arts, I have found just what they wanted me to find—happiness and fulfillment.

What are the solutions to these divisions? Should I limit my pursuit of education to stay physically and emotionally closer to my family? Will my advances bring long-term benefits to my family? There are no simple answers to these complex questions. It is good that education gives individuals the skills to tackle tough questions, rationally consider a wide range of answers, develop opinions, and articulate feelings and ideas. In other words, although education may have created a chasm between my family and me, it also provides me with the skills to resolve or transcend this chasm. I am sure my progression is in the right direction. I am lucky my unselfish, intelligent, and loving parents recognize this and, despite new divisions and conflicts, support my adventure into education.

John Adams, the second president of the United States, once said, "I must study war and politics, so that my son may study mathematics and science, so that his son may study art and music." Adams's plan presupposes that not all professions are equally valuable or enjoyable and that parents must work diligently to provide their children access to those professions that are most rewarding. The way he frames his plan for family progression also exposes his gender partiality; he feels men have worked and now work to benefit the men of the future. In the Hunter family, however, the women are not invisible non-factors; my grandmother and mother are equally responsible for my family's progression and deserve equal thanks for putting me in a position to study the literary arts. Art—and literature in particular—is one of the best vehicles humans have for self-realization and heightened social consciousness. I believe, as the Mormon president Brigham Young said, "The greatest and most important labor we have to perform is to cultivate *ourselves.*" Receiving as much education as possible is fundamental to this cultivation. Therefore, first-generation college students must not feel irresponsible or selfish when we dismiss family expectations and pursue higher education. So to all of you first-generation college students: the work required in class can be even more difficult than the work required in our families, but I know from experience that academic study is some of the most important work we will ever do—it is one of the purposes of our existence.

NARRATIVE TEN: NATALIE JIMENEZ

I remember getting ready for my first day of school, sometime in September 1988. My mom had packed me some tacos that were wrapped in shiny aluminum foil. It was cloudy that day. I was so anxious to go to school. Actually, I didn't really know what school was at the time, but anything was better than staying at home playing the same games over and over. I was excited that I would finally be able to play with other girls. My brother was an infant; he would play with his baby toys that were no fun to me anymore.

I was looking forward to my first day and was ready to go. I remember the teacher was really nice and helped me out a lot. It was only years later that I realized I was different, that my skin color was different: it was brown.

My family immigrated to the United States in search of the American Dream. I was only two years old when I had to leave Mexico. I didn't know what was going on at the time because I was just a baby. When we arrived in Texas in June of 1985, my parents experienced culture shock. The change of culture and language was difficult. We lived in Texas for one year in a mobile home in the back yard of my aunt's house. She took care of us financially until we were somewhat stable. My dad, who was the only one working, found it hard to live in Texas. The jobs did not pay enough to support a family, and my mom was pregnant. After my brother was born in Texas, my parents decided to seek opportunities in California, where two of my uncles lived. We moved to California in 1987. It was hard at first since we didn't have a place to live and my uncle's apartment was too small. My dad started working with my uncle in the fields. Since 1987 my family has lived in Sonoma County.

I remember someone looking at me and talking to me that first day of kindergarten. She was a middle-aged woman who was speaking to me in a language that I did not understand, English. My first school was Piner Elementary in Santa Rosa. I did not know at the time that I wouldn't finish elementary school there. In kindergarten I was the only Mexican girl in my class. The lack of a bilingual program obligated me to pay attention even more to how people talked. At some point in the first year of kindergarten I had a bilingual tutor who helped me with anything I didn't understand. Children learn much faster when they are young, and I picked up the language very quickly. Just when my family's situation seemed stable, we moved. That year it was raining a lot and we lived along the Russian River. My parents decided they had to move because of the constant floods. It was then that we moved to Windsor, a town a few miles away, and I was transferred to Windsor Elementary School in the second grade. In Windsor there was a more diverse group of students. Because of rent problems and work issues, my family moved several times during my elementary school years. I went to six different elementary schools. I spent two years in schools in Mexico, for the third and fifth grades. Every time we moved, I lost friends but made new ones.

My family is composed of six members, my parents, my three brothers, and me. I am the oldest and the only girl. I have always been the one my brothers look up to. My mother finished elementary school but got married when she was fifteen. My father also only finished elementary school. They have been together for twenty years now. My parents knew nothing of the university system in the United States. When I told them I wanted to apply to various campuses in the California State University (CSU) system, they told me they didn't have money to pay for my education and that I would have to wait for them to raise money for me. They were very supportive and encouraged me to apply. I felt that I was putting pressure on my parents, so I started going to information meetings about how to get into a CSU campus. My family felt pride in having their daughter go to a university. I was the first one from our family to go to college.

My secondary school history is fairly normal. I graduated from Elsie Allen High School in June 2001. High school was fun until the last year, when I was filling out all kinds of papers and getting recommendation letters from all my teachers. It was only then that I found out I wasn't told about the advanced placement (AP) courses that would help me to go to college. The high school staff assumed everyone knew about AP courses. Well, I didn't even know what "AP" meant. I felt like an outcast; all my friends were just relaxing and having fun with the celebrations and rallies that the school provided for seniors. I was busy with paperwork. I tried to get my friends to apply to colleges too, but they refused to waste their lunch time in the library. I was isolated, but I knew college was what I wanted. I applied to SSU because it was the only university that was near my home. I knew my parents weren't going to let me leave California for another state, and I didn't want to leave home anyway. I had already moved too much during my younger years.

During summer school after my senior year, I met the best teacher I had had up to that point. His name was Fernando Nugent, and he taught at a school in Geyserville, California. Fernando was very outgoing and enthusiastic. He was the person who believed in me and helped me apply to SSU. He was a great mentor, and I know that if it hadn't been for him, I would probably not be at Sonoma State right now. There are people who care, and he was one who cared a lot for his students.

Sonoma State always sounded nice to me, but I had never visited the campus before the first orientation. I was unaware of what kinds of people attended and what kind of campus it was. I walked onto a campus that was very different from what my high school looked like.

My family did not know where the campus was located; in fact, they didn't even know there was a university in Sonoma County. They were always too busy working, and they never had time to take me to visit the campus even though we lived only thirty minutes away. I had no clue what to expect, but I was anxious to start my college education.

It was the first day of school, which began in the morning and wasn't finished until 7:00 p.m. My classes were all spread out, and there was no lunch bell or anyone to tell you what to do. I had no idea school was going to be both so fun and so hard. The first few days, I had trouble. I was excited and scared at the same time. I didn't know how to take good notes, so the first few weeks I struggled in class. At the same time I was working thirty hours a week. I soon realized I needed to concentrate more on school and less on work. However, I needed money, so I had to continue to work. Later, I discovered that my GPA was falling. I started working less and eventually recovered. This was a transitional moment in my life where new things were thrown at me, and I was expected to catch them.

I am currently a junior at Sonoma State. You could say I have held on to my education. I am now a declared economics major with a minor in business. I have met many people who have become true friends over the past three years. Struggling through the first year was difficult, but it was worth it. It felt like I was blindfolded during that first year, but now I can see a clear path. I know what courses I'm supposed to take and feel confident about my academic program. I never thought I would enjoy school as much as I do, but I have found that if you study something you really like, you'll enjoy it more. When you really want to do something in life, as long as you're willing to sacrifice the time, you'll be sure to reach your goals.

NARRATIVE ELEVEN: CARLOS SOSA

My name is Carlos Sosa, and I am Salvadoran. I was born and raised in a neighborhood full of problems in Los Angeles. I grew up in what everyone calls the ghetto, between Compton and Watts. Growing up in that kind of environment forced me to work hard so one day I would be able to leave and go to college. Growing up in Los Angeles was difficult because I had to deal with gang members on the streets and make sure I lived to see the next day. My neighborhood was not all bad, however, and certain positive characteristics of my community kept kids like me out of trouble.

My family has impacted my life greatly. I learned much from school but have also learned a great deal from my family. I thank God for letting me have both my parents with me. My parents are very strict, and at first I did not understand why. I have just now come to realize they did it to make sure I could succeed in life. I love my parents so much that it hurts at times to think I am not with them now. I have three brothers, and all of them taught me different things in life in their own little ways. One of them is my twin brother, which makes me feel special, knowing that he is my best friend and that we have known one another from the start of life. My twin brother has had a very difficult life, and I have learned from his problems. I believe that having a twin is hard because we always try to make ourselves different from each other, and sometimes that means taking the wrong path in life. My older brother has taught me to never give up on anything, and he also has provided me with some tools that I will be able to use in life. I admire my older brother because he has gone through so much. He is one of the many reasons I have decided to continue with my education. My younger brother has taught me to be more understanding toward people and to help others by setting aside any differences or problems. My younger brother and I are not as close as I would like. I hope that we can be closer later on in our lives. Sometimes I feel guilty because I know I am harsh toward him, but it's not to be evil to him. I am harsh at times toward him in order to help him learn how to deal with problems by himself, instead of relying on other people. I want him to see me as a role model, so that he will go to college like me and accomplish his dreams in life.

I am the first in my family to attend college. The decision to attend college was the hardest one I have made in my life because it required me to leave my family behind and move to Northern California. My family did not understand why I was going so far away, and they wondered why I chose SSU. Because my family has no experience with how to get into college, I had to do everything myself—everything from applying for financial aid to researching colleges. It took a while for my family to understand my decision and a while for my parents to support me. My older brother made some sacrifices, like taking time off work to bring me here during spring break so that I could see the campus. He also bought me a laptop computer for college.

My parents have also made a big sacrifice by letting me go to school so far away from home. They support me when I need money, and they canceled their Christmas trip to El Salvador so that I could spend time with them.

I remember when I had to leave home for college the first time. I was saying goodbye to my whole family, and then it was time to say goodbye to my dad. I couldn't do it, and I broke down in tears. I believe it takes a true man to cry in front of people, especially if those people are family. My mom came with me to drop me off so that I wouldn't be alone and sad during my trip here. It was so hard to finally say goodbye. My heart ached, full of pain, and I did not want to let them go. I always knew, though, that one day this moment would come. I still have not learned how to live without them.

I attended King/Drew Medical Magnet High School in Los Angeles, which really prepared me to attend a university. Their focus is to send students to colleges and to prepare them for life. Being an SSU student feels almost like attending my high school, because my high school teachers gave us a great deal of homework in one night, and we had to learn how to balance our time wisely. I took some honors classes in high school, which makes me feel proud of myself. Being in honors classes made me feel like I could do anything in life. Attending a Medical Magnet High School made me grow up mentally, but also helped me to be aware that anything in life is possible if we take the time to focus. In order to graduate, I had to meet entrance requirements for the University of California system. I also went to night school, which made going to high school a little harder because I would sometimes have to stay up until the morning to finish my homework. This experience helped me prepare for college.

I was very involved with extracurricular activities in school as well. I improved my leadership skills by becoming a member of the Site Management Council, a program that allowed another student and me to become the representative voice of all the students in the school. I also became the French Club president, and I planned the club's trip to Canada. I was also involved with the Drama Club, the Swing Dance Club, Just SO, a student-created club dedicated to the celebration of diversity, and BrainWorks, a club designed to help King/Drew's future doctors and surgeons receive a better understanding of how the human body works. I was also involved in two programs outside of school, MAPS and YouThink. MAPS helps students who are planning to go to college get a better understanding of what they need to do in order to accomplish their dreams. YouThink provides community service in the form of mentor programs and other programs. I am still involved with this program and am going to be a camp counselor for them this summer. All the friends I hung out with throughout high school were planning to attend college, and some of us made a promise to attend college together, which has happened.

There have been many people in my life who have contributed to the idea of attending college. My friends are my most important support because they believe it's important for us, the future of this country, to become educated. Of course, my college counselor and my academic counselor helped me very much, and I thank them for that. Ms. Moody, a high school counselor, helped me the most by meeting with me often and calling colleges for me to get information that I wanted. In addition, all my teachers from high school gave me the idea that I could do as they did and attend college. The program MAPS and the Educational Opportunity Program (EOP) have helped me to accomplish my dreams.

I applied to five universities, and all five accepted me. I plan to major in nursing. The other four schools I applied to have nursing programs, but everyone I talked to said that SSU had the best nursing program. When I came to see the campus, it was just what I always wanted college to be like—peaceful, relaxing, and surrounded by wildlife and beauty. I am from the city, so I wanted to be in a completely new type of environment. Being accepted to the EOP program encouraged me to attend SSU because the EOP staff provides a great deal of support, plus I had made many friends during the Summer Bridge program. Because my parents are busy people, they could not come with me to visit the campus. I had my brother with me, which is always good because he has always made me feel confident with the decisions I make. As a result of the Summer Bridge program and other SSU orientations I knew a great deal about this university before the first day of classes arrived.

When the first week of classes was over, I knew that college was going to be somewhat difficult, but I looked forward to the new experiences. I have learned to interact with people from different backgrounds, and to balance my work and my social life. The hardest thing for me has been becoming accustomed to the fact that I am away from my home, family, and childhood friends. I had to open up and make new friends and start my life all over in this new place. I did not want to make friends, at first, because I am a shy person, but I made it somehow to this day without giving up. Living on campus was and still is exciting because there is always something different going on. It was hard to move in with strangers because I did not know one thing about them, and I had to trust them without really knowing them. However, I am getting to know them and am still learning things about them. It has also been difficult to get used to the weather because in Los Angeles it does not get too cold or rain much. At first, the food made me feel sick because it wasn't what we ate at home. I had to figure out ways to get used to this new environment, which has not been easy, and I am still working on it. It took me a long time to feel comfortable at SSU because it is not as diverse as Los Angeles.

I look forward to starting the nursing program. I am not, however, in a rush to graduate because I feel a certain fear about life, and I do not want to start it right away. I want to take my time, but I do not plan to stay in school for an overly long time. My first impressions of college life have not changed much. One big shock was the amount of money I had to spend on books. When I started college, I did not know how much money I would need to spend on schoolbooks. They are crazy expensive. I think incoming students should be aware that they will need to spend a great deal of money on books.

Getting a college degree means that career doors will open, but also that you will gain a new meaning of the word "knowledge." With a degree, you will be able to accomplish a great deal, as well as gain a career. Attending college as a first-generation student can be very hard because we have to deal with getting into a university and also deal with our families' reluctance to let us go. You have to make them understand why you have to do this for yourself. First-generation students must do everything for themselves because family members might not know the process of applying to school and that there is money available for them. Never give up if you think it will not work out, because you can make it happen if you just give it a chance and use all the resources available to you. Also, talk to people about the way you are feeling because it can help you let go of some of the stress that you will have. Always ask for help when you need it. Do not think people are not there for you because there are many people willing to help you. When you feel homesick, do not think it's time to give up; think of it as a test: once you overcome it, you will be able to accomplish your goals. Also, think about your life, about your future; always ask yourself what you want to do with your life. For those who are thinking about applying to college, my advice for you is to get help from your peers and your counselors; use all the resources around you, but most importantly, apply. If you think your parents cannot afford to pay for college, apply for financial aid to get grant money; you may also be able to get scholarships and loans, but you have to apply. Apply for the EOP program; they help first-generation students make it to college, as well as offer support during college. Finally, I hope that you follow what is right for you; do not force yourself to do what others want you to do—remember that going to college is for you and your future.

NARRATIVE TWELVE: YOLANDA ORTIZ

We inevitably go through change throughout our lives. We complete many cycles throughout our lifetimes. These are never-ending cycles of self-transformation. These transformations are like that of the butterfly: Like Butterfly, you are always at a certain station in your life activities. You may be at the egg stage, which is the beginning of all things. This is the stage at which an idea is born but has not yet become a reality. The larva stage is the point at which you decide to create the idea in the physical world. The cocoon stage involves "going within," doing or developing your project, idea, or aspect of personality. The final stage of transformation is the leaving of the chrysalis and birth. This last stage involves sharing the colors and joy of your creation with the world.

—Native American Medicine Cards

I was born in Tucson, Arizona, on September 15, 1952, to Josefa Borboa and Ernesto M. Noriega. I was the first child of a family of six (I have a brother and four sisters). I am of Native American and Mexican American descent—a product of the colonized working class. My father finished elementary school, worked, and then was drafted into the service to fight in World War II in the Pacific theater. My mother did not get to finish elementary school because she had to work and help support the family. On my father's side of the family, there were no college graduates, and I believe that no one on his side finished high school. On my mother's side of the family, her oldest brother, Gildardo, went to a community college and earned an A.A. degree. My mother never expressed directly how she felt about college; she never said whether she approved of it or not.

In my working-class family, graduating from high school was all that was required. As we knew, the law mandated it. After graduation my parents encouraged my siblings and me to secure well-paying jobs with benefits, preferably with the city, county, state, or federal government. My mother mainly seemed concerned about what type of job would result from our educations, and whether we would earn a good salary. She influenced my life a great deal—directing my thoughts and activities and concerning herself with my physical appearance. Any participation in activities outside the family was limited unless I was with my *Tio* (uncle) Pilo and *Tia* (aunt) Jenny. They would take my cousins and me to San Xavier Mission, the park, movies, and swimming. I cannot remember any time that my parents took us to the library or museums, asked how our day went in school, did arts and crafts with us, or read to us. Our family time was spent watching television together, participating in occasional family picnics with our relatives, taking cherished vacation trips to California, and planning the many holiday gatherings. Our family stressed work, family obligations, and graduation from high school.

> *Egg and Larva Stage: At the egg stage the idea or thought is planted and in the larva stage the decision is made to follow through with the idea or thought.*
>
> —Native American Medicine Cards

I found it tough going in high school. Due to my parents' limited education I did not have any help with my homework. My essays were poorly written because of my limited vocabulary and my weak reading abilities. We could not afford tutors, and I was very shy and did not ask for help from the teachers. I would not participate in class discussions because giving the wrong answer really embarrassed me. I was not able to participate in extracurricular activities because my mother did not believe in them. I was required to come directly home from school so that I could help my mother with chores and care for my siblings. Not many of my friends were considering attending college, and neither was I. One of my high school counselors, however, told me that I could make it in college. I did not believe it at first, but she eventually convinced me. I received a $300 scholarship to attend the University of Arizona. Even so, I had scored low on the SAT test and did not believe I was smart enough to attend college.

Cocoon Stage: Developing and doing something to make the idea a reality.
— Native American Medicine Cards

I gave college a try anyway, and at the University of Arizona enrolled in a college success program. It included an English preparatory course, and a class that gave tips on studying, taking notes, and test-taking strategies. The college environment was so free, compared to home, that I did not know how to act. I was so used to my life being controlled by strict school management and my family that I went wild and did not attend my classes or do my homework. I was sliding through school for two semesters, until I finally dropped out because I could not focus. That first year in college was disastrous.

I returned to the University of Arizona after seven years of marriage and four children. After two more semesters, however, I had to drop out again, this time due to marital difficulties. In 1988 I enrolled in Ventura Community College to get certification in the Psychiatric Technician Program. With a great deal of support from a friend, I completed the program with a 3.8 GPA. I knew that this was only the beginning, and that I wanted to continue with school. In 1996 I enrolled in the Licensed Vocational Nursing Program at Santa Rosa Junior College (SRJC), completed that program, and made the dean's list. At SRJC my sense of self-worth was given a boost when I led an informal study group that increased the test scores of all the participating students. I continued with school, hoping to get into the Physician's Assistants Program. I ended up not pursuing that career path because, in order to qualify, the program required a total of 4,000 hours of work experience in the medical field. Although I had worked more than 5,000 hours as a Psychiatric Technician, the department would only count 1,000 hours of my experience. To make up those hours would have meant postponing my education for two years. I continued with my education in biology and graduated from SRJC with associate of arts and associate of sciences degrees. I then transferred to SSU and could not get into the biology department because of my past grades from the University of Arizona. I eventually declared sociology as my major and Native American studies as my minor.

While attending SSU, I worked as a teacher's assistant (TA) for Professor Elaine Leeder for two semesters in the Introduction to Sociology class. During the first semester, I was terrified at the prospect of facilitating the discussion section, so I spent half my time fighting my fears and felt that I did not contribute my best to the class. I became a TA for the second semester because I knew I needed the experience to get over my low self-esteem and fears of public exposure. I also worked as a TA in a tai chi class, assisting the instructor with directing the class in breathing and meditation. These TA positions helped me overcome my low self-esteem and fears. I also had the pleasure of assisting Professor Edward Castillo of the Native American studies department in a research project. This project entailed gathering statistics, data about domestic violence and addictions, and researching treatment centers tailored to Native American communities. I also helped *Project Censored* in a promotion to encourage local libraries to stock Project Censored books. I am presently helping Professor Peter Phillips in a fundraising project for the sociology department. For the spring semester 2004, I have applied to the JUMP program in hopes of participating in the Alternative Spring Break Trip that involves tutoring Navajo students in the elementary and junior high grades.

Birth Stage: Sharing a completed idea.

—Native American Medicine Cards

Being a first-generation college student has been very difficult because I entered the college setting with low self-esteem, no self-control, lack of familial support, and lack of college preparatory classes. I felt that I could not succeed and that I was not smart enough because of low to average grades in high school and my low SAT scores. Coming from a controlled environment (where individualism is not encouraged and the value of one's identity is based on one's employment status) contributed to the insecurity and lack of self-control that I experienced once I was able to make decisions on my own. My family, having had no educational background, could not help with my homework; furthermore, they did not offer emotional encouragement or monetary support. My high school did not prepare me for college.

Many non-first-generation students seem to have the support of their families and the school system. Their parents have the educational background to facilitate their writing skills, reading abilities, and can offer financial support. Generally, the schools they attend seem to better prepare them for higher education, offering college preparatory courses sponsored by local universities or junior colleges.

What I have realized in pursuing my college degree is that my parents did the best they could. My parents learned what their parents, grandparents, great-grandparents emphasized. They were taught to think differently from the way their ancestors thought. When the colonizers came to their land, they were forced to survive the best way they could. Oftentimes that meant being submissive and invisible in public; they learned not to verbalize their opinions, and they developed a slave mentality, assimilating and accepting the fate that was handed down to them. My parents grew to believe that land ownership and capital gains determined the value of the individual. This identity secured them a comfortable existence with minimal discrimination—or so they believed. They accepted that way of life because they figured it could have been worse. Breaking away from this slave mentality makes it extremely difficult for me, a first-generation college student, because I must fight against the effects of generations of colonization. I have learned to survive in the college setting, which expects students to be assertive, verbalize opinions, and be visible in public. It has been a difficult journey, but the rewards of respect, dignity, and self-esteem are worth it. This segment of my long, sometimes grueling, but incredibly fruitful journey is now coming to a close. This is my last semester at SSU, and I will be graduating in May 2004.

NARRATIVE THIRTEEN: ELIZABETH ORDAZ

I live by these words: "If I made it through that, I can make it through this." Throughout my life, I have balanced two different worlds—my home life and my school life. At an early age I learned some difficult lessons in my old home in Richmond, California. When I was ten, my family was torn apart by my father's drug addiction. I saw directly how drugs can ruin addicts' lives and the lives of those close to them. Our mother moved in with our grandmother to escape the abuse of my father. Life became a living nightmare. Nobody really understood the things we had to handle. The water, the electricity, and the phone were cut off. Mice and rats infested the house. It was difficult to sleep. Most of the time my older sister, younger brother, and I were on our own, and we had to learn how to take care of ourselves. My sister assumed the parental role. She made sure we were up and ready in the morning for school. I will never forget the things she sacrificed for our well-being at the young age of fourteen.

I went to a Catholic school from kindergarten through the eighth grade. My mother did everything she could to keep us going to that school, which meant working in the cafeteria to receive a tuition discount and holding down extra jobs, all the while trying to hide her black eyes. She too had to carry on and act as though everything was fine. Through all of these difficulties, it was my mom who stressed the importance of getting an education, no matter what it took. My two siblings and I eventually moved in with my grandmother as well, whose house became our refuge. Later, we moved into our own apartment. Though our family went through many changes, I was still very fortunate to be able to graduate from the school I had attended for nine years.

It is difficult to explain to people my previous schooling when they only know parts of my story. I was truly privileged to have attended Saint Mary's College High School (SMCHS). It is extremely competitive, receiving over 400 applications for 160 spaces. During the application process, my grandmother, who had taken my family in when we had no place to go, passed away. She would never know that I was accepted as the first woman in my family to attend SMCHS. For the first year, with scholarships, I was able to handle the still-expensive tuition with some money that was left by my grandmother. It was not just a battle academically, but financially as well, with the tuition being over $10,000 a year, plus books. I was able to keep a steady job and at certain points three jobs, as well as participate in sports. It was very difficult to handle all of these things, but also rewarding because it prepared me for college.

I almost had to leave St. Mary's College High School in the middle of my junior year because the financial burden was just too much. The athletic director, Mr. Shaughnessy, saw how hard I was working. One day, he pulled me out of class to talk. I explained to him that I work every day after school and give all of my paychecks to my mother. He was able to get me a full scholarship for the remainder of high school. Shag, as we called him, always encouraged me to keep on working hard and made sure I was doing OK. Without his support I would not have been able to stay at Saint Mary's.

I decided I wanted to be a kinesiology major when I was a junior in high school. I did a lot of research on different kinesiology programs. Sonoma State was at the top of my list. When it came time to choose, I considered only campuses that were not too far away for the most part. I needed a place from where I could easily go home if something had to be taken care of. On the other hand, I wanted to get the full college freshman experience. To understand college expectations better I enrolled in EOP's Summer Bridge program. A week before I had to go to Summer Bridge, I made the decision to attend Sonoma State. It was a great choice to be able to make for myself.

I knew about the nice dorms and campus environment, but I never actually set foot on the SSU campus until Summer Bridge. My mom did not attend the orientation with me, but that was OK because it did not take long for me to meet my fellow classmates and friends. I got better acclimated with the campus and learned how to utilize the resources that were there for me. Summer Bridge was absolutely great! I was able to meet so many wonderful people like professors, peer mentors, and classmates. We went to many workshops and seminars to better understand how to use what is available and how the university works.

What I imagined college to be like was immediately proven wrong. Although they told us at Summer Bridge that SSU was a majority White school, for some reason I still thought it was going to be diverse. Not only did I quickly pick up on the disproportionate male-to-female ratio, but, ethnically, SSU is not like where I am from at all. I can remember walking into the dorm cafeteria and having a sea of faces staring at me and my friends. It's always difficult to begin as a new student, but imagine looking different from everybody else and hearing remarks like, "They like to stick together."

Many of the majority students at SSU did not seem very receptive to anything that was different from themselves and their experience. The way I see it, I brought an open mind to college. I was told at Summer Bridge about all of the things I could do to help ease the transition, but what about the attitudes of other people? Being half Filipino and the other half German and Irish, I found myself doing things to keep my cultures close to me. I refuse to compromise who I am, despite the huge pressure to conform many students face when coming to college.

So, my first impressions of the SSU campus were bittersweet, but at least they warned me at Summer Bridge. When I started going to class, I noticed the campus was absolutely beautiful. I can honestly say that I love living in the dorms. I am happy with having a bed to sleep on because at home I don't have a room and I sleep on the floor. I appreciate what I have, when I have it. I have learned that things could easily just be gone. It took me until the end of the year to even believe I was here, in college, something many people did not think I could do. I found myself going to the library a lot because it was so convenient and nice. I do not think many students use what is there for them. Salazar Hall was great, too. I can remember when it was under construction during the summer. Upon my arrival in the fall, I had classes, advising, and EOP right there in the same building. I knew how to utilize all of the resources that were there for us. I was also able to help others who were not as knowledgeable about how the campus worked. One of the biggest fears I had before coming to college was having roommates who were completely different than me. I didn't move in with a lot of stuff. I did not have money coming in every month from my mom. In fact, I was sending my financial aid refunds home. Just a few weeks into school I was shocked to hear my suitemate say, "You wouldn't be in college if you were poor." I felt very different from those around me, even if I was just walking to class or in my suite. I lived with two other girls in a room and was very lucky to have met my roommate Danielle. She was from San Diego. When everybody else in our dorm would go home on the weekends, she was still at school. I did not go home until we had vacation, partly because I wanted to challenge myself. We got to know each other pretty well and became really good friends during our first year in college.

Classes were not too difficult for me with the exception of math. I have a visual processing disorder—a learning disability—and so mathematics has always been difficult for me. I am a very diligent student and did not miss a single class my first year of college. I earned a 3.5 GPA at the end of my first semester. My second semester, I had nineteen units, no books, and really enjoyed each class I was taking. They all had something interesting and different for me to learn about.

I became involved in the Residential Students Association (RSA) during my freshman year. It was good to have some say in the activities of the residential community. I can remember trying to sell candygrams in the Zinfandel Quad when it was raining. I took a boom box out and would sing for people to buy a friend some candy and help us out. I also assisted in recruitment and tabling. This year I have assumed the publicity duties for the organization. We make flyers and posters for different activities. Next year, I will be the vice president of RSA. It feels good to have a position where I can be a leader. What I love the most about RSA is the traveling we get to do. The Pacific Affiliates of College and University Residence Halls held a conference at UC Santa Barbara this past fall, and I represented Sonoma State. It was great to meet people from other residence hall associations and learn about campus programs. A week after finals this semester, I will be going to the University of St. Louis for the national conference. I can't help but feel excited because it will be my first time traveling out of California. I never was able to travel like this before. It is just another opportunity I am glad to have experienced here at Sonoma State. At the beginning of my sophomore year, I got a job working for the Student Union event staff. I am one of those people who check your bags at bowling nights, and I work at the dances in the Commons. It is good for me because it's mostly night and weekend hours. Sometimes the night hours will go until 3:00 in the morning, and then I have 8:00 a.m. classes. I really enjoy the non-conventional work environment. It is not an office-type setting, and I get to work with my peers. Each day of the week there is something different going on. When I came to college, I wanted to be involved in many different things. I have been able to do a good job of balancing my engagements at SSU, and learning how important it is to be responsible for myself. I am glad I don't just go to class and go back to my dorm, and I am taking as much as I can from the opportunities given to me.

Being the first person in my family to go to college is a unique position to be in. I am paving the way for those who come after me like my younger brother and my children. I would like to help make a better life for my loved ones. Going to college, educating myself, creates more opportunities for my future. Receiving a college degree will be an achievement that proves I have triumphed over the adversity I have faced throughout my life. I will not only have handled the coursework, but I will have done so in an environment that was different and challenging to me. I will have done what many said I could not do, but what the few who I cared about helped me to do. It is as much their accomplishment as it is my own because they were supportive no matter what.

NARRATIVE FOURTEEN: PHILLIP HAMMER

I was a toddler and my brother was on the way when my family left San Francisco. In 1962 we moved to Rohnert Park, a remote outpost of suburbia, for one reason: no down payment was required to buy a brand-new home in a brand-new town. Outside the door of this home, the tall fields stretched without obstruction to the site that would later become Sonoma State University (SSU). My own path between that home and the SSU campus was not nearly so uninterrupted.

My dad, a brash, city-wise San Francisco kid, left high school without graduating to make it on his own. He eventually became an intensely hard-working Teamster, a furniture mover. He had Popeye forearms and a machine-gun laugh bigger than his muscles. My mother went to Fresno State for one unexciting year. She was not unhappy when her mother told her the money had run out and she needed to get a job. She moved to San Francisco and became a secretary. When my parents met, he offered to take her to dinner. Less than three years later, they had two sons and their new home on Bonnie Street.

I can't say that education wasn't important growing up, but it wasn't a first priority either. School was easy for me, and I did well without working hard. My family probably placed more emphasis on athletics than on scholastics. They considered my grandfather's baseball tryout, with the San Francisco Seals of the Pacific Coast League in the 1930s, to be one of our family's great accomplishments. Dad's emphasis can be easily determined by a conversation I remember from elementary school. I asked him which one of two activities I should pursue (for some reason, I couldn't do both)—basketball or band. He said, "Son, either you can be up in the stands playing for someone down on the gym floor, or you can be the guy down on the floor they are playing for." Making my choices simple, Dad both coached and avidly watched my own sporting career, which was hindered only by my ponderous lack of athletic ability. I would later wonder (sometimes angrily) what might have happened had he given academics, at which I excelled, the same attention he applied to athletics, at which I did not. He has since explained that as a youth he had always wanted his own father to be involved in something he was good at—that he was trying to provide what he was not given. Now that I am a father, I know he was doing the best he could. I am increasingly grateful for the sound of him pounding the basketball against the concrete of our driveway—a sound that said, "Come play with me, come be with me."

From Waldo Rohnert elementary school through Santa Rosa Junior College (SRJC), I was an uninspired "B" student. At SRJC, I decided I wanted to write and became editor of the student newspaper there, the *Oak Leaf.* I received my A.A. in two years and cruised along until I arrived at the University of Oregon (UO) in the fall of 1980. My first foray into the bookstore told me I was in trouble. I needed more books for one upper-division history class than I had needed for an entire semester of courses at SRJC. My economics book was biblical in both proportion and scope. I felt absolutely unprepared to put in the kind of effort required to manage this desperate situation. So I did what seemed sensible at the time. I poured alcohol on it. The concoction was implosive. I began to have panic attacks, except I didn't know what they were called. I only knew that in the middle of class I would rush outside in paroxysms of anxiety fueled by excess adrenaline—and that I couldn't go back in or tell anyone.

I grimly clung to academic life—getting "A's" and "B's" if the class seemed easy to me, or getting an assortment of letters below "B" if it didn't. Though I majored in English, I became more a student of drama. In my worst moment, yet greatest performance, I played the part of a distraught son grieving the loss of his father. This was a challenging role, since my real father was alive and well—in fact, no one close to me had ever died. And yet I soldiered on, playing to a riveted audience of one: an academic counselor trying to tell me I was finished at UO. An adherent of method acting, my motivation was to follow up my placement on academic probation with another quarter of grinding failure. My persuasive staging of this fictional event earned me another chance at failure, which I soon achieved. Like Oedipus, I had killed off my father, but for what?

I married my high school sweetheart (who, ironically enough, had only gone to college because I was going, but went on to graduate with honors from Chico State) and we left on a lark to teach English in Japan. I dove into teaching conversational English. For my co-workers, it was a job. For me, it was redemption—a chance for success in the classroom. Responding to my students' shyness, I brought energy and humor to our lessons. I reveled in turning a group of men and women who were frightened to say, "Hello, my name is . . ." into boisterous English stunt pilots.

After two years in Japan, despite my enjoyment of our life there, my wife and I wanted to start our own family and could not foresee bringing them up as *gaijin*—the Japanese term for non-Japanese. We returned to Sonoma County. I took the first secure job I could find, delivering Wonder Bread in a big white truck with blue, red, and yellow balloons. Though not spiritually or intellectually elevating, it provided a steady union income. I quit drinking soon after Paige, our first daughter, was born. It had become painfully apparent that alcohol thoroughly impaired my ability to be the kind of husband and father my family needed. We soon gave Paige a sister, Lisa. As our girls reached elementary school, my wife decided she, too, needed to go to school. She earned her master's in counseling and became a licensed marriage and family therapist—an incredible accomplishment. I helped edit her papers and read many of the books she brought home. Something began stirring inside me. I started to write children's stories, but I was still openly weeping from the self-inflicted wounds of my academic failure—until my dying grandmother tricked me into going back to school.

I spent an afternoon with her—what turned out to be one of the last afternoons of her life. She was clear-headed and thoughtful and had propped herself up in her hospital bed, her blue eyes dazzling beneath the folds of her ancient skin. She repeatedly asked me when I would finish my degree. To appease her, I promised to look into what it would take to finish, but I said, specifically, that I was *not* promising to go back to school. This seemed to satisfy her, and we spent the rest of our time together discussing other matters. She passed away just a few days later. At the funeral, after consoling each other, family members who had talked to her between my visit and her death congratulated me. They told me how proud she had been that I promised her I would graduate. My disbelief turned to wry amusement. I wagged a finger at the dazzling blue sky. She knew what I meant but she had the last word. How could I let down my dead grandmother?

It took several attempts and finally one very dedicated University of Oregon academic advisor (mercifully, the counselor who was under the impression my father was no longer among the living had retired) to wade through the debris field left by my collision with UO. Somehow I needed just three classes to complete my B.A. in English! Now I could begin preparing for my first day as an SSU student. Two common acronyms for the word "fear" come to mind at this point—Feeling Excited And Ready, and Forget Everything And Run. Neither excited nor ready, I fought against the flight impulse as waves of adrenaline and failure physically surged through my body. My feet, followed unwillingly by the rest of me, walked through the classroom door at SSU, my first college class in fifteen years! Though spent in a bread truck, those years had prepared me in ways I hadn't considered. I had learned that hard work was the surest route to anything important—at home or on the job. When I had been in school the first time around, it had seemed way too demanding to make it to every class. But now, after having never missed a workday in fifteen years of employment with Wonder Bread, getting to class seemed a fairly simple process. The same was true for preparation.

Before, it had been a real challenge to complete all the reading or work required for each class session, but now I couldn't imagine *not* being prepared. Most importantly, I had grown up enough to realize there was something called joyful work that was not to be avoided, but diligently pursued.

I also realized that what was stirring inside me was an impassioned voice awaiting escape. By my second semester, in a course in rhetoric with an outstanding professor, Scott Miller, I began to feel that, by expressing myself, I was giving life to a part of myself that had become wilted and withered after many winters of disuse. At the end of the semester, Dr. Miller suggested that I apply to the graduate program. I was stunned.

I received my B.A. (UO, class of 2000) and have taken four courses as a graduate student—two of them with SSU's Dr. Julie Allen, who somehow manages to both accept my limitations and challenge me to exceed them. I love the library. I appreciate having the opportunity to read and write about great literature. My biggest obstacle is learning to discuss literature. Though I have been gaining a command of the vocabulary necessary to feel comfortable expressing myself verbally at the graduate level, I still feel hindered by a lack of confidence—perhaps it is the passing of a shadow from my earlier experiences.

When asked, I have difficulty answering what I hope to accomplish by going back to school. I'm not self-assured enough to tell people about my emerging voice, or a good enough storyteller to engagingly portray my mischievous grandmother. Becoming an English instructor certainly isn't the recommended first step toward increased personal wealth—maybe this is why most people appear so mystified when they inquire into the practicality of studying English. And my rationality, as well as my practicality, would be called into question if I described in detail my meandering path through the tall fields toward this campus. Perhaps I should just smile and let them figure it out for themselves. After all, I don't have as much time as I used to.

I have joyful work to do.

Although books like this one must generalize about the people they claim to describe, in this case first-generation college students, they must also find a way to make visible the specific people who in their daily activities, social interactions, and private worries exist outside the generalization. The 14 narratives included in this chapter do just that, I think; they present a whole range of specific details pertinent to the first-generation student experience we cannot expect researchers to focus on.

The process of describing the first-generation student experience outside these generalizations continues in chapter 5, which honors the actual words of these students in attempting to bring out common themes and characteristics. If the experiences of these students were easy to comprehend and appreciate, chapter 5 would not be necessary. That it is necessary is more evidence of the complicated nature of the first-generation student experience. Complicated and nuanced, the difficulties these students encounter tend to have a lot to do with their internal states, how they think about being disadvantaged if they feel disadvantaged, how they think about their family members and friends left behind in the home culture, and how they think about what it means to be an educated person. Higher-education researchers and scholars can learn much from the statistical data, from surveys, interest inventories, and the like, but to access peoples' internal states, you have to listen to them talk about themselves. The narratives in this chapter are as close as we can get in this format to sitting down with one of these individuals and listening to him or her talk about going to college. Without chapters 4 and 5, this book would be inadequate, if not outright irresponsible, in claiming to describe the first-generation student experience.

5

Narrative Analysis

THIS CHAPTER PARSES the student narratives presented in chapter 4 and places them in context. It also places the writers' personal observations of their own condition in and among the observations of the relevant scholars and researchers. Finally, it compares and contrasts the 14 accounts that these students have so graciously shared with us. If reading the narratives is not enough to change the minds of those postsecondary officials who still regard first-generation student status as something of a nonissue, this chapter should help those readers question their assumptions.

In the same way that the chapter 4 narratives are not case histories in the strict social science sense, chapter 5 is not strictly a case history analysis. The organization of this chapter corresponds to the order in which the narratives appear in chapter 4 and is not meant to bring out one theme or another, nor is it designed to make connections between narratives more easily. The themes that do emerge and are catalogued at the end of the chapter will not be unexpected, but their relationship to the lived experience of the individual writers likely will be, and this is the point. If the narrative writers had the training to write the chapter 5 analysis, I believe it would look something like this.

Referring to and expanding on the chart that appears in chapter 3, chapter 5 also seeks to develop further the important distinctions between the college experience of first-generation-only students, low-income students, and non-first-generation students. From time to time throughout this chapter, then, I use the language included in the chart to emphasize certain characteristics of the individual narratives.

Finally, this chapter also demonstrates why including Sonoma State University as a point of reference is so valuable; SSU provides a place where we can imagine how higher-education officials engage with first-generation students. The chapter 4 narratives describe many specific interactions among SSU students, faculty, and staff, and chapter 5 starts where the students leave off, repackaging this specific experience for more general consumption.

NARRATIVES ONE–THREE: AVILA, HALVERSON, AND KNIGHT

Not every first-generation college student has the kind of chaotic upbringing that Rosa Avila describes in her narrative. In the way she handles her family difficulties, however, Rosa does exhibit the single-minded determination to succeed that is characteristic of her peer group. Rosa does not consider herself a typical member of her family, she writes, explaining that many of her family members become parents early in life and do not go to college. Even if some of them manage to attend college intermittently and part time, she continues, they usually struggle and are not able to complete a program of study. Rosa's sister Katrina is the key figure here who has diagnosed the problem and who tries to set up a support system for her younger sister so she will not follow the family pattern. Katrina is the change agent who, even while she struggles herself, finds the wherewithal to help Rosa financially and, more important, helps her move toward what this book defines as the *intuitive orientation toward college.*

Although Rosa clearly had made some strides in orienting herself toward college before enrolling at SSU with the help of her sister and high school advisors, like most first-generation college students, she clearly has a way to go. As the previous chapters show, it is not possible for first-generation students to achieve the intuitive orientation. This would make them *non*-first-generation students. Although they may not be able to achieve the intuitive orientation, and experience college from a truly privileged perspective, they can approximate it. Rosa knows, for example, that it is better for her to attend a private high school than the apparently low-performing public school in her neighborhood, but her decision-making process for choosing the private school over the public one is different from the decision-making process that results in many non-first-generation students attending private school rather than public school. Students with the intuitive orientation are unlikely to show any hesitation in making this decision; the superiority of private school is regarded as a natural fact of life to many non-first-generation students and their families and not open for discussion or examination. Often accompanying this natural appreciation for private school is the expressed belief that public schools are not only *not* superior but are always inferior. Rosa is obviously proud of her private school attendance, as well she should be, but she exhibits this pride outside the typical discourse about choosing a good private school over a bad public one. She does not criticize the public school she would have attended, for example, or provide any detail about how private school attendance helped her become accepted at SSU. So it appears that she does not fully understand the dichotomy the way many children of privileged families do—that is, she does not fully recognize that many children attend private school because their parents think the public school system is not good enough academically and in other ways.

Rosa's pride in her accomplishments, including attending a private high school, is so intense that it is easily converted to anger and resentment toward the father who evidently abandoned her. Although the desire to show people that they are worthy does drive many first-generation college students, this extremely negative attitude toward a parent is unusual. Rosa clearly harbors very strong feelings toward her father.

On the surface, Rosa appears confident in her abilities and in her college preparation, but you do not have to dig very deeply to find insecurity and perhaps a low level of self-efficacy, psychological traits that unfortunately are also characteristic of first-generation college students (Clauss-Ehlers & Wibrowski, 2007; Longwell-Grice, 2008). Rosa writes a great deal in her narrative about the process of applying to colleges and universities. She does everything right, she is told, and has produced a solid application package. It may come as a surprise to the reader, therefore, to find out that Rosa expects her applications to be rejected. She expects to fail. But this contrary thinking is common among first-generation students, too; even when they are doing well, they expect to fail. Even with a 3.0 GPA and a good secondary school education behind her, Rosa still believes she will be rejected by a not particularly selective state college.

As a reentry student with a 14-year interval between high school attendance and college attendance, Crystal Halverson's comprehension of the postsecondary school environment is quite different from that of Rosa Avila. Whereas Rosa is only beginning to grasp the unique schedules and daily triumphs and failures of a contemporary college student, Crystal, with her life experience and community college attendance, has achieved a more practical understanding. Even with such a background, however, becoming acclimated to the campus culture at SSU was an ordeal, as she describes it, and considerably more difficult than it was for Rosa. Perhaps Rosa's youth was an advantage, allowing her to plow ahead without dwelling on whether she fit in, while for Crystal, who appears to require a more extensive support network, her self-consciousness and feelings of isolation almost caused her to drop out before she had a chance to succeed. Crystal's narrative shows how first-generation college students are more at risk of being derailed by the anxiety that most people feel when they are trying to infiltrate an in-group that does not necessarily desire them.

As is often the case with first-generation college students who are also reentry students, Crystal's path to a postsecondary education is long and circuitous. After one reads several of these narratives, it begins to become fairly obvious that the eventual enrollment of a student such as Crystal has as much to do with chance as with any causal factor. There appear to be any number of ways that Crystal's odyssey could have been prematurely terminated. She mentions divorce, financial issues, health issues, and a late-diagnosed learning disability, any one of which by itself could have derailed her progress. If she had not found what appears to be an extremely dedicated staff of support professionals at Santa Rosa Junior College (SRJC), who supplied her with the academic assistance she needed and who built up her sagging confidence, she likely never would have been prepared to earn a bachelor's degree at SSU. For Crystal and many other first-generation students like her, the community college environment is the best place to begin a postsecondary education, a starting point that gave her the skills and confidence to be able to manage the structural disadvantages of a public four-year institution.

Another trait Crystal shares with many first-generation students is the absence of a strong sense of entitlement, although it is clear she does feel "Relatively Entitled" to a college education, to use the language developed in the chart in chapter 3. She knows that she is entitled to the academic support available at postsecondary institutions, for example, but she also knows that such support does not just fall into a student's lap. Contemporary students must be self-advocates. Crystal also appears to know that academic support is usually provided by dedicated people who do their jobs well. She wastes no time acknowledging and thanking the staff at SRJC, for example, appearing to truly appreciate and value their help. Crystal includes a final message to other first-generation students who would follow her: Seek out academic and other assistance and make good use of it. Whereas "Fully Entitled" non-first-generation students may take a top-notch tutor for granted, first-generation students rarely do. They are more likely to appreciate the extra help they receive and to share their success with the people who helped them.

Any first-generation college student would do well to study Crystal's story. It pays to know who your friends are, she seems to be saying. It pays to know where help can be found and how to ask for it. Unfortunately, many first-generation students simply are not psychologically predisposed to be able to follow this advice. Calvin Knight is a good example. His narrative begins with the image of a young boy taking screwdriver and wrench to a favorite toy. The reader thinks maybe he will be an engineer. Maybe he will be a designer. What we find out as we get deeper into the narrative, however, is that the boy's actions are not so much a demonstration of mechanical aptitude as a representation of an extreme kind of self-reliance. The little boy is taking apart his Big Wheel, not because he is particularly interested in its internal machinery but because he wants to play with it, wants it to work for him. What we find out is that the boy's actions are more the result of dysfunctional family dynamics than mechanical curiosity. His family members have taught him that toys, cars, and perhaps even relationships do not work properly unless he tends to them himself. This is likely not the kind of child, in other words, who is going to find it easy to ask for help as an adult. He is not likely to be able to follow Crystal Halverson's advice.

One gets the feeling while reading Calvin's narrative that he would have liked to have asked for help from time to time, but something, perhaps "Irish pride," as he calls it, always prevents him from doing so. Again, this is not unusual. It has been my experience working with first-generation college students for many years that some of them can become almost addicted to self-reliance, often to their own detriment. They do not use support units, under the false belief that they can do everything that needs to be done by themselves. This is why even though the professionals who run effective support units make their services easy to access, they still must do internal-to-the-institution outreach to help the students they are charged to serve. Many non-first-generation students, on the other hand, can be very comfortable asking for help, having heard from degree-holding parents and other family members that asking for extra help from professors and other institution officials is the best way to succeed. As we all know, self-sufficiency is a highly regarded trait in American culture, and many first-generation students get pleasure from the attention and compliments they receive for being self-sufficient. Sometimes a highly developed ability to be self-sufficient is the only advantage first-generation students have over their non-first-generation student peers. But just as often—perhaps even more often—self-sufficiency masks other problems. Yes, the kind of childhood Calvin describes as being outside the in-group can build character, but it can also be a breeding ground for feelings of alienation and a nonproductive kind of world-weariness. As Calvin writes, he became adept at socializing with many different kinds of children during his K–12 schooling, but being around non-first-generation students who possessed a wide range of options for college attendance and other opportunities became harder and harder to take. In fact, it became "hellish," he writes.

Although it is true that many first-generation college students gravitate toward majors that are perceived as having the potential for producing a large income (Bui, 2002; Chen & Carroll, 2005), some first-generation students—students like Calvin, who has experienced much difficulty on his road to a bachelor's degree—have a much different attitude. Calvin writes that the death of his father and grandmother and his estrangement from other friends and family members had the effect of freeing him. He became free, in other words, to view his education in a more traditional light, as a way of improving himself, as a way of learning how to really appreciate, experience, and be comfortable in the world. At the time of his writing he was working toward a bachelor of science degree in business, but he mentions that later, after he graduates, he is likely to pursue a second degree in environmental studies. This kind of education plan is characteristic of first-generation college students and should be differentiated from the behavior of low-income students, who with their "Survivalist" orientation toward developing a college-student identity and their "Future Focused" relationship to the period of college attendance, are much more likely to enter the job market after getting a business degree. It is easy to see why good academic advising is so important for first-generation students, given this tendency to have an open attitude toward education planning. Yes, good advising is necessary so first-generation college students do not make mistakes that can interfere with academic progress because of their novice status, but first-generation students also represent an *opportunity* for academic advisors. They can be the students who choose majors for the purest reasons. They receive information from advisors the way advisors would like the information they convey to be received.

NARRATIVES FOUR–SEVEN: BRAVOS, CAMACHO, GOMEZ, AND PETERSON

As Calvin's narrative demonstrates, some first-generation college students come from families that have lived in the United States for many years or even generations. They may be full participants in American life, generally speaking, but that does not necessarily mean, as we have seen, that they know their way around a college campus. For first-generation college students who are also first- or second-generation Americans, attaining a postsecondary degree can be even more arduous. The narratives of Maria Bravos and Erica Camacho show how being a member of an American family with immigrant parents can complicate being a first-generation college student.

Maria became the official interpreter for her Spanish-speaking parents at an early age. She was the one who took the important phone calls and wrote the checks that kept the household running smoothly. She appears to have taken this role very seriously, and this seriousness is reflected in her writing style. Her style is very concise and clear, with no room for flowery descriptions or overstatement; Maria wants to be understood, first and foremost. Like Calvin, she needed to become self-sufficient at an early age, albeit for very different reasons.

Even if Maria's parents had been well educated in their native Mexico, they still would have been of limited help in developing their daughter's orientation toward college. For example, they were not able to help with their children's homework, not for lack of desire but simply because they did not speak English well enough. Since they were not able to help much with the K–12 education of their children, it would be unfair to expect them to offer much help with preparation for a postsecondary education. Certainly, Maria's parents were able to offer their unqualified love and support, but Maria appears to have made her own decisions about her schooling—for example, which college to attend and why. It is a tribute to her parents' love and support that she chose to attend a college close to home. Maria is not very interested in living far away from her mother and father.

Maria's narrative is the shortest in the collection, and she does not mention the impact of her K–12 schooling on her desire and ability to attend college. Again, one suspects that keeping the possibility of attending college alive in their daughter is one of the chief contributions Maria's parents made to the process that ended with her enrolling at SSU. The shortness of her narrative is perhaps a reflection of another characteristic of first-generation students; in addition to the absence of flowery description and overstatement is the absence of a discussion of the existential question about college attendance and, on a larger scale, the absence of a discussion of identity in general. Maria does not include this in her narrative, perhaps because she is very sure who she is. She demonstrates one way the "Skepticist" orientation toward developing a college-student identity manifests itself—some first-generation students arrive on campus as fully formed adults—and, having read her story, one can easily imagine that she will consider herself the same person after attaining her bachelor's degree. Maria's parents do deserve a lot of credit, though, for keeping hope alive is no small thing.

Erica Camacho's parents do not appear to have been able to help with their daughter's K–12 homework either, for reasons similar to those of Maria's parents, but Erica did get help by participating in middle and high school and college outreach programs. Although the precollege histories of these two young women are similar in many ways, there are significant differences as well. One does it all on her own, and the other uses assistance, but this assessment is not to suggest that Maria is internally strong or that Erica is not. On the contrary, Erica shows the same determination to achieve a four-year degree that Maria does; it is just that Erica is wise enough to know that taking advantage of assistance is itself a kind of strength. Although we should admire Maria's determination and ability to get things done on her own, we also must recognize Erica's ability to use the system to her own benefit.

Sonoma State University, like many American colleges and universities, is a predominantly White institution. For the fall 2008 semester, for example, only 23.1% of the undergraduate population reported ethnic minority status. Most ethnic minority students, for better or worse, find they are more aware of their minority status when they are on the SSU campus than when they are in their home environment. Although documented instances of overt racism at SSU are few, they do occur. Erica's narrative confirms this; she describes the comments White students made to her friend when they saw a child's safety seat in the back of her friend's car. Fear of such treatment no doubt adds to the feelings of alienation and negative self-worth that many first-generation students bring when they arrive on a college campus for the first time, even if first-generation student status is the majority background at the institution, as it is at some American colleges, community colleges in particular (Phillippe & Patton, 2000). Although Erica does not hesitate to describe her nervous apprehension about having minority status in her narrative, some first-generation students who are also members of ethnic minority groups downplay the effect their minority status has on their academic performance, believing, perhaps, that they already have enough to contend with. Remember, having first-generation-*only* status is no small thing, in and of itself.

Some students may downplay ethnic minority status, but few ethnic minority students attending college today are able to avoid thinking about potential racist treatment entirely. Jessica Gomez, for instance, the next narrative writer, is not nearly so direct in describing her first days on the SSU campus as a member of an ethnic minority group. You have to read between the lines, and when you do, you will see that having ethnic minority status on a predominantly White campus definitely made Jessica's acclimation process during those critical first few months more difficult than it should have been. She writes that she was intimidated by all the "new faces," and when she tells us she felt more comfortable among the more "familiar faces," it is hard not to imagine that those more familiar faces contained more pigment than the ones that seemed so intimidating.

At the same time, however, one gets the impression that Jessica is not the type to be intimidated easily. Growing up in the impoverished Canal Area of the city of San Rafael, some 40 miles south of SSU, in a single-parent household, does not make getting to college any easier; yet she made it with room to spare. Jessica did well at the K–12 schools she attended and accessed the appropriate support organizations, receiving several scholarships as a result. Even with such a history, however, she resembles Rosa Avila in being surprised that she was accepted at not just one but six different California State University campuses. This very competent young woman cannot believe her "good luck" upon receiving something that had nothing to do with luck and everything to do with hard work.

Although some first-generation college students may be able to muddle through, say, the first month of college attendance and start to demonstrate a limited familiarity with the campus culture, the full acclimation process almost always takes a fairly long time, even for someone like Jessica with all her confidence and ability, as well as what appears to be a very outgoing personality. After having read just the first two-thirds of her overwhelmingly positive narrative, the reader might expect her to be able to put the difficulties that go with first-generation student status behind her after the first few weeks of freshman composition, but this is not what happens; the psychology of first-generation student status runs deeper than this. Jessica writes that it was not until the beginning of her sophomore year that she really felt comfortable as a college student. Imagine the acclimation process for more introverted students; they can take two years or more to become confident in the college environment. Jessica's "Skepticist" orientation toward developing a college-student identity seems less intense than Maria's, and one can easily imagine after having read her story that she might very well consider herself a different person after attaining her bachelor's degree.

One of the purposes of the narratives that make up chapter 4 is to demonstrate that it is not always easy to measure the impact of first-generation student status on students and their quest for a four-year degree. Education researchers and other educators examine retention and graduation statistics, GPAs, and reports from academic support units to measure impact, and we should continue doing this. These measures and others already in place can shed light on the often subtle difficulties and challenges that most first-generation students face. We can do all this and more, but we will never fully understand the dynamics in play unless we really listen to and analyze what the students themselves are saying about the first-generation student experience. And what they are saying should cause the higher-education establishment to examine certain deleterious practices described more fully in chapter 6. As has been mentioned in previous chapters, being a first-generation student is more difficult than many professional educators have been ready to admit. It is hard not to be touched, for instance, by how often these student writers evoke their own children when summing up the first-generation student experience, by how often they say they do not want their existing and future children to face what they have had to face. More than any other evidence, perhaps, these statements should give us pause before we echo the sentiments of too many college faculty and staff when they claim that first-generation student status really does not amount to much of a hardship. Jeff Peterson, in his narrative, puts it plainly: "I will make my children's experience much better than mine." And he will, too, but Jeff's conscious intent and actions may not have much to do with it. What Jeff may not realize is that he has already made the most important contribution toward that end that he can make. After he earns his degree, his children will not be first-generation college studentswhen they start college.

Because so much of the difficulty first-generation students face is subtle and embedded in deep-seated habits of mind having to do with identity and one's place in the world, academic advising is critically important, as mentioned earlier. We can see how academic counseling at the high school level failed Jeff by not describing for him the larger context for his develop-ment, interests, and future opportunities. Evidently, to his counselor, Jeff appeared to be a typical jock not worth the extra time needed to educate him to the harsh realities of making a living as a professional athlete. Luckily, Jeff did receive some excellent advice at a critical moment in his academic and emotional development, and it came from an unlikely source, his girl-friend. It is no accident that this individual came from a "long line of college graduates," making her able to deliver the kind of information that many non-first-generation students get just by growing up in a more-privileged family. Her "Fully Entitled" attitude toward getting a college education appears to have influenced Jeff very much. Although academic advisors do not have to have been first-generation students themselves to advise first-generation students successfully, a similar background can be a benefit.

Although Jeff clearly has affection for his parents, it is not difficult to locate a certain resentment expressed in his narrative as well. He seems to have come to terms with his parents' inability to assist him in his pursuit of a higher education, but one wonders. Jeff demonstrates the kind of compli-cated relationship many first-generation students have with their parents in the context of acquiring a postsecondary education. He shows why so many of his peers are "Present Focused" when considering the time spent in col-lege; his past, which includes little information about what college is like, just is not that helpful. It is never easy to accept the fact that your parents are not able to help you in the way you need to be helped. Remember, what Jeff needed—what all first-generation students need—usually is not delivered directly by non-college-educated parents. That is not the way it works. The intuitive orientation toward college that Jeff lacks is produced by growing up in a non-first-generation household and receiving college-oriented direction and information, conscious and unconscious, formal and informal, from just being there. In that sense, then, it is unfair for Jeff to resent his parents, because even if they had been aware that they were not supporting their son adequately, there was no way for them to do so; theirs was a first-generation college student household. You cannot communicate to others what you do not know yourself, and, as Jeff writes, his parents do not fully comprehend the difficulty and value of acquiring a college education.

NARRATIVES EIGHT–ELEVEN: GUTIERREZ, HUNTER, JIMENEZ, AND SOSA

Jeff's family may not fully comprehend the value of a college education, but they did not consciously erect barriers against Jeff's becoming a university student. In contrast to the lack of support Jeff and students like him experience, Anna Gutierrez has had to contend with an entirely different kind of difficulty, the wholly conscious and manifest barriers of traditional Mexican culture against women attending college. Because first-generation college students are statistically more likely to be members of minority groups than are non-first-generation students, it follows that first-generation students are more likely to experience difficulties caused by rigid cultural views of family relationships and friends.

Similar to the way Jeff benefited from having an important advisor at a critical time in his life, Anna benefited from an important event at a critical time in her educational development. She describes winning a prestigious scholarship to attend a private Mexican high school upon finishing junior high. Although she appears to have been exposed to the best teachers and curriculum at this school, which was sufficiently well known to enroll the son of the then-Mexican president, something more subtle than these largely material benefits allowed her to earn a four-year degree from SSU and make plans to attend graduate school in the United States. Again, it is about the intuitive orientation toward college: Attending such a high school placed Anna in an environment that fostered the idea of college attendance as a given, and there is evidence in her narrative that she learned to give a "Personal" answer to the existential question about college attendance, the kind of answer given by non-first-generation students. Students at her high school likely were not told they should study hard so that they could attend college; they were told to study hard so that they could attend the *best* college. At these types of prep schools in both Mexico and the United States, students are inundated with the signs and signals of college attendance from the moment they step on the school grounds in the morning to the time they leave to go home in the evening. One wishes Anna had included more information about how this institution communicated views about gender difference, but suffice it to say there was likely a double standard at play in a number of ways. Although the students attending this prestigious high school probably were not as subject to rigid cultural norms as were students attending less-privileged Mexican high schools, male students likely still benefited from the different expectations for boys and girls.

As a result of her "Personal" relationship with the idea of college and her somewhat "Past Focused" orientation to the period of her college attendance, perhaps caused by her exceptional high school experience, Anna may be the most unusual of the first-generation students profiled here. She appears to have shown exceptional aptitude in the sciences from an early age. She has the benefit of a first-class secondary school education. And although she married and created a new family right after high school (which is not unique, sadly), she did not postpone her postsecondary education. Having acknowledged all of this, Anna's story contains a number of important tips for any first-generation college student. Perhaps first among these is that she did not allow her lack of support and financial resources to divert her from her goals. In an age when low- and high-income students alike have credit cards, cell phones, and direct access to the American consumer culture, Anna earned her four-year degree without ever owning a car or a computer. She is unique, indeed.

In contrast to Anna's uniqueness, John Hunter begins his narrative by writing, "You have heard this story a million times." It would be a mistake, however, to take this statement at face value without looking deeper into its larger implications, because in his ability to write it, John demonstrates his own uniqueness. Being able to write, "You have heard this story a million times," to describe your own autobiographical narrative means you have a fairly well-developed sense of your identity and your place in the world. It means, among other things, that you may not struggle so much when you are placed into environments that are foreign to you. The skeletal outline of the triumphant story John tells does sound similar to many of the other stories in the narrative collection: Immigrant family moves to the United States; family members work hard to be successful with little time for post-secondary education; eventually family produces first-generation college student; and so on.

But there is something different, something more here, and it is not in the facts of the story. What is different is that John appears to have fully accepted first-generation student status. He has accepted all the difficulties and challenges and made them his own. With his opening statement, John shows that he *has* asked himself the question, "Will I feel like I don't fit in when I start attending Sonoma State?" And he has answered, "Yes, I will feel that way." He has asked himself, "Will I have difficulty deciding on a program of study?" "Yes, I will," is his answer. "Will I find academic study challenging?" "Yes." "Will my parents and I drift apart?" "Yes."

In his ability to fully accept the difficulties and challenges of being a first-generation college student, John's upbeat narrative shows us what the first-generation student experience can be. His is the experience we wish more first-generation college students could have, an experience and a concomitant state of mind visible in his opening sentence, but we cannot know for sure how he got this way. We can see in his narrative, however, that his "Skepticist" orientation toward developing a college-student identity gradually gives way to something like the "Assumptionist" orientation more characteristic of *non*-first-generation students. It could be that he experienced some life-changing epiphany, perhaps triggered by one of the books he read in his liberal arts program. It could be that he was just born this way. Or it could be that the family of this particular first-generation student was just so generally supportive that John did not feel he had to wrestle with family ghosts every time he took a step in one direction or the other. It was probably a little bit of all of these things. One thing is for sure, however; the benefits of a resilient psychological makeup are clear and can be seen in a statement toward the end of the narrative: "There are no simple answers to these complex questions," John writes, referring to the complex fundamental questions of identity.

More than other first-generation college students, it seems, John is able to accept the idea that things will not always work out. Even if he wanted to be as close to his family as he was when he was five years old, he knows this is impossible. After a first-generation student receives a college education, he or she often cannot go home—not because home is any different but because the student is different. Unlike John, many first-generation students straddle the home world and the college world because they find comfort in the belief that they *can* straddle both worlds, find comfort in not having to make a choice. At some point, however, most of them discover that such a position (and identity) is untenable. Some, like John, will choose the college world, and some, unfortunately, will choose the home world—that is, they will drop out. One thing John's story tells us is that college advisors and counselors can help first-generation students stay in college by pointing out that if they do return to the home world, it probably will not be the same.

We have heard this story a million times, as John says. Well, maybe . . . but reading the narratives of Natalie Jimenez and Carlos Sosa reminds us just how amazing and how worth our attention the first-generation student experience truly is. Neither of Natalie's parents continued education after elementary school, and although Carlos does not describe his parents' level of education specifically, it is a pretty good bet, given other details of his story, that they didn't progress much further than elementary school, either. Natalie's mother could not have been much older than 15 when Natalie was born. Her parents came to the United States with few skills with which to make a living in this country and worked as agricultural laborers, and they may still work in agriculture. Carlos's family left El Salvador during the time of the death squads and settled in one of the most impoverished and blighted areas of the West Coast of the United States, the area of Los Angeles between Compton and Watts. For many individuals, we know, these circumstances are recipes for lifelong poverty, but somehow, in Natalie and Carlos, the seeds for college achievement were planted.

It can be difficult for non-first-generation students to understand why so many first-generation students choose to remain so closely tied to their families throughout college, even when they know their families are dysfunctional. As we have seen, sometimes these strong family ties are enough by themselves to cause first-generation students to drop out. Carlos loves his parents so much, he writes, "that it hurts at times to think I am not with them now." Reading the narratives of Natalie and Carlos, it becomes easier to see why these family ties are often so strong. Not to underestimate or slight the positive feelings most everyone has toward their family, but in the case of Natalie and Carlos and children like them, the harsh conditions under which they grow up require their family to be much more than the place where they spend their leisure time and get their meals. It must be the sanctuary to which they can escape when the outside world becomes too inhospitable. In writing about this, the two emphasize the low-income dimension of their lives, an emphasis that may sometimes cause them to resemble low-income students on a college campus rather than first-genera-tion-only students, especially in terms of their "Survivalist" orientation toward developing a college-student identity.

Although the upbringing of most first-generation college students includes more financial wherewithal than that of Natalie or Carlos, as shown in chapter 1, the sense of "us against the world" visible in both their stories is almost always in place regardless of family income. Yes, the first-generation experience is amazing. So amazing, it is hard to come up with a simile to describe the huge leap of circumstance that the families of Natalie and Carlos will have made once those two receive their bachelor's degrees. And it has happened in one generation. It is like writing with pencil and paper and then being introduced to a word processor. It is like buying a home in California for $26,000 25 years ago and being able to sell it now for half a million dollars or more. It is like being born in a log cabin and later becom-ing president of the United States. It is like . . . well, I guess it *is* like rags to riches, an American success story.

NARRATIVES TWELVE–FOURTEEN:
ORTIZ, ORDAZ, AND HAMMER

Not only do the stories of many first-generation college students recount the archetypal American rags-to-riches success story, as we have seen, but many first-generation students and their families, in their development and prog-ress as families, recapitulate the development of what is often referred to as the American "national character" itself. I am speaking of the countless immigrant families who arrived in the United States at the end of the 19th century and the beginning of the 20th century, with little in the way of material possessions or money but much in the way of determination and a huge capacity for hard work, who created an environment of success and achievement for themselves and their children (Pferdehirt, 1997). I am speaking of families like the family of Yolanda Ortiz—in her case, a Native American family with a long history of disenfranchisement—who in their struggles and perseverance, their determination to make national diversity a virtue, provide much of the liveliness and energy visible in this "national character" we speak of. When we talk about the first-generation student experience, we sometimes forget that first-generation students come from people very accustomed to getting things done on their own. Much of the discussion that takes place in the research literature, including this book as well, necessarily addresses what colleges and universities can do for first-generation students, but that does not mean we should not consider the flip side of the coin. What can first-generation students do for colleges and universities? It is easy to see from Yolanda's narrative that they bring a different worldview and a wealth of experience to college campuses. Although they may sit quietly in classrooms and avoid raising their hands when the instructor asks a question, they are not sitting quietly because they do not have anything to say. Yolanda's experience is far different from the experience of the privileged students sitting next to her in class, with their indifference and "Fully Entitled" perspective. When Yolanda lends her opinion to the discussion, it is an opinion to be valued highly.

So Yolanda's wealth of experience travels with her when she enrolls at SSU. One of the striking features of her narrative is that she seems driven to make sure this already full and diverse experience becomes even more full—full to the point of bursting, it would seem. Fighting through feelings of low self-esteem and shyness, Yolanda becomes a teaching assistant to not just one but two professors; assists a different SSU professor with a research project; becomes a student employee working on an SSU publication, *Project Censored*; helps with fundraising for the sociology department; and on and on. This is exactly the kind of energy and enthusiasm that first-generation students bring to college and university campuses. And they bring so much more as well.

In addition to abundant energy and the capacity for hard work, Yolanda has other qualities and experiences that are characteristic of first-generation college students. The pursuit of a four-year degree does not always go so smoothly. There will be setbacks, we know. First-generation student readers of her narrative should pay close attention when she writes about her first year of study at the University of Arizona. The repercussions from first-year blowups like the one Yolanda describes sometimes are not confined to that first year. They have a way of following students as they develop and mature. The low grades from those first semesters, for example, prevented Yolanda years later from pursuing a biology degree, her first choice of major at SSU. It is a shame when such circumstances drive the choice of major for first-generation students—or any student. As we saw in chapter 2, the process of choosing a major is often far different for first-generation students from that of their non-first-generation counterparts, another example of how first-generation students feel "Relatively Entitled" to a college education. Until the fundamental processes of college achievement such as choosing a major become more similar for both groups of students, first-generation students will benefit less from a college education than will their non-first-generation counterparts.

Through having to work to help support her impoverished family, Elizabeth Ordaz finds out what Yolanda Ortiz seems to have known before she arrived at SSU: Getting a college education is more than just going to classes and receiving passing grades. It is no accident that, once first-generation students get over the radical dislocation of the first semester of study, they can become more engaged in campus events and college student life, like Yolanda has, than can non-first-generation students, even though they almost always have less time for extracurricular activities. Sometimes, as in Elizabeth's case, they are initially dazzled by what they regard as the super-abundance of college student life. If they recover from the shock, and many do not, as the literature shows, they can become enthralled with the idea of participation. They cannot get enough of it. Correspondingly, they do not find it pleasant to sit in their residence hall rooms by themselves and waste time when so much is going on. First-generation students possess no more virtue, generally speaking, than do their non-first-generation counterparts, nor are they more or less likely to conform to student affairs ideals. What they do often possess more of, however, is an experience of the world that includes living in close, critical proximity with numbers of people, which allows them to be comfortable in complex relationships with a variety of different people. Although they are used to helping others, they are not used to solitary contemplation, by and large, and to the degree that solitary contemplation is necessary to do well in academic activities, they may struggle. But first-generation students are not easily scared off. Whereas more-self-absorbed students may bristle at the thought of checking coats at a college dance, Elizabeth does not bat an eye. She thinks of it not only as an opportunity to make money but also as an opportunity to engage in yet another aspect of college life.

As we have seen, first-generation students often come to college with a different opinion of American life and a different view of the world from that of their non-first-generation counterparts; in Elizabeth's case, this different view of the world is a product, for the most part, of the harshness and poverty of her home life. The courage this young woman demonstrates in overcoming the difficult realities of her precollege life should cause us to applaud her effort. Elizabeth's first-generation student status is complicated by so many other difficulties and barriers, including, of course, the difficulties of poverty. One of the purposes of this volume is to show that the first-generation student experience of college and the low-income student experience of college are not the same. First-generation students are also low-income students at a higher rate than are non-first-generation students, we know, but their low-income status, if they have that status, may not be what is keeping them from excelling at college. It may be in fact their first-generation student status that is responsible for adjustment problems and poor academic performance. Still, we can learn something about the first-generation student experience from students like Elizabeth, who is both a first-generation student and a low-income individual. As a low-income student, for example, Elizabeth perceives her residence hall facilities as almost perfect for her. She has a room and a bed, after all, and this is more than her personal experience would lead her to believe was possible. When not in her dorm room or in class, Elizabeth finds herself going to the library a lot because, as she writes, "it was so convenient and nice." The library, too, is probably more comfortable than her sometimes unheated, sometimes unlighted home. When Elizabeth calls the SSU library "convenient and nice," she is speaking as a first-generation student. When she imagines that it is also "warm and comfortable," she is thinking as a low-income individual, playing out the "Survivalist" attitude. Comparing the perceptions of low-income students with those of first-generation students, the core relationship to the college experience becomes more visible for each group of students. For low-income students, college attendance is closely linked to thoughts of surviving in the world (Delpit, 1995; Payne, R. K., 2005; Zhou, 1997); for first-generation-only students, it is closely linked to thoughts of expanding the world (Chaffee, 1992; Choy, 2001; London, 1992). First-generation students almost always mention the library when they talk about their college experience, and they are usually puzzled: "How come there are so few students in the library?" they ask. They think the absent students are taking the library for granted.

First-generation college students do not take college for granted. Perhaps this short statement is the best way to describe how first-generation students are different from other kinds of students. They do not take the library for granted. They do not take the happy unruliness of residence hall living for granted. And what should be of most interest to the faculty and staff of American universities, they do not take the process of acquiring an education for granted. Why they do not take college for granted is more complicated than saying they are new to college. Yes, the college experience is new to these students, by definition, but the newness can wear off fairly quickly. The narratives in chapter 4 demonstrate, I believe, that first-generation students value and appreciate their time in college in a more intense way than do many of their non-first-generation counterparts; they are "Present Focused" while in college managing the process of acquiring a postsecondary education. Putting it bluntly, "Past Focused" non-first-generation students are more likely to be bored by the college experience; they are more likely to need present-time stimulation. In the end, it comes down to possessing a fundamentally different view of college and education. It comes down to having a precollege experience that may not have prepared them well for getting an "A" in freshman composition or a "B+" in chemistry 1A but has prepared them well for truly appreciating how a college education can be a life-changing experience.

I did not choose to place Phillip Hammer's piece last in the narrative collection because it so clearly demonstrates that acquiring an education has changed Phillip's life. Phillip appears to be the kind of person who would be living a full life even if he never attended college, maintaining a decidedly "Skepticist" orientation toward developing a college-student identity throughout his education journey. He appears to have a happy and healthy attitude toward family life and toward his work life and has already spent two years in Japan teaching English. If you asked him, Phillip might say that acquiring an education *has* changed his life, or he might say it has not. I do not know. But what we can assume after reading his narrative, I think, is that like most first-generation college students, he has directly addressed the process of acquiring an education. He contemplates its meaning in the present time. He has intellectually investigated the possibilities of higher education and incorporated some of these possibilities into his life. He certainly does not take education for granted.

I think considering Phillip's well-written narrative is a good way to finish this chapter analyzing what first-generation college students say about the first-generation student experience. As we have seen in so many of the narratives, all of the typical characteristics of the first-generation student experience are present: the lack of preparedness; of self-confidence in the academic environment; and of a clear, straightforward plan for getting from point A to point B, academically speaking. It is my hope that considering Phillip's narrative now also brings to mind the world of possibilities presented by the first-generation student experience and the large number of first-generation students who will be enrolling in American colleges and universities in the upcoming years. Progressive institutions will acknowledge both the possibilities and the numbers and start making preparations to serve these students better. Finally, in considering Phillip's narrative, I would have readers ask themselves the following question: Is this the kind of student you would like to have in a class you are teaching? Most of the instructors and professors I know would reply with a resounding yes.

Chapter 5 concludes that part of this book that seeks to present a more mature definition of the first-generation college student. The profile that has emerged is more various and complicated than many might have imagined, I would wager, but it is worth repeating that, as various and complicated as these different accounts of the first-generation student experience may be, there is a core experience universal to all these students, one that all first-generation students and their families would recognize and one that non-first-generation students and their families perhaps cannot recognize. That core experience contains the following five elements:

- A lack of sophistication about K–12 education that carries over into the postsecondary environment.
- A location in the psychological landscape of the postsecondary environment that establishes first-generation students as outsiders.
- A complicated identity development process—produced from having to straddle two cultures, the home culture and the campus culture—

that can terminate enrollment during the first two years of study and that often can add to anxiety about the unknown.

+ A family dynamic concerning college attendance that is often much different from the family dynamic of non-first-generation students.

+ The ability to triumph over challenges and barriers, which speaks to a special kind of determination to succeed.

Now that we have a full picture of who first-generation college students are and what the first-generation student experience is, it is time to figure out what college professors, administrators, and other education professionals should do with this picture. It is my hope that this book spurs more research on and draws more attention to this student demographic category. More and more scholars of education are researching and writing about performance outcomes for both students and the institutions that educate them. More attention is being paid to problems such as dissatisfaction with institution policies and institution fit, alienation from the education process, student lack of success, and more. These are surely large, complicated problems, but they can be solved. It is my contention that if the movement toward performance outcomes is linked to a better understanding of the first-generation student experience, solutions to many of these seemingly intractable problems of the American higher-education system will come into focus.

My hope is that college professors, administrators, and other education professionals make the connection: Focusing on assisting first-generation students can transform your institution. Chapter 6 makes recommendations for just how higher-education institutions can construct polices and practices so that first-generation students can begin graduating at a rate approaching that of their non-first-generation counterparts.

6

Recommendations

CHAPTER 1 OF THIS BOOK sounded the alarm: A new wave of first-generation college students is on the way, and those students will be enrolling in American colleges and universities in increasing numbers in the next few decades. Chapters 2 and 3 established the definition: First-generation students are a distinct group, and the research literature clearly shows that they behave differently from traditional non-first-generation students. The first three chapters, then, urge postsecondary education officials to count first-generation students and to learn about them. Progressive educators will put the findings of chapters 1, 2, and 3 together and recognize that being better prepared to serve first-generation students is one key to their institutions' success in the near future.

Chapter 6 follows up on these findings and makes recommendations. Some college and university officers already know they need to start educating their first-generation students more effectively, but few of them recognize that educating first-generation students more effectively along the lines suggested in this chapter can serve the more general aims of their institutions at the same time (Brown, 2008; Fuller, 2007). For instance, one of the most important issues facing the American postsecondary school system in the early 21st century is how to improve graduation rates. The consensus represented in the literature is that graduation rates have become stagnant and are simply too low (Carey, 2008). Many American institutions have realized few, if any, gains since 1991, when national statistics on the six-year graduation rate began to be collected: The national average for the six-year graduation rate for the years between 2001 and 2007 is 57% (Carey, 2008).

Because the graduation rate is the ultimate measure of an institution's effectiveness, and in a sense everything an institution does is at least tangentially related to the goal of graduating students, stagnant and low graduation rates are caused by a combination of factors—institutional philosophy, poor student preparation, the effectiveness of instruction and support services, and even changing public attitudes about four-year degrees, to name just a few (Astin & Oseguera, 2005; Carey, 2008). People can disagree about what is to blame, but there is little disagreement about how costly low graduation rates can be. Considering the problem from a limited perspective to make a point, a 50% graduation rate means half the money an institution spent on educating students during the previous six years went to waste.

The successful colleges and universities of the future are in the process of creating policies to improve graduation rates and will be implementing these policies soon. It may be true that there is no easy way to improve graduation rates, but it is also true that some ways are easier than others. Progressive colleges and universities will recognize, for example, the fundamental correlation between overall graduation rates and the success of first-generation students. The graduation rate of first-generation students at some institutions lags so far behind the graduation rate of all four-year-degree-seeking students that, in many cases, institutions need do nothing more than address the academic success of their first-generation students to improve the overall graduation rate significantly. As cited in chapter 1, the 2005 National Center for Education Statistics (NCES) study shows that first-generation students enrolling in American postsecondary institutions in 1992 were only half as likely to achieve a bachelor's degree *eight* years later than were their non-first-generation counterparts—34% and 68%, respectively (Chen & Carroll, 2005). This study did not report on the six-year graduation rate, but had the researchers calculated the six-year rate, it would have been lower than 34%, of course.

Similar to so many of the other findings in this book, the above statistic speaks for itself; but let us apply it to the actual graduation numbers of a specific institution to show what is at stake. What would Sonoma State University's overall six-year graduation rate be if its first-generation students graduated at the same rate as its non-first-generation students? The logic demonstrated here could be applied to any postsecondary institution, even to community colleges, which, of course, would have to use a measure of success other than the six-year graduation rate. When using the national statistics in considering the question, we should keep several factors in mind. In applying the national statistics, we are assuming, for example, that SSU's first-generation students graduate at half the rate of its non-first-generation students. This may not be true. SSU's first-generation students may be graduating at a rate higher than this, but as is the case at almost every American postsecondary institution, SSU officials cannot know for sure, because they are not certain how many first-generation students they have.

The calculation that follows is based partially on what was reported in chapter 1 about SSU, that at least 34.5% of SSU undergraduates have first-generation status. This figure is probably a little low for SSU (as has already been discussed), and it is certainly lower than the first-generation student population in many community colleges and other four-year institutions located in urban or rural areas.

SSU's most recently reported six-year graduation rate is 50.0%. (The average of the last 10 years is 47.6%.) In other words, first-time freshmen enrolling at SSU in the fall semester 2002 graduated at a rate of 50.0% six years later. If SSU's first-generation students are graduating at a rate of 34.0% (the *eight-year* graduation rate for first-generation students nationally from the 2005 Chen and Carroll study), its non-first-generation students are graduating at a rate of 58.4%. This means that SSU's overall graduation rate would increase by over 8.0 percentage points, from 50.0% to 58.4%, if its first-generation students graduated at the same rate as its non-first-generation students. What is more, if SSU improved the performance of its first-generation students by a more modest amount—let us say that it starts graduating them at a rate that is 75.0% of the rate for non-first-generation students, or 43.8% instead of 34.0%—SSU could improve its overall graduation rate by more than 3.0 percentage points, to 53.4%. As anyone who has studied what it takes to raise a four-year institution's graduation rate by even 1.0% knows, these are very significant numbers. Again, gains would be much higher at community colleges or four-year institutions with a higher proportion of first-generation students.

Before moving on, let us engage in just one more bit of speculation on how first-generation student performance interacts with and affects a postsecondary institution's overall graduation rate. Using SSU as an example again, if 44.5% (10 percentage points higher than the NCES 34.5% figure) of SSU's undergraduate population are first-generation students—likely closer to reality than the 34.5% figure used in the above calculation—the improvement in the overall graduation rate is even more dramatic. If 44.5% of the undergraduates enrolled for the fall semester 2002 were first-generation students, and they graduated six years later at a rate of 34.0%, the graduation rate for *non*-first-generation students would be 62.8%. If that 44.5% of the undergraduate population (first-generation students) had graduated at a rate *only* 75.0% of that of non-first-generation students, 47.1% instead of 34.0%—a modest goal—SSU's overall graduation rate would have been 55.8% (as opposed to the 50.0% figure actually reported).

Given such a statistical reality, the obvious next question is, how can colleges amend their procedures and policies to improve the postsecondary experience and academic performance of first-generation students, which may be the best and easiest way to raise overall graduation rates? Suffice it to say, many things can be done. Some of these things are easy for colleges and universities to do, some are moderately easy to do, and some are difficult to do. The rest of this chapter discusses what can be done to improve the postsecondary experience and academic performance of first-generation college students. The range of potential actions by cost is visible in each of the recommendations. By "cost" here, I mean not only the estimated additional financial expenditure (including hiring new employees) necessary for following the recommendation, but also the cost in terms of the time and effort of employees already working at the institution. Although it is likely that spending more money to address the issue would result in the most effective change in student performance, that is not always going to be the case. Much will depend on the individual character of the college or university itself. Much will depend on whether the institution is a community college or a bachelor's degree-granting college, on whether the institution is public or private, and on whether the institution is a research university granting doctoral degrees or a teaching college. This is to say, some institutions will be able to effect a big change in the academic performance of its first-generation students by enacting a low- or moderate-cost way of addressing the issue. Finally, the cost of identifying first-generation students will come into play in many of my recommendations, given that the officials at most American postsecondary institutions have not yet developed a process for determining exactly how many first-generation students they have. Although what needs to be done to identify individual first-generation students, and the cost of this procedure, will vary from institution to institution, there are a number of standard ways to do this: Admissions applications can be changed so that all applicants must disclose their parents' level of education (this would work at SSU); surveys can be filled out in classes that all first-year students must take; or family background information can be gathered as part of an administrative procedure to which all students must submit, such as granting a student ID card. (See chapter 1 for more suggestions on how institutions can count first-generation students.) Institutions undoubtedly will be able to design many other mechanisms for establishing first-generation student status. Once the status of the student is determined, that information should be entered into the institution's data system so that academic departments and all other campus units can determine with a keystroke who is a first-generation college student and who is not.

The 14 recommendations that follow are arranged to coincide with the organization of chapters 2 and 3, which describe the characteristic behaviors, internal psychology, and academic performance of first-generation college students. That organizational structure is as follows: (1) Learning at College, (2) Campus Presence, (3) An Extended Campus Acclimation Process, and (4) The Importance and Impact of Personal Relationships.

SECTION ONE: LEARNING AT COLLEGE

Issue 1: First-generation college students need remediation in higher numbers, proportionally speaking, than do non-first-generation students.

Most postsecondary institutions include some remedial course offerings, particularly in math and English. As discussed earlier, a higher proportion of first-generation students take remedial courses because of their weak cognitive skills and poor academic preparation, particularly in math, and for many of these students, remedial coursework represents their first taste of postsecondary education (Chen & Carroll, 2005; Horn & Bobbitt, 2000). What's even worse, the need for remediation is strongly correlated with dropping out (Hoyt, 1999; Pulley, 2008). Pulley (2008) reported that as few as 10.0% of students who take remedial courses ever achieve a four-year degree. Of the 14 student writers whose narratives make up chapter 4, nine of them had to take remedial English, remedial math, or both at SSU. This may come as a surprise to some readers as many of the student writers describe fairly successful high school careers. Only Crystal Halverson and Elizabeth

Ordaz disclose learning disabilities that may have accounted for their need for remediation, but as far as the other writers go, one conclusion we might make is that their first-generation student status somehow interfered with their ability to test out of remediation.

Many students enrolled in remedial courses, including first-generation students, of course, can feel like less-than-full-fledged students until after they have completed remediation, so stigmatization is a concern (Martinez, Sher, Krull, & Wood, 2009). No system that includes remedial course offerings can completely avoid the issue of student status hierarchies, given the highly structured advancement protocol of most postsecondary institutions, but faculty and staff can do a lot to make students feel more comfortable. Faculty who teach remedial courses should be trained to validate the presence of first-generation students enrolled in these courses. They should be trained in student development theory and should understand that the success of their remedial students is linked to their own well-being as educators and to the well-being of their institution as well. For instance, faculty probably will have more engaged and engaging postremediation students in the nonremedial courses they teach—when these students advance—if they validate the presence of remedial students.

With the noteworthy exception of some community colleges, the institutional culture of many colleges and universities does not place a high priority on remedial course offerings. At many four-year institutions, part-time adjunct faculty and graduate students teach most of the remedial classes, and even though the instruction these individuals deliver is often excellent, the symbolism of these assignment practices is not lost on first-generation college students. All University of California campuses employ this strategy, as do California State University campuses, albeit to a lesser degree. This arrangement has more than just a symbolic impact, however, when administrators regard remedial courses as "money makers" because of their low overhead compared to more "academic" courses, further decreasing the status of developmental education (Pulley, 2008). Because some institutions do not value remedial study highly enough, they often create and implement draconian policies—especially if there is not a positive relationship between the four-year institution and the local community college—and students can be dismissed if they do not complete remediation quickly enough. Although intra-institution discussion about class size can become very contentious, pitting academic departments against one another, every effort should be made to limit the size of remedial classes so the greater numbers of first-generation students registered in those classes receive the attention they need to succeed.

Some contemporary, progressive high schools have discovered that having their most accomplished teachers teach "low ability" students is a good way to effect a positive change in the school graduation rate (Hess, 2004). It has been much more common, however, for high schools to allow their most accomplished teachers to teach "high ability" students or honors students as a kind of reward. The same is true at many postsecondary institutions. Progressive postsecondary institutions should adopt the same contravention of the conventional wisdom that progressive high schools do. Sometimes the more accomplished high school teachers have to be encouraged to teach "low ability" students by a small increase in pay or some other incentive. Although most institutions are unlikely to adopt an increase in salary for faculty willing to teach remedial courses, other incentives such as a lighter teaching load can be offered. Whatever the method, pay increases, lighter teaching loads, or other incentives, progressive colleges and universities should encourage their most talented professors to teach remedial course offerings and the high number of first-generation students populating them. Another option is for academic departments to adopt a rotating course assignment system that provides all appropriate faculty the opportunity to teach remedial course offerings from time to time. This idea has the virtue of exposing an entire department's faculty to first-generation college students. If this enlightened attitude toward teaching remedial courses is coupled with smaller class sizes, colleges and universities will see not only higher graduation rates but also improved academic performance across the board.

Issue 2: First-generation college students need instruction in study skills.

As described in chapter 2, many faculty, especially those faculty at large public four-year institutions, do not teach study skills (Polansky, Horan, & Hanish, 1993; Weinstein & Mayer, 1983). Some instructors think study skills cannot be taught; some think study skills should not have to be taught; and some do not think about the issue at all, probably because they are more interested in their discipline's content than with how students learn that content (Hattie, Biggs, & Purdie, 1996; Wingate, 2006). Because first-generation students are much less likely to have been exposed to serious study habits than have their non-first-generation counterparts, this institutional attitude affects them more adversely. Faculty should be trained to teach study skills, and they should teach them in lower-division, high-enrollment courses containing large numbers of first- and second-year students, so first-generation students more likely to drop out in their first or second year can perform better academically and, therefore, be retained. Institutions might develop and adopt a standard study skills unit that faculty can plug into their lecture schedules early in the semester and revisit from time to time as the semester goes on. This is easier to do at smaller private institutions that have a universal vision of student development, but most institutions can benefit from some kind of serious study skills programming.

All first-generation college students should be enrolled in study skills workshops in addition to their regular coursework. The familiar pattern, described by narrative writers Yolanda Ortiz and Phillip Hammer, of giving postsecondary education a try after high school and quickly flaming out probably has something to do with a lack of study skills. It is no accident that both Ortiz and Hammer became successful students only after many years had passed between college classes. Although a higher level of maturity that comes with age likely had something to do with their success the second time around, learning how to process information better during their hiatus also was a probable contributing factor. Institutions should consider something like three one-hour study skills workshops during the first semester of study and a single refresher and/or checkup workshop during the second semester, but some students probably will need more attention. The study skills workshops can be taught by student development professionals or interested faculty. These instructors must be trained, however, so the curriculum they teach does not reflect the negative attitude most institutions have toward teaching study skills. Students who need help with study skills need more than to be given a couple of worksheets about budgeting time; they need to develop the complicated cognitive processes of serious study.

In addition, all first-generation students who fall below a certain level of performance—first-, second-, and third-year students—should automatically be enrolled in mandatory refresher workshops. Again, this sort of system is easier to implement at smaller, often private institutions that can monitor student participation carefully and follow up on progress, but the gains are worth the trouble and expense for any institution. These mandatory study skills workshops should not be treated as punitive in the institution culture or linked to academic probation workshops. They should be treated as something the majority of students (not only first-generation students) need to attend to maximize their potential.

Issue 3: Many first-generation college students need to be placed in study groups.

For many postsecondary institutions, it is relatively easy and inexpensive to help students form study groups attached to certain high-enrollment, low-GPA courses, so-called parent courses. This organization of resources is often called Supplemental Instruction, but it may go by different names at different institutions. For the most part Supplemental Instruction employs students to help students. The work of Treisman (1992) has shown that many nontraditional students need the example of other students to develop good study habits. Faculty and staff can make announcements in the "parent" class, arrange for locations, and generally encourage the formation of study groups. Fully engaged faculty may even drop in occasionally and offer suggestions to the group (Hodges & White, 2001).

As any postsecondary administrator should know, making an activity voluntary rather than mandatory will result in many students not attending—often those students who would benefit most from the activity. Because first-generation students often do not accurately perceive their own need for activities such as study groups and Supplemental Instruction, institutions have to monitor access and attendance carefully (Hodges & White, 2001). Although all students do benefit from these kinds of activities, first-generation students benefit more, as we have seen. Some institutions foster the attitude that study groups are only appropriate for "difficult" courses and/or that spending long hours studying alone in the library is the only way to be a good student. Many first-generation students need the example of other students, so these kinds of attitudes should be addressed and challenged; it should be explained to them that the work that goes on in study groups might be the most important work they do in terms of truly mastering content.

Participating first-generation students can monitor mandatory study groups themselves. For example, the students can take roll and, perhaps with the help of the faculty member teaching the "parent" course, can decide what the format of the study group should be and which topics participants should discuss. The best way to make sure the study group will produce the desired learning outcomes, however, is to hire a study group leader. The leader will establish consistency of study and an orderly presentation of supplementary material and, most important, monitor attendance and contact students who are doing poorly in the "parent" course or not attending the study group regularly. Community colleges may hire any student who has taken the "parent" course before and has done well in it as the study group leader, and institutions with graduate programs may hire a graduate student.

Issue 4: First-generation college students need specialized academic advising.

As described in chapter 2, first-generation students must be identified as having first-generation student status before academic advising takes place. Their academic advising needs are often very different from the needs of their more traditional counterparts (Kocel, 2008; Payne, K. K., 2007). To give just one specific example, the research of both Terenzini and associates (1995) and Chen and Carroll (2005) shows that first-generation students take longer to choose a major and often make their choice based on different criteria from those of their traditional counterparts. These different criteria can result in a choice of major that is not right for the student, which can lead to longer time to graduation when the major is changed or even to the student's dropping out. Many of the chapter 4 narrative writers mention difficulty surrounding the choice of a major, but what is even more illustrative is that many of them describe a feeling of well-being after they finally choose the "right" major and have a clear path in front of them. For example, John Hunter writes that he is "sure" that his decision to abandon the kinesiology major and a career in chiropractics for the English major is the "right direction," and that academic study and the pursuit of the arts is nothing less than "one of the purposes of our existence." Academic advisors should be trained to understand the differences between first-generation students and their non-first-generation counterparts and make appropriate adjustments to their advising practices when advising first-generation students.

At many large public four-year institutions, students must be proactive in scheduling time with an academic advisor, and many students fall through the cracks, meeting with an advisor once a year or not at all (Lau, 2003;

Sickles, 2004; Varney, 2007). At such institutions, where a high level of specialization in the staff pool has been adopted as a cost-saving measure, designated academic advisors are often the only people "allowed" to deliver academic advising. One advising appointment a year is not enough attention for first-generation college students because there is so much to cover. A good academic advising meeting addresses more than simply deciding on a major, more than can be addressed adequately in one 50-minute meeting a semester or a year. Progressive institutions will monitor student progress more carefully and require that first-generation students meet with academic advisors more often than do non-first-generation students.

Finally, to have a positive impact on the graduation rate of first-generation college students, most postsecondary institutions will need to hire more academic advisors. Or, if hiring more staff in advising positions is impossible, they will need to train more existing staff to deliver academic advising.

SECTION TWO: CAMPUS PRESENCE

Issue 5: First-generation college students need help overcoming the "imposter phenomenon."

The imposter phenomenon, described in chapter 2, refers to a special kind of self-esteem challenge that can impede the academic progress of first-generation college students more than it can other kinds of students. Typically, the imposter phenomenon shows up most clearly in regard to classroom behavior. For example, many first-generation students allow other students to dominate classroom discussions, believing that these "real," nonimposter students know what to do and what to say, unlike themselves, who, they believe, have little to say that anyone in the classroom, especially the instructor, wants to hear (Hayes, 1997; McConnell, 2000; Strayhorn, 2006). Chapter 4 narrative writer Phillip Hammer describes such a severe case of the imposter phenomenon that he tells an academic advisor that the reason for his below average academic performance the previous semester was the death of his father, who actually was alive and well.

Faculty and staff should be trained to recognize the imposter phenomenon and to enact classroom procedures that encourage the classroom participation of first-generation students. Perhaps the best way to encourage first-generation students to participate is to make classroom procedures as transparent as possible, so first-generation students feel they are on an even footing with non-first-generation students. For example, faculty should be very clear about how papers are turned in, how to format a paper, and how to prepare for a visit during office hours. Preparation should go beyond such concrete issues, however, and touch on the kind of abstract cognitive processing involved in preparing for class. What is commonly called "thinking on your feet" is a skill that can be learned, but first-generation college students must be shown what to do and given an opportunity to practice such skills.

These kinds of feelings probably are less intense for first-generation students at community colleges and most intense at private four-year institutions, especially highly selective ones. The imposter phenomenon should be identified by name and discussed during preregistration orientations and even in classrooms with high numbers of first-generation college students.

Another way to address the imposter phenomenon is to show first-generation students that non-first-generation students and even some faculty and staff suffer from it as well. An institution's counseling center can organize group discussions for first-generation students to nip low self-esteem in the bud. The group might include a panel of faculty and staff, highly regarded officers of the institution who discuss the imposter phenomenon as an almost necessary step in the development of a college-student identity. In an academic environment, opportunities for representing oneself as an authority are many, including becoming expert in a school of thought, in the jargon of an academic discipline, and in a category of research. First-generation students should be shown how to capitalize on these opportunities.

Progressive institutions should have some mechanism in place for identifying the negative feelings associated with the imposter phenomenon in new first-generation students, and in serious cases be able to facilitate a transfer to a community college without depriving the student of his or her enrollment privileges. When students become more comfortable in their abilities and have shown good progress at the community college, they should be allowed to register for classes at the first-choice institution without having to reapply.

Issue 6: First-generation college students need to be enrolled in a "University 101" course.

You will recall from chapter 2 that Hayes (1997) wrote that the so-called University 101 courses "provide students an in-depth orientation to college life, including help with study skills, test and speech anxiety, as well as career counseling and a general overview of the university structure" (p. 2). The curriculum also can include how to behave in a tolerant manner toward people with different religious beliefs and different sexual orientations; how to avoid getting sick, including how to avoid sexually transmitted diseases; and how to manage new freedoms when living away from parents for the first time. First-generation college students often come from home environments where information in these categories and others is scarce. The curriculum of the course will vary depending on the institution; for example, community colleges with few if any residential students may have less need for a full-blown course, but even they should consider how they deliver this important information to first-generation students. Although all students can benefit from such a course, usually paid for and taught by the student affairs division of the institution, first-generation college students benefit more than traditional students.

Enrolling in a University 101 course should be mandatory for all first-generation students in their first semester of study, especially at large public four-year institutions where delivery of the kind of information taught in such a course can be inconsistent. In addition, progressive colleges and universities should develop and initiate a plan to incorporate the University 101 course into some structural correspondence with academic departments. One of the problems with University 101 courses is that students often perceive them as outside their regular course of study, when just the opposite should be the case. The ideal structure is to team-teach the University 101 course using student support professionals with knowledge of first-generation student concerns and a rotating group of faculty from different academic departments so students are introduced to the different theoretical approaches and discipline-specific methodologies of knowledge that are characteristic of the different fields of study. Given their family histories, first-generation students often have significant gaps in their knowledge base, so they may lack knowledge of the organizational philosophy and historical purposes of the postsecondary education system. Institutions with already functioning University 101 courses should take this project to the next level to create a truly coherent first-year experience for first-generation students. Remember, the research (Filkins & Doyle, 2002; Smart & Umback, 2007) clearly shows that first-generation students can be skeptical of institutional initiatives that appear to be outside the academic goals and purposes of the institution.

Many institutions have recognized that enrolling first-generation students in University 101 courses may not be enough. Sonoma State University, along with many other institutions across the country, provides what is typically called a "Summer Bridge" program. In SSU's case Summer Bridge is for first-generation students from low-income families, and the curriculum covers much of what usually is delivered in University 101 courses along with other material. Several of the chapter 4 narrative writers describe their Summer Bridge experience as central to their successful transition to college life, including, for example, Erica Camacho, who writes that the program "really helped me understand living on the campus and all the issues around succeeding in college."

Issue 7: First-generation college students need a program that models the procedures and protocols of academic discussion and debate.

Progressive institutions will find ways to model the life of the mind. First-generation students come into contact with their professors and other academics in the classes they take, of course, and in most cases they can learn fairly quickly how to receive information through the standard activities of the traditional classroom environment. But if this is all they see of their professors, they can develop a very limited view of what academics do. Given their backgrounds, they may not be acquainted with the principles of rhetoric or even comfortable discussing abstract ideas. This is illustrated in a humorous way by narrative writer Jeff Peterson, who begins his narrative by quoting his father saying, "Oh, stop that," during a discussion about ideas Jeff was having with another family member. Many first-generation students have lived in a world much different from the world their teachers and advisors live in. They may not understand that academics often disagree with each other on substantive issues in their field, for example, and they may not understand the different strata of authority and different subspecialties in an individual field of study. Becoming familiar with these can only strengthen their motivation to learn, instilling in them the desire to become lifelong learners and perhaps continue their education as graduate students. First-generation students currently are very underrepresented in American graduate schools (Choy, 2001; Raymond & Black, 2008).

In addition to making academic discussion and debate as transparent as possible in the traditional classroom environment, institutions should schedule monthly or even weekly demonstrations of academics in action for a student audience. They should enlist the services of relevant faculty, for example, to represent various positions in a number of academic discourses that all students should know something about. For example, one kind of demonstration might feature a campus "difference" feminist debating a campus "equality" feminist about the future direction of feminist philosophy or some other interesting topic in contemporary feminist thought. Some of these demonstrations should simply showcase an interesting discussion, but others should intentionally demonstrate the metaprocesses at play in the interchanges between faculty. For example, first-generation students should see how one party in a debate responds to another, how to construct and deliver an authoritative comment, and how to accept disagreement graciously. Although the parents of non-first-generation students may not have overtly schooled their children in the finer points of rhetoric, they are more likely than the parents of first-generation students to have communicated the principles of logical discourse during daily exchanges and conversations seeking to influence certain kinds of behavior.

Because engaging in debate and discussion is only one facet of being an academic, first-generation college students should be exposed to the other duties and behaviors of faculty, including how they prepare for teaching, how they write and publish reports and scholarly articles, and how academic departments function. This information can be conveyed in workshops, public demonstrations, or regularly scheduled colloquiums to which scholars from other campuses are invited.

SECTION THREE: AN EXTENDED CAMPUS ACCLIMATION PROCESS

Issue 8: First-generation college students need a preregistration orientation to the institution.

Many institutions hold some sort of postenrollment, preregistration orientation for incoming students and their families in the summer. Orientation organizers should plan to group first-generation students and their families together so the material can address their specific concerns. The orientation material for first-generation student groups should be different from the material for the non-first-generation student groups. As mentioned in chapter 3, however, these orientations cannot hope to educate parents so they can be academic advisors to their children, but they can present material that addresses the issues that cause the most anxiety.

For some institutions, the orientation will be the only activity for parents of first-generation students, and given the unique interpersonal dynamics between first-generation students and their parents, this is an opportunity that cannot be missed. If a separate first-generation student orientation is not possible, at the very least institutions need to make addressing first-generation student needs a major part of the general orientation, and staff delivering the orientations need to start using the term "first-generation college student." For example, officials running the orientations should spend time describing how the lack of familiarity with postsecondary education can be a serious hindrance to doing well at the institution, and that views on the importance of this lack of familiarity and on the first-generation student category itself are changing.

In addition to the one- or two-day summer orientation described above, progressive institutions should create a more extensive orientation for first-generation students, similar to the Summer Bridge program at SSU mentioned earlier. Most institutions with such a program in place generally accommodate only the most at-risk students, but these programs should be expanded to include as many first-year first-generation students as possible. It is a shame that institutions resort to charging students and their families large sums of money for these activities. Too many institutions demand the same rates for room and board as they get from corporate clients renting space for a conference. Officials need to think through all the barriers specific to first-generation students; for instance, some parents may not want to come to orientations because *they* feel out of place on a college campus. Narrative writers Jeff Peterson, Carlos Sosa, and Elizabeth Ordaz all say their families were not able to accompany them to orientation activities. It is not always about money, but when it is, institutions need to realize that they will recoup such expenditures when graduation rates improve.

Issue 9: First-generation college students need help from the institution to resist the pressure exerted by family members, friends, and the familiar to return to the home culture without a four-year degree.

Complementing the previous recommendation, institutions should consider follow-up orientations specifically for first-generation college students and their families that seek to weaken the ever-present lure of returning to the home culture without a degree. Many times, it is not a single event involving family members and/or friends that causes the student to drop out, but the gradual grinding down and undermining of the student's motivation and confidence by home culture attractions, parental misunderstanding, or other reasons. Often, parents and family members do not intend to make a postsecondary education more difficult for students, but their subtle nonsupport does the trick anyway. To prevent such difficulties before they happen, progressive institutions will create and implement events such as a follow-up to the preregistration orientation for which parents of first-generation students can come to the institution and find out what is going on. Institutions should consider such meetings for parents of first-generation students at the beginning of the second year of study to discuss problems that occurred during the first year. Narrative writers Maria Bravos and Carlos Sosa illustrate the desire for parent contact: Maria has planned her postsecondary education so she will never have to be too far from home, and Carlos struggles with homesickness but is able to manage it so it does not interfere with his studies.

Multiple mandatory meetings with campus advisors is often the best first line of defense against homesickness's affecting academic performance, but progressive institutions should go beyond this. Perhaps through psychological service units, institutions should facilitate peer group meetings in which first-generation students can talk with their peers about issues such as homesickness and the lure of the home culture. When first-generation students understand that what they are experiencing is common among students like themselves, they will be better able to keep such pressure in context and remain enrolled. Other peer group members also may offer tips on how to deal with troublesome family members and friends. Much of this issue depends on whether the student is living on campus, commuting from home, or living on his or her own.

Although community colleges traditionally enroll a higher percentage of first-generation students than do public or private four-year institutions, so they might be expected to be better able to address the allure of the home culture, they also enroll a higher percentage of commuter students. It may be that first-generation students attending community colleges and living at home, as many of them do, are at a higher risk for dropping out due to pressure and interference from people in the home culture. In other words, more separation between the campus culture and the home culture might be what is required. This perhaps controversial view is ripe for new research, and if it does turn out that first-generation students at community colleges who live at home are at higher risk of dropping out, this is a serious matter as community colleges are often at the beginning of the pipeline to a four-year degree, as we have seen.

As reported in chapter 3, first-generation college students are much more likely to live off campus, even when on-campus housing is available and reasonably affordable. Living on campus makes initiatives such as collaborative learning and learning communities much easier for students to access (Smith, B. L., & MacGregor, 1992, Smith, K. A., & MacGregor, 2000). Some smaller private four-year institutions may be able to create a system that gives first-generation students priority for on-campus housing, thus placing them in a better position to manage difficult home relationships, but this is unlikely at large public four-year institutions. In any event, local and state programs that help first-generation and low-income students pay for on-campus housing should be maintained at levels that permit every first-generation student who is able to live on campus.

Issue 10: First-generation college students need to be involved in the campus life.

As the research surveyed in chapter 3 demonstrates, first-generation students are much more likely to be on the outside looking in when it comes to campus activities, both curricular and extracurricular (Terenzini et al., 1996). Being fully integrated into campus life, we know, leads to higher levels of academic achievement, including higher GPAs (Martinez et al., 2009). It can affect general well-being, too, as narrative writer Jessica Gomez demonstrates when she writes that her sorority is her "second family." All campus promotional activities and advertisements encouraging students to become involved in campus clubs (community service, departmental, and social clubs), student government, campus employment opportunities, and campus-sponsored social events should be developed with first-generation students in mind. For example, because first-generation students so often feel like outsiders, they can be sensitive to restrictive activities and campus clubs that accept only certain kinds of students; therefore, institution administrators should monitor campus event planning to remove all evidence of an exclusionary ideology from advertising and club/event procedures. Institutions should do everything they can to validate participation in campus life as standard behavior for all students as a means to get first-generation students involved. Pascarella et al. (2004) confirmed that first-generation students are much less likely than their non-first-generation peers to be involved in extracurricular activities, but their analysis went one step further: "Ironically, first-generation students derived greater outcome benefits from extracurricular involvement and peer interaction than other students *even though they were significantly less likely to be engaged in these activities during college* [emphasis in original]" (p. 278).

Although many institution administrators and business officers will shiver at the thought of allocating more money to campus clubs and other campus life activities, preferring instead to allow student contributions and associated student financial organizations to bear the load, institutions should develop and fund campus life activities in the gaps when other funding sources have dropped the ball. In other words, institutions that seriously want their first-generation students to participate in campus life activities need to have this goal in mind when designing activities.

The desire to work, the need to make money, may be the single biggest impediment to first-generation students' participating in campus life activities. Because of their backgrounds, many first-generation students work more than their non-first-generation counterparts. Also given their backgrounds, I do not think it is unreasonable to conclude that many work even when they do not really *need* to work, when it would be better to take out a student loan, for instance (Somers et al., 2004). Progressive colleges and universities will encourage first-generation students who must work to work on campus. Few will be able to balance the need to work, involvement in campus life, and maintaining good grades like narrative writer Elizabeth Ordaz, but that should be the goal. First-generation students who do not need to work to stay enrolled at the institution should not work at all; instead, they should become involved in campus life activities. Institutions should be heavily involved in helping first-generation students make decisions about how much to work and about how much money they will truly need during their matriculation. In concordance with this advising and counseling, institutions should invest in ensuring that there are enough employment opportunities on campus to support the students who truly need to generate income to stay enrolled. You cannot be involved in campus life activities if you are not present on the campus because you work 30 hours a week at a downtown department store. At the very least, institutions with high numbers of first-generation college students should make full use of federal work-study funding, and any other grant support they can obtain, to keep working students on campus.

Issue 11: First-generation college students need more unstructured, informal public spaces on campus.

As everyone who works in postsecondary education knows (or should know), the gradual corporatizing of American colleges and universities has resulted in, first, the reassignment, then the scaling down, and finally the disappearance of public spaces on many campuses. At some colleges and universities, financial affairs officers appear to regard any office, classroom, or public space for students that is not being used 12 hours a day as a loss of revenue. What they do not understand is that public spaces for students need to be unoccupied from time to time to be fully functional as public spaces. Solitary study and private contemplation, which students must practice at least part of the time, are not compatible with public spaces that are packed solid with bodies from 9:00 a.m. to 5:00 p.m. It used to be that assigning certain spaces on campus for unsupervised and unstructured student use, whether students actually used the spaces 12 hours a day, was just a cost of operating a postsecondary institution. Not any more. Lounge and study areas and empty rooms are becoming harder and harder to find. This cost-driven philosophy of human geography hurts first-generation students more than it does non-first-generation students, because, in addition to needing somewhere for solitary study and private contemplation, the former need to make contact with students like them as part of the process of acclimating to college life. Institutions must slow down the corporatizing process so that students have places on campus to gather or to be by themselves. This is easier to do at well-endowed private schools, of course, but all postsecondary institutions have to begin fighting the good fight with financial officers if they are going to help their first-generation students become better, higher-achieving students.

Not every public space on campus needs to be reserved for unsupervised and unstructured student use. Faculty and staff should be involved in constructing public space with certain aims in mind. For example, certain spaces on campus should be designated as student gathering places where students can get together and talk about their studies, successes, and failures; in addition, some spaces should be identified as first-generation student gathering places. Simply having empty public spaces available is enough for many students, but not for first-generation college students. They have more difficulty constructing and claiming spaces as their own; they may even be intimidated by the emptiness of a space. This is a fine line to walk, I know; public spaces for students need to be unsupervised and unstructured most of the time, as mentioned earlier, but sometimes first-generation students will need help and advice on how best to use these unsupervised and unstructured spaces. First-generation students are more likely to allow a lack of self-confidence to interfere with the free flow of ideas that can occur in the kind of public spaces I am imagining. They need to practice. As we have seen with other issues, the more an institution validates this kind of activity, the more first-generation students will participate.

Truly progressive colleges and universities will not regard public space for students as a waste of money but as absolutely necessary for the success of students, especially first-generation students. They will include public spaces for students in any expansion plans. The disappearance of public spaces on campus should be made a public issue and be discussed through the student newspaper and by other means, and those institutions that are sincere about improving the graduation rates of their first-generation student charges should attempt to reverse this process and create more public spaces for all students.

SECTION FOUR: THE IMPORTANCE AND IMPACT OF PERSONAL RELATIONSHIPS

Issue 12: First-generation college students need to develop personal relationships with faculty and nonfaculty staff members.

After learning how to identify the first-generation students in their classes, faculty members should look for opportunities to develop relationships with these students. For example, they should look for opportunities to pay special attention to the student during class time or to stop the student in the hall to exchange greetings and brief comments. As demonstrated in chapter 3, research (Filkins & Doyle, 2002; Smart & Umback, 2007) shows that developing a personal relationship with a faculty member is an extremely important factor in becoming comfortable in the postsecondary environment and is highly correlated with academic success among first-generation students. The symbolic impact of being able to say, "I know Professor Smith," cannot be underestimated. Many parents (as well as friends and other family members) of first-generation students will regard postsecondary professors with such respect that any such report from their child will be received as proof that he or she is a full-fledged college student. Remember that many parents, other family members, and friends of non-first-generation students will have communicated their own college and university experiences in terms of relationships with professors, what this professor or that one might have said, etc. The idea behind this recommendation is that first-generation students, too, should be able to develop this kind of family mythology about college attendance.

Academic departments should create structured activities and gatherings during which faculty members can meet and get to know first-generation college students. Once institutions establish a procedure for entering first-generation student status in the student-record database, this database should be available to all academic departments. These meetings might take the form of social mixers at which nonacademic issues are discussed, or more academically oriented meetings at which professors describe what they do in terms of professional duties and academic activities to small numbers of students. Any kind of meeting at which faculty members talk directly to individual first-generation students rather than aim their discussion at an imagined ideal student, which is what usually happens in the traditional classroom environment, is very beneficial to first-generation students, who often do not consider themselves ideal students and so are quick to feel excluded in large group discussions.

Another technique for putting this recommendation into place is for faculty members to hold *mandatory* office-hour meetings with first-generation students. If such meetings are made mandatory, first-generation students are more likely to be able to dismiss any feelings of inadequacy—which might cause them to believe they are wasting the faculty member's time—and actually take advantage of office hours. This issue transcends the differences among institution types, community colleges, public/private four-year for-profit professional schools, etc. Those institutions that train faculty or suggest to faculty that they follow an institutional model for interacting with students are in a better position to communicate well with first-generation students.

Although we all know that the average professor's time is already highly impacted by numerous duties, the intensity of relationships with first-generation students is very important. Whenever possible, these relationships should extend beyond simply saying hello in the hallways (although I am not disparaging this kind of contact, which is also important). Progressive institutions will find ways to match faculty in mentor relationships with appropriate first-generation students as often as possible. Special consideration should be given to students' backgrounds and academic interests. Research (Hahs-Vaughn, 2004) on mentor programs indicates that when female faculty are matched with female first-generation students, for example, and Latino faculty are matched with Latino first-generation students (not to mention first-generation faculty with first-generation students), each party gets the most out of the relationship. Many institutions must rely on grant funding to operate these kinds of mentor programs, and that is fine; but making them part of the institutional fabric will guarantee the biggest possible impact and reward. If institutions cannot afford to give interested and committed faculty a financial stipend for taking on first-generation protégés, they should offer service credit or other promotion-track benefits to faculty who agree to participate in a mentor program.

I recommend that institutions facilitate the development of personal relationships between first-generation students and nonfaculty staff for many of the same reasons they should facilitate personal relationships between first-generation students and faculty. This does not mean to suggest there are no differences between the two types of relationships, however, differences that stem mostly from the realization that the average faculty member cannot be expected to have studied the latest student development theory or the latest research on the success of first-generation college students. It is interesting to note that the chapter 4 narratives mention relationships with nonfaculty staff much more often than they do relationships with faculty. This might have something to do with the methodology we used to recruit the student writers, or with the project being hosted by a student support unit and not an academic department. Student support professionals assisting first-generation students, however, should realize that they cannot replace the relationships students must have with faculty. On the one hand, we should applaud narrative writer Crystal Halverson for the intensity with which she develops and organizes her support staff network, but on the other hand, student support professionals shouldn't enable such students into becoming addicts, so to speak, of support units.

Academic advisors and other nonfaculty staff, including administrators, who have significant contact with students should be able to discuss all of the issues mentioned in this chapter in the context of their personal relationships with first-generation students. Because these issues touch all areas of the first-generation student's life, as we have seen, nonfaculty staff should be able to foster a more well-rounded relationship with first-generation students. They should be prepared to discuss home-culture, work, and campus-culture acclimation issues, for instance, in addition to standard advising topics. This is not to say that nonfaculty staff should know every detail about every first-generation student's life—this obviously is not practical; but in their chance meetings and brief conversations with first-generation students, they should be able to draw on the research on first-generation student challenges. Personal relationships with faculty and nonfaculty staff are an important component of the validation process discussed elsewhere in this volume.

Issue 13: First-generation college students need help in advancing their personal relationships with family members and friends from their home culture.

Part of understanding the first-generation college student experience is understanding the special relationship that first-generation students often have with family members and friends from their home culture. As discussed in chapter 3 and illustrated in chapter 4, these personal relationships can be very positive, very negative, and every place in between, but they are rarely irrelevant to the success of the student. Academic advisors and counselors should be trained to intervene in these relationships and to bring about a positive outcome for the student when problems arise. Because of the various barriers and challenges described throughout this book, first-generation college students are more likely to suffer from depression and other emotional problems, and these emotional issues often are related to relationships with family and friends from the home culture. "Survivor guilt" and other unproductive thought patterns can weigh heavily on first-generation students, who may need assistance in keeping everything in perspective (Somers et al., 2004). One of the saddest things an advisor or counselor is likely to see is a capable first-generation student who would rather return to home-culture family and friends than finish a four-year degree just because he or she never felt comfortable in the campus culture. Institutions can benefit by being proactive in breaking the chain of non–college attendance in first-generation student families.

Potential difficulties caused by family members and friends from the home culture should not be addressed solely through the student; institutions should anticipate such difficulties and prevent them as much as possible through contact with family members and even friends. The easiest way to do this is by producing and distributing promotional material describing the first-generation student experience for incoming students and families that brings these issues to light. Such material should be mailed home to potential first-generation students before class registration and should be included in any summer orientation presentation. Many parents who cause problems for their children do so unconsciously; they subtly communicate to their children, for example, that they would rather have them around the house than attending college.

Narrative writer John Hunter gets this phenomenon just right, describing the relationship between the college culture and his home culture this way: "Each time I visit home, I am reminded I do not fully understand their world and they do not fully identify with mine." He goes on to write, "My family has not ostracized, disowned, or even criticized me," and his parents do sound like the accepting type, but that does not mean his relationship with his family has not weighed on his mind and interfered with his academic performance. Even for well-meaning, benign parents like John's, an orientation workshop specially for them can be a big help. They can learn which behaviors do not help a student acquire a postsecondary education and which do. The sensitive areas can be explained to them, so they can avoid the most deleterious behaviors. Many parents of first-generation students have never thought of their child as a "first-generation college student," so it should come as no surprise that they do not know how to anticipate first-generation student problems; postsecondary institutions do not have this excuse.

Issue 14: First-generation college students need role models.

Creating nonfaculty mentor programs on campuses is very much in fashion these days in student affairs circles, and mentor programs can be very valuable for sure. Because the outsider dimension of the first-generation student psychology can be a benefit (as well as a deficit), however, mentor programs for them need to be thought through and implemented carefully. As mentioned earlier, students benefit most from a mentor who is like them: A student of color benefits most from a mentor who has experienced the difficulties of being a student of color on a predominantly White campus; a female student studying in the sciences benefits most from a mentor who has experienced the difficulties of being a female professional in a field dominated by males; and a student with physical disabilities benefits most from a mentor who has experienced the difficulties of getting from one place to another on a hilly campus or working with a learning disability in a demanding job. By the same token, first-generation college students need mentors who were also first-generation college students. Existing mentor programs, therefore, should be able to match first-generation students with mentors who have had the same experience of college attendance. Notice how few of the chapter 4 narrative writers tell of receiving advice from people like them. Jeff Peterson, for example, illustrates how people in need of role models sometimes can have them fall in their laps, as if out of nowhere, so institutions need to keep this in mind. Making sure that first-generation students have many opportunities to network and meet students like them, as well as students unlike them, cannot be underestimated. Jeff gives a lot of credit to his girlfriend for modeling how a college student should think and behave, and although she comes "from a long line of college graduates," she appears to have been able to keep her boyfriend on the right track.

Progressive institutions should create mentor programs that specialize in first-generation college student issues. Not only should the mentors be first-generation students as undergraduates, but the programs also should include meetings and workshops that address the barriers and challenges of being a first-generation student. The "guide philosophy" for assisting first-generation students described in chapter 2 is key here. The term "guide information" seems appropriate because what first-generation students need most is to become comfortable in the postsecondary environment, which is an ongoing and sometimes lengthy process, a process through which they need to be guided.

Student mentor programs can also be a help, but the student mentors need to be trained to be more interventionist and involved than what is usually required. If the mentor program provides student mentors whose main purpose is to show mentees where the financial aid office is, remind them of deadlines, and describe where the best parties are, these mentors are not going to help first-generation students much. They need more. They need to hear how professors really perceive their students. They need to be shown what life with a college education is like. They need discussions about what non-first-generation college students think about college.

Finally, to have an impact on low retention and graduation rates among first-generation students, mentor programs need to be mandatory. After all, this is what all non-first-generation students have received from growing up in a household where one or both of the parents have graduated from college. They were not given a choice, either; receiving this information was in a sense mandatory. It takes a long time (about 18 years, in most cases) to become *intuitively oriented toward college*, as most non-first-generation students are, by absorbing stories, opinions, and attitudes about college from parents, other family members, and family friends. Progressive college and university administrators should construct an educational environment in which their first-generation charges can catch up, an environment in which these students can approximate being intuitively oriented toward college. A mandatory mentor program could be one element in a larger plan to achieve this goal.

Conclusion

To CONCLUDE, I would like to draw special attention to two fairly recent, very important studies by researchers who have long been at the forefront of describing and explaining how disadvantaged students experience college, *Moving Beyond Access: College Success for Low-Income, First-Generation Students* by Engle and Tinto (2008) and "First Generation College Students: Additional Evidence on College Experiences and Outcomes" by Pascarella, Pierson, Wolniak, and Terenzini (2004).

The first thing to point out about these two studies is that they define the term *first-generation student* in different ways, which makes their findings and conclusions, sadly, hard to compare. The Engle and Tinto (2008) study defines first-generation college students the same way this book does: Individuals can claim first-generation student status if neither one of their parents or guardians has earned a four-year degree. The study by Pascarella and associates (2004) employs a three-part scheme for arriving at a definition: (1) students whose parents have both completed a bachelor's degree or above (high parental postsecondary education); (2) students having one or more parents who have completed at least some college, but no more than one parent who has attained a bachelor's degree or above (moderate parental postsecondary education); and (3) students whose parents have no more than a high school education (first-generation college students). To make all of this even more complicated, the Engle and Tinto (2008) study did not separate the first-generation student category from the low-income student category. More to the point, Engle and Tinto did distinguish between the two student categories, but their study's methodology is such that this distinction is not useful to researchers who are interested in understanding the college experience of first-generation-*only* students. Similar to the Pascarella et al. study, Engle and Tinto compare three categories of students: (1) not low-income and not first-generation students, (2) low-income *or* first-generation-only students, and (3) low-income first-generation students (Engle &

Tinto, 2008). As it turns out that "or" in the second category is all important. It means that the findings about the students in the second category
cannot be assigned to either low-income students or first-generation-only
students; the findings can only be assigned to the two kinds of students as a
group excluding one or the other without revealing which one is excluded.
The result of this methodology is that readers and researchers who want to
learn about first-generation-only students are not given much specific data.

The authors of these studies have good reasons for dividing up students
into these various mutually exclusive categories, no doubt, but their good
reasons also point out a bad problem: The higher-education community
does not have a universal definition for the term "first-generation college
student," and it needs one. Without a universal definition, we cannot count
students, and without the ability to count students, we cannot advocate well
for policies and practices that will benefit first-generation college students.

Despite these problems, these two studies do contain useful information
for understanding the first-generation student experience. Both of them are,
in fact, very useful, as I show below, but they are not as useful as they could
have been to designing postsecondary education policies and practices had
they shared the same definition of the subject of their inquires.

The Engle and Tinto (2008) study puts forward *again* the very gloomy
statistics about the lack of success of first-generation college students (and
low-income students). According to the study, "After six years, only 11 percent of low-income, first-generation students had earned bachelor's degrees
compared to 55 percent of their more advantaged peers" (p. 2). Engle and
Tinto suggest that the main reason for this large disparity is the types of
institutions first-generation (and low-income) students usually attend:
"Low-income, first-generation students were actually more than seven times
more likely to earn bachelor's degrees if they started in four-year institutions,
but only 25 percent of them did so" (p. 2). Now the picture is getting a
little clearer. Engle and Tinto found that "a large number of low-income,
first-generation students began—and ended—their studies at public two-
year and for-profit institutions" (p. 2).

Unfortunately, the picture that is getting clearer here is a familiar one.
First-generation college students are much more likely to attend nonselective
institutions, and they are poorly integrated into the overall postsecondary
education system in this country as well. As has been shown, they are much

more likely to attend, for example, community colleges, which is not necessarily a problem if not for the fact that these students who start out at
community colleges are also much less likely to earn a bachelor's degree later
in their postsecondary education careers. Pascarella et al. (2004) confirmed
these dire statistics: "Our findings suggest that compared to other students,
first-generation college students tend to be significantly handicapped in
terms of the types of institutions they attend and the kinds of experiences
they have during college" (p. 275). First-generation students, please notice,
are not just mildly affected by their poor integration across the postsecondary
education system, they are *significantly* "handicapped."

Being significantly "handicapped" recalls the language at the beginning
of the introduction to this book. Although the people who run the American
postsecondary education system have made some strides in terms of access,
facilitating instead of hindering the attendance of more ethnic minority individuals and more individuals with disabilities, for example, they still have
much work to do. Yes, the doors to academe are open a little wider at the
beginning of the 21st century, but it is fairly obvious that they are not open
wide enough. The Engle and Tinto (2008) and Pascarella et al. (2004) studies reveal, among other things, that the American postsecondary education
system is deeply segregated along class lines. This is a major structural problem that, if not corrected, will have sweeping, national ramifications for years
to come. First-generation students have access to some kinds of postsecondary institutions, but they do not have full access to others. Pascarella et al.
put it this way: "Family cultural capital plays a significant role in informing
the choices students make about the types of institutions they attend and
the kinds of experiences they have once enrolled" (p. 277). Once again, it
appears that first-generation college students are caught in the middle; on
the one hand, their limited cultural capital prevents them from getting into
the kinds of institutions that will lead to a four-year degree; and on the other
hand, they cannot acquire the needed cultural capital unless they can get
into the kinds of institutions that will lead to a four-year degree.

It does come down to cultural capital. The stories, anecdotes, and other
information about college attendance—cultural capital—conveyed to children in non-first-generation student families really do matter. Being intuitively oriented toward college really does matter. As this book has
demonstrated again and again, being a first-generation college student is no

small thing. In fact, it is a very big thing . . . and it affects every dimension of being a contemporary college student.

After reading the narratives that comprise chapter 4, you know that first-generation college students are often the heroes of their families. Younger siblings look up to them, parents see their own hopes and dreams realized through them, and aunts and uncles brag about them. Although being a hero has its fringe benefits, it also comes with potentially crushing responsibilities and pressures.

Every first-generation college student has a different story to tell. The stories are different, that is true, but they are also the same. Overcoming adversity when the deck is stacked against you, as we have seen, is something with which all first-generation students are familiar. The time to get the word out about first-generation students has arrived. It is my hope that *The First-Generation Student Experience: Implications for Campus Practice, and Strategies for Improving Persistence and Success* shows how postsecondary faculty and staff can tailor instruction and other services so that as many first-generation students as possible can realize the dream of a timely graduation. Many professional educators believe the success of the American postsecondary education system, which is so integral to the success of the American economy, depends on universal access. If this is true, helping first-generation students succeed is more important than ever.

References

Alessandia, K. P., & Nelson, E. S. (2005). Identity development and self-esteem of first-generation American college students: An exploratory study. *Journal of College Student Development, 46*(1), 3–12.

Almanac Issue 2008–09. (2008). *The Chronicle of Higher Education, 55*(1).

Astin, A. W. (1984). Student involvement: A developmental theory for higher education. *Journal of College Student Personnel, 25*, 297–308.

Astin, A. W. (1993). *What matters in college: Four critical years revisited.* San Francisco: Jossey-Bass.

Astin, A. W., & Oseguera, L. (2005). *Degree attainment rates at American colleges and universities* (Rev. ed.). Los Angeles: Higher Education Research Institute, UCLA.

Baxter Magolda, M. B. (2001). *Making their own way: Narratives for transforming higher education to promote self-development.* Sterling, VA: Stylus.

Baxter Magolda, M. B. (2003). Identity and learning: Student affairs' role in transforming higher education. *Journal of College Student Development, 44*(1), 231–247.

Bean, J. B., & Metzner, B. S. (1985). A conceptual model of non-traditional undergraduate student attrition. *Review of Educational Research, 55*(4), 485–540.

Boyd, V. S., Hunt, P. F., Kandell, J. J., & Lucas, M. S. (2003). Relationship between identity processing style and academic success in undergraduate students. *Journal of College Student Development, 44*(2), 155–167.

Braxton, J. M. (2000). *Reworking the student departure puzzle.* Nashville, TN: Vanderbilt University Press.

Brown, C. (2008, April 8). Farm pushes economic diversity: Bridge program may be option for future admits. *The Stanford Daily,* p. 1.

Bryant, A. N. (2001). Community college students: Recent findings and trends. *Community College Review, 2*(3), 77–93.

Bui, K. (2002). First-generation college students at a four-year university: Background characteristics, reasons for pursuing higher education, and first year experiences. *College Student Journal, 36*(1), 3–12.

Burd, S. (2002). Bridging the gap. *The Chronicle of Higher Education, 48*(48), 1–25.

Cabrera, A. F., & La Nasa, S. M. (2001). On the path to college: Three critical tasks facing America's disadvantaged. *Research in Higher Education, 42*(2), 119–149.

California Postsecondary Education Commission. (1995). *Tidal wave II.* Report on the Projected Enrollments of the California Community College system, the California State University system, and the University of California system to 2005. Los Angeles: California Higher Education Policy Center.

Camarota, S. A. (2007). *Immigrants in the United States, 2007: A profile of America's foreign-born population.* Washington, DC: Center for Immigration Studies.

Carey, K. (2008). *Graduation rate watch: Making minority student success a priority.* Washington, DC: Education Sector.

Chaffee, J. (1992). Transforming educational dreams into educational reality. In L. S. Zwerling & H. B. London (Eds.), *First-generation students: Confronting the cultural issues* (New Directions for Community Colleges, No. 80, pp. 81–88). San Francisco: Jossey-Bass.

Chen, X., & Carroll, C. D. (2005). *First-generation students in postsecondary education: A look at their college transcripts* (NCES 2005-171). Washington, DC: U.S. Department of Education, National Center for Education Statistics.

Chin, H. K. (Ed.). (2003). *Open doors: Report on international educational exchange.* New York: Institute of International Education.

Choy, S. (2001). *Students whose parents did not go to college: Postsecondary access, persistence, and attainment* (NCES 2001-126). Washington, DC: U.S. Department of Education, National Center for Education Statistics.

Clauss-Ehlers, C. S., & Wibrowski, C. R. (2007). Building educational resilience and social support: The effects of the educational opportunity fund program among first- and second-generation college students. *Journal of College Student Development, 48*(5), 574–584.

Delpit, L. D. (1995). *Other people's children: Cultural conflict in the classroom.* New York: W.W. Norton.

Dennis, J. M., Phinney, J. S., & Chuateco, L. I. (2005). The role of motivation, parental support, and peer support in the academic success of ethnic minority first-generation college students. *Journal of College Student Development, 46*(3), 223–236.

Duggan, M. (2001). *Factors influencing the first-year persistence of first-generation college students.* Paper presented at the 2001 NEAIR Conference, Cambridge, MA.

Easterlin, R. A., Schaeffer, C., & Macunovich, D. J. (1993). Will the baby boomers be less well off than their parents? Income, wealth and family circumstances over the life cycle. *Population and Development Review, 19*(3), 497–522.

Engle, J., Bermeo, A., & O'Brien, C. (2006). *Straight from the source: What works for first-generation college students.* Washington, DC: The Pell Institute for the Study of Opportunity in Higher Education.

Engle, J., & Tinto, V. (2008). *Moving beyond access: College success for low-income, first-generation students.* Washington, DC: The Pell Institute for the Study of Opportunity in Higher Education.

Fenske, R. H., Porter, J. D., & DuBrock, C. P. (2000). Tracking financial aid and persistence of women, minority, and needy students in science, engineering, and mathematics. *Research in Higher Education, 41*(1), 67–93.

Filkins, J. W., & Doyle, S. K. (2002). *First-generation and low-income students: Using the NSSE data to study effective educational practices and students' self-reported gains.* Paper presented at the 2002 Association for Institutional Research Annual Conference, Toronto, Ontario, Canada.

Fuller, A. (2007, June 7). Admissions department seeks rise in low-income students: Socioeconomic diversity data gets tabulated for the first time this year. *The Stanford Daily*, p. 1.

Galor, O., & Weil, D. N. (1996). The gender gap, fertility, and growth. *The American Economic Review, 86*(3), 374–387.

Hagy, A. P., & Staniec, J. F. O. (2002). Immigrant status, race, and institutional choice in higher education. *Economics of Education Review, 21*(4), 381–392.

Hahs-Vaughn, D. (2004). The impact of parents' education level on college students: An analysis using the beginning post-secondary students' longitudinal study 1990–92/94. *Journal of College Student Development, 45*(5), 483–500.

Harbour, W. (2008). *AHEAD 2008 report on disability services and resource professionals in higher education.* Huntersville, NC: Association on Higher Education and Disability.

Hardin, L. (2007, January 31). Minorities maintained: While percentages at most schools are decreasing, Stanford's students remain diverse. *The Stanford Daily*, p. 2.

Harrell, P. E., & Forney, W. S. (2003). Ready or not, here we come: Retaining Hispanic and first-generation students in postsecondary education. *Community College Journal of Research and Practice, 27,* 147–156.

Hattie, J., Biggs, J., & Purdie, N. (1996). Effects of learning skills interventions on student learning: A meta-analysis. *Review of Educational Research, 66*(2), 99–136.

Hayes, L. L. (1997). Support from family and institution crucial to success of first-generation college students. *Counseling Today, 40*(2), 1–4.

Hess, F. M. (2004). *Teacher quality, teacher pay: To improve schools, reward excellence.* Retrieved from www.hoover.org/publications/policyreview

Hodges, R., & White, W. G. (2001). Encouraging high-risk student participation in tutoring and supplemental instruction. *Journal of Developmental Education, 24*(3), 2–10.

Horn, L. J., & Bobbitt, L. (2000). *Mapping the road to college: First-generation students' math track, planning strategies, and context of support* (NCES 2000-153).

Washington, DC: U.S. Department of Education, National Center for Education Statistics.

Horn, L. J., & Carroll, C. D. (1997). *Confronting the odds: students at risk and the pipeline to higher education* (NCES 93-091). Washington, DC: U.S. Department of Education, National Center for Education Statistics.

Hoyt, J. E. (1999). Remedial education and student attrition. *Community College Review, 27*(2), 51–73.

Hsiao, K. P. (1992). *First-generation students.* (ERIC Document Reproduction Service No. ED 351 079).

Inman, W. E., & Mayes, L. (1999). The importance of being first: Unique characteristics of first-generation community college students. *Community College Review, 26*(4), 1–20.

Ishitani, T. T. (2003). A longitudinal approach to assessing attrition behavior among first-generation students: Time-varying effects of pre-college characteristics. *Research in Higher Education, 44*(4), 433–449.

Ishitani, T. T. (2005). *Studying educational attainment among first-generation students in the United States.* Paper presented at the 45th Annual Forum of the Association for Institutional Research, San Diego, CA.

Johnston, T. (2004). *Family firsts.* Retrieved from www.stanfordalumni.org/news/magazine

Kocel, C. K. (2008). Advising first-generation college students for continued success. *The Mentor: An Academic Advising Journal, 10*(1), 1–4.

Lau, L. K. (2003). Institutional factors affecting student retention. *Education, 124*(1), 126–136.

Lohfink, M. M., & Paulsen, M. B. (2005). Comparing the determinants of persistence for first-generation and continuing-generation students. *Journal of College Student Development, 46*(4), 409–428.

London, H. B. (1989). Breaking away: A study of first-generation college students and their families. *American Journal of Education, 97*(2), 144–170.

London, H. B. (1992). Transformation: Cultural challenges faced by first-generation students. In L. S. Zwerling & H. B. London (Eds.), *First-generation students: Confronting the cultural issues* (New Directions for Community Colleges, No. 80, pp. 5–12). San Francisco: Jossey-Bass.

Longley, R. (2005). *College degree nearly doubles annual earnings.* Retrieved from usgovinfo.about.com

Longwell-Grice, R. (2008). *First-generation students: Status quo is not enough.* Retrieved from www.starfishsolutions.com

Lynch, J. W., Kaplan, G. A., & Shema, S. J. (1997). Cumulative impact of sustained economic hardship on physical, cognitive, psychological, and social functioning. *The New England Journal of Medicine, 337*(26), 1889–1895.

Martinez, J. A., Sher, K. J., Krull, J. L., & Wood, P. K. (2009). Blue-collar scholars?: Mediators and moderators of university attrition in first-generation college students. *Journal of College Student Development, 50*(1), 87–103.

McAdams, D. P., & Josselson, R. (Eds.). (2001). Moving up and the problem of explaining an "unreasonable" ambition. In R. Ochberg & W. Comeau, *Turns in the road: Narrative studies of lives in transition* (pp. 121–144). Washington, DC: American Psychological Association.

McCarron, G. P., & Inkelas, K. K. (2006). The gap between educational aspirations and attainment for first-generation college students and the role of parental involvement. *Journal of College Student Development, 47*(5), 534–549.

McConnell, P. J. (2000). What community colleges should do to assist first-generation students. *Community College Review, 28*(Winter), 75–87.

McCubbin, I. (2003). *An examination of criticisms made of Tinto's 1975 students integration model of attrition.* Retrieved from http://www.psy.gla.ac.uk/~steve/localed/icubb.pdf

National Center for Education Statistics (NCES). (1993). *Baccalaureate and beyond longitudinal study.* Retrieved from http://www.nces.ed.gov/surveys/b&b/

National Center for Education Statistics (NCES). (2007). *Digest of Education Statistics: 2007.* Retrieved from http://nces.ed.gov/programs/digest/d07/

National Coalition for Women and Girls in Education. (2008). *Title IX at 35: Beyond the headlines.* Washington, DC: National Coalition for Women and Girls in Education.

Nuñez, A. M., & Cuccaro-Alamin, S. (1998). *First-generation students: Undergraduates whose parents never enrolled in postsecondary education* (NCES 98-082). Washington, DC: U.S. Department of Education, National Center for Education Statistics.

Oakes, J. (1989). *Lost talent: The underparticipation of women, minorities, and disabled persons in science.* Santa Monica, CA: The Rand Corporation.

Padron, E. J. (1992). The challenge of first-generation college students: A Miami-Dade perspective. In L. S. Zwerling & H. B. London (Eds.), *First-generation students: Confronting the cultural issues* (New Directions for Community Colleges, No. 80, pp. 71–80). San Francisco: Jossey-Bass.

Pascarella, E. T., Pierson, C. T., Wolniak, G. C., & Terenzini, P. T. (2004). First-generation college students: Additional evidence on college experiences and outcomes. *The Journal of Higher Education, 75*(3), 249–284.

Pascarella, E. T., & Terenzini, P. T. (2005). *How college affects students, volume 2: A third decade of research.* San Francisco: Jossey-Bass.

Pascarella, E. T., Wolniak, G. C., Pierson, C. T., & Terenzini, P. T. (2003). Experiences and outcomes of first-generation students in community colleges. *Journal of College Student Development, 44*(3), 420–429.

Payne, K. K. (2007). First-generation college students: Their challenges and the advising strategies that can help. *The Mentor: An Academic Advising Journal, 9*(1), 1–4.

Payne, R. K. (2005). *A framework for understanding poverty.* Highlands, TX: Aha! Process.

Pferdehirt, J. (1997). *One nation, many peoples: Immigration in the United States, a resource book.* Madison, WI: Knowledge Unlimited.

Phelan, D. J. (2000). *Enrollment policy and student access at community colleges. A policy paper.* Denver, CO: Education Commission of the States, Center for Community College Policy.

Phillipe, K. A., & Patton, M. (2000). *National profile of community colleges: Trends & statistics* (3rd ed.). Washington DC: Community College Press.

Pike, R. G., & Kuh, G. D. (2005). First- and second-generation college students: A comparison of their engagement and intellectual development. *The Journal of Higher Education, 76*(3), 276–300.

Pizzolato, J. E. (2003). Developing self-authorship: Exploring the experiences of high-risk college students. *Journal of College Student Development, 44*(6), 797–812.

Polansky, J., Horan, J. J., & Hanish, C. (1993, May/June). Experimental construct validity of the outcomes of study skills training and career counseling as treatments for the retention of at-risk students. *Journal of Counseling & Development, 71*, 488–492.

Popenoe, D. (1993). American family decline, 1960–1990: Review and appraisal. *Journal of Marriage and the Family, 55*(3), 527–542.

Pryor, J. H., Hurtado, S., Saenz, V. B., Korn, J. S., Santos, J. L., & Korn, W. S. (2007). *The American freshman: National norms for fall 2006.* Los Angeles: Higher Education Research Institute, UCLA.

Pulley, J. L. (2008). *In need of remediation: The challenge of remediating ill-prepared students continues to confront community colleges.* Retrieved from www.ccweek .com.

Raymond, K. J., & Black, K. (2008). Assessing the graduate school readiness and preparation needs of low-income, first-generation and minority college students. *Opportunity Matters: A Journal of Research Informing Educational Opportunity Practice & Programs, 1*, 44–55.

Rendón, L. I. (1995). *Facilitating retention and transfer for first-generation students in community colleges.* Paper presented at the Rural Community College Initiative, Espanola, NM.

Richardson, R. C., & Skinner, E. F. (1992). Helping first-generation minority students achieve degrees. In L. S. Zwerling & H. B. London (Eds.), *First-generation students: Confronting the cultural issues* (New Directions for Community Colleges, No. 80, pp. 29–43). San Francisco: Jossey-Bass.

Ryu, M. (2008). *Minorities in higher education 2008: Twenty-third status report.* Washington, DC: American Council on Education.

Saenz, V. B., Hurtado, S., Barrera, D., Wolf, D., & Yeung, F. (2007). *First in my family: A profile of first-generation college students at four-year institutions since 1971.* Los Angeles: The Foundation for Independent Higher Education.

Seburn, M., Chan, T., & Kirshstein, R. (2005). *A profile of the Ronald E. McNair postbaccalaureate achievement program: 1997–1998 through 2001–2002.* Washington, DC: American Institutes for Research for the U.S. Department of Education.

Sickles, A. R. (2004). *Advising first-generation students.* Retrieved from www.nacada .ksu.edu/Clearinghouse/AdvisingIssues

Smart, J. C., & Umback, P. D. (2007). Faculty and academic environments: Using Holland's theory to explore differences in how faculty structure undergraduate courses. *Journal of College Student Development, 48*(2), 183–195.

Smith, B. L., & MacGregor, J. (1992). What is collaborative learning? In A. Goodsell, M. Maher, V. Tinto, B. L. Smith, & J. MacGregor (eds.), *Collaborative learning: A sourcebook for higher education.* University Park, PA: National Center on Postsecondary Teaching, Learning, and Assessment at Pennsylvania State University.

Smith, K. A., & MacGregor, J. (2000). Making small-group learning and learning communities a widespread reality. In J. MacGregor (Ed.), *Strategies for energizing large classes* (New Directions for Teaching and Learning, No. 81, pp. 77–88). San Francisco: Jossey-Bass.

Somers, P., Woodhouse, S., & Cofer, J. (2004). Pushing the boulder uphill: The persistence of first-generation college students. *NASPA Journal, 41*(3), 418–435.

Strayhorn, T. L. (2006). Factors influencing the academic achievement of first-generation college students. *NASPA Journal, 43*(4), 82–111.

Terenzini, P. T., Springer, L., Yaeger, P. M., Pascarella, E. T., & Nora, A. (1995). *First-generation college students: Characteristics, experiences, and cognitive development.* Paper presented at the meeting of the Association for Institutional Research, Boston, MA.

Terenzini, P. T., Springer, L., Yaeger, P. M., Pascarella, E. T., & Nora, A. (1996). First-generation college students: Characteristics, experiences, and cognitive development. *Research in Higher Education, 37*, 1–22.

Thayer, P. B. (2000, May). Retention of students from first-generation and low income backgrounds. *Opportunity Outlook: The Journal of the Council for Opportunity in Education, 3*, 1–8.

Tinto, V. (1975). Dropout from higher education: A theoretical synthesis of recent research. *Review of Educational Research, 45*(1), 89–125.

Tinto, V. (1993). *Leaving college: Rethinking the causes and cures of student attrition* (2nd ed.). Chicago: The University of Chicago Press.

Treisman, U. (1992). Studying students studying calculus: A look at the lives of minority mathematics students in college. *The College Mathematics Journal, 23*(5), 362–372.

U.S. Census Bureau. (1999). *Summary measures of college enrollment: October 1999.* Washington, DC: U.S. Census Bureau, Current Population Survey.

U.S. Census Bureau. (2000). *Motherhood: The fertility of American women, 2000.* Washington, DC: U.S. Census Bureau, Population Profile of the United States.

U.S. Census Bureau. (2006). *School enrollment: Social and economic characteristics of students.* Retrieved from http://www.census.gov/population/www/socdemo/school/cps2006.html

U.S. Census Bureau. (2008). *Projections of the population by selected age groups and sex for the United States: 2010 to 2050.* Retrieved from www.census.gov/population/www/projections/2008projections.html

Varney, J. (2007). *Intrusive advising.* Retrieved from www.nacada.ksu.edu/Clearinghouse/AdvisingIssues

Warburton, E. C., Bugarin, R., & Nuñez, A. M. (2001). *Bridging the gap: Academic preparation and postsecondary success of first-generation students* (NCES 2001-153). Washington, DC: U.S. Department of Education, National Center for Education Statistics.

Weinstein, C. E., & Mayer, R. E. (1983). The teaching of learning strategies. *Innovation Abstracts, 5*(32), 1–4.

Wingate, U. (2006). Doing away with "study skills." *Teaching in Higher Education, 11*(4), 457–469.

Yorke, M., & Thomas, L. (2003). Improving the retention of students from lower socio-economic groups. *Journal of Higher Education Policy & Management, 25*(1), 63–74.

Zhou, M. (1997). Growing up American: The challenge confronting immigrant children and children of immigrants. *Annual Review of Sociology, 23,* 63–95.

About the Author

JEFF DAVIS has been an English professor, academic counselor, and administrator at Sonoma State University in California for more than 10 years.

He received bachelor's degrees in journalism and in English from San Jose State University in 1982, a master's degree in English from San Jose State University in 1987, and a Ph.D. in English studies from the University of California at Santa Barbara in 2002.

Davis became interested in the plight of first-generation college students when he was exposed to the work being done with nontraditional students on the Sonoma State campus, specifically, the services provided by federal TRIO grant projects, and eventually he became the director of a TRIO Student Support Service project and a TRIO McNair Scholars project. Student Support Service projects assist low-income students, first-generation students, and students with disabilities to earn their bachelor's degrees in a timely manner. McNair Scholars projects assist low-income and first-generation students and students belonging to ethnic minority groups underrepresented in graduate education to become enrolled in graduate schools.

As a result of his work in TRIO projects, Davis is designing an institute for the study of the first-generation student experience to be housed at Sonoma State. He is also interested in the growing academic discipline of evolutionary psychology. He and colleagues at Sonoma State are preparing a book on composition pedagogy that will attempt to apply the principles of evolutionary psychology and contemporary brain research to the processes involved in learning how to improve writing.

Index

ACPA
College Student
Educators International

Stylus is the official publisher of the books program of ACPA's Books and Media Board.

The Aims of the Program

Chair of Editorial Board: Ellen M. Broido

ACPA books are designed to appeal to a broad, interdisciplinary audience of researchers, scholars, and practitioners in the areas of college student development and student affairs theory and practice, and are intended for use by individual student affairs professionals, in graduate courses, and by student affairs divisions and departments.

Forthcoming titles:

Building Bridges, Revisioning Community
Multicultural Student Services on Campus
Edited by Dafina Lazarus Stewart

Transformational Tapestry Model
A Comprehensive Approach for Assessing and Improving Campus Climates for Underrepresented and Underserved Populations
Susan R. Rankin and Robert D. Reason

Theoretical Frameworks in Student Affairs Research
Courtney H. Thornton and Audrey J. Jaeger

Difficult Conversations
Enacting the Core Values of Inclusion in Student Affairs
Edited by Vasti Torres, Jan Arminio, and Raechele Pope

Empowering Women in Higher Education and Student Affairs
Theory, Research, Narratives, and Practice from Feminist Perspectives
Edited by Penny A. Pasque and Shelley Errington Nicholson

22883 Quicksilver Drive
Sterling, VA 20166-2102   Subscribe to our e-mail alerts: www.Styluspub.com